# GRAMMAR
## Form and Function

Milada Broukal

McGraw-Hill

# Acknowledgements

The publisher and author would like to thank the following individuals who reviewed *Grammar Form and Function* during the development of the series and whose comments and suggestions were invaluable in creating this project.

- Tony Albert, *Jewish Vocational Services, San Francisco, CA*
- Leslie A. Biaggi, *Miami–Dade Community College, Miami, FL*
- Gerry Boyd, *Northern Virginia Community College, VA*
- Marcia M. Captan, *Miami–Dade Community College, Miami, FL*
- Yongjae Paul Choe, *Dongguk University, Seoul, Korea*
- Sally Gearhart, *Santa Rosa Junior College, Santa Rosa, CA*
- Mary Gross, *Miramar College, San Diego, CA*
- Martin Guerin, *Miami–Dade Community College, Miami, FL*
- Patty Heiser, *University of Washington, Seattle, WA*
- Susan Kasten, *University of North Texas, Denton, TX*
- Sarah Kegley, *Georgia State University, Atlanta, GA*
- Kelly Kennedy-Isern, *Miami–Dade Community College, Miami, FL*
- Grace Low, *Germantown, TN*
- Irene Maksymjuk, *Boston University, Boston, MA*
- Christina Michaud, *Bunker Hill Community College, Boston, MA*
- Cristi Mitchell, *Miami–Dade Community College-Kendall Campus, Miami, FL*
- Carol Piñeiro, *Boston University, Boston, MA*
- Michelle Remaud, *Roxbury Community College, Boston, MA*
- Diana Renn, *Wentworth Institute of Technology, Boston, MA*
- Alice Savage, *North Harris College, Houston, TX*
- Karen Stanley, *Central Piedmont Community College, Charlotte, NC*
- Roberta Steinberg, *Mt. Ida College, Newton, MA*

The author would like to thank everyone at McGraw-Hill who participated in this project's development, especially Arley Gray, Erik Gundersen, Annie Sullivan, Jennifer Monaghan, David Averbach, Kasey Williamson, and Tina Carver.

---

**Grammar Form and Function 2**

ISBN: 0-07-008231-6 (Student Book)
ISBN: 0-07-111067-4 (International Student Edition)

Editorial director: Tina B. Carver
Senior managing editor: Erik Gundersen
Developmental editors: Arley Gray, Annie Sullivan
Editorial assistants: David Averbach, Kasey Williamson
Production manager: Juanita Thompson
Cover design: AcentoVisual
Interior design: AcentoVisual
Art: Eldon Doty

**Photo credits:**

All photos are courtesy of Getty Images Royalty-Free Collection with the exception of the following: *Page 30* © Bettmann/CORBIS; *Page 31* © 2003 Estate of Pablo Picasso/Artists Rights Society (ARS), New York, and © Francis G. Mayer/CORBIS; *Page 34* © Hulton-Deutsch Collection/CORBIS; *Page 44* © Archivo Iconografico, S.A./CORBIS; *Page 171* © DOCWHITE; *Page 352* © Bettman/CORBIS; *Page 366* © John Springer Collection/CORBIS; *Page 368* © AFP/CORBIS.

The **McGraw-Hill** Companies

# Contents

## UNIT 4 NOUNS, ARTICLES, AND QUANTITY

## UNIT 5 PRONOUNS

## UNIT 6 THE PERFECT TENSES

## UNIT 7 QUESTIONS AND PHRASAL VERBS

## UNIT 8 MODAL AUXILIARIES AND RELATED FORMS

## UNIT 9 GERUNDS AND INFINITIVES

## UNIT 10 COMPARATIVE AND SUPERLATIVE FORMS

## UNIT 11 THE PASSIVE VOICE

## UNIT 12 CONJUNCTIONS AND NOUN CLAUSES

## UNIT 13 ADJECTIVE AND ADVERB CLAUSES

## UNIT 14 REPORTED SPEECH AND CONDITIONAL CLAUSES

## APPENDICES

# Welcome to Grammar
# Form and Function!

In **Grammar Form and Function 2**, high-interest photos bring basic grammar to life, providing visual contexts for learning and retaining new structures and vocabulary.

Welcome to **Grammar Form and Function 2**. This visual tour will provide you with an overview of the key features of a unit.

❖ *Form* **presentations** teach grammar structures through complete charts and high-interest, memorable photos that facilitate students' recall of grammar structures.

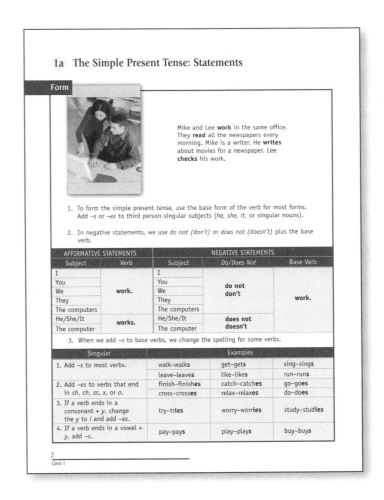

1a   The Simple Present Tense: Statements

**Form**

Mike and Lee **work** in the same office. They **read** all the newspapers every morning. Mike is a writer. He **writes** about movies for a newspaper. Lee **checks** his work.

1. To form the simple present tense, use the base form of the verb for most forms. Add –s or –es to third person singular subjects (*he, she, it,* or singular nouns).

2. In negative statements, we use *do not (don't)* or *does not (doesn't)* plus the base verb.

| AFFIRMATIVE STATEMENTS | | NEGATIVE STATEMENTS | | |
| Subject | Verb | Subject | *Do/Does Not* | Base Verb |
|---|---|---|---|---|
| I | | I | | |
| You | | You | do not | |
| We | **work.** | We | don't | |
| They | | They | | **work.** |
| The computers | | The computers | | |
| He/She/It | **works.** | He/She/It | does not | |
| The computer | | The computer | doesn't | |

3. When we add –s to base verbs, we change the spelling for some verbs.

| Singular | Examples | | |
|---|---|---|---|
| 1. Add –s to most verbs. | walk–walks | get–gets | sing–sings |
| | leave–leaves | like–likes | run–runs |
| 2. Add –es to verbs that end in *sh, ch, ss, x,* or *o.* | finish–finish**es** | catch–catch**es** | go–goes |
| | cross–cross**es** | relax–relax**es** | do–does |
| 3. If a verb ends in a consonant + *y,* change the *y* to *i* and add –es. | try–tri**es** | worry–worri**es** | study–studi**es** |
| 4. If a verb ends in a vowel + *y,* add –s. | pay–pay**s** | play–play**s** | buy–buy**s** |

2
Unit 1

❖ **Form presentations** also include related grammatical points such as negatives, yes/no questions, wh– questions, and short answers.

4. Two verbs are irregular in the simple present tense, *be* and *have*. Also, *be* forms its negative differently from other verbs.

| | AFFIRMATIVE STATEMENTS | | | NEGATIVE STATEMENTS | | |
|---|---|---|---|---|---|---|
| | Subject | Verb | | Subject | Negative Verb | |
| Be | I | am | late. | I | am not<br>'m not | late. |
| | You<br>We<br>They | are | | You<br>We<br>They | are not<br>'re not<br>aren't | |
| | He/She/It | is | | He/She/It | is not<br>'s not<br>isn't | |
| Have | I<br>You<br>We<br>They | have | a problem. | I<br>You<br>We<br>They | don't have | a problem. |
| | He/She/It | has | | He/She/It | doesn't have | |

**Function**

1. We use the simple present tense when we talk about habitual actions and for things that happen all the time or are always true.

   Mike **talks** on the phone a lot.
   He **writes** movie reviews on his computer every day.

2. We use the negative contracted forms *don't* and *doesn't* in speech and informal writing. We use the full forms *do not* and *does not* in formal writing and in speech when we want to emphasize the negative.

   INFORMAL:　　　　　　　I'm sorry. I **don't** have time to help you now.
   FORMAL OR EMPHATIC:　The president **does not** want this report to be late.

3
The Present Tenses

❖ **Function** explanations and examples clarify when to use grammar structures.

❖ **Extensive practice** through topical exercises guides students from accurate production to fluent use of the grammar.

❖ **Your Turn** activities guide students to practice grammar in personally meaningful conversations.

---

1 Practice

Complete the sentences with the correct form of the verb in parentheses. Make the verb negative if the word *not* is in the parentheses.

1. Mike (live) _____*lives*_____ in New York City.
2. He (have) _____ an apartment near the office.
3. He (not, take) _____ the bus to work.
4. He (walk) _____ to work.
5. Mike (like) _____ his job.
6. He (not, be) _____ an office worker.
7. He (be) _____ a writer.
8. He (write) _____ about movies.
9. He (go) _____ to the movies every day.
10. He (see) _____ new movies.
11. He (have) _____ a small computer.
12. He (take) _____ his computer with him to the movies.
13. He (not, go) _____ home at 5:00 in the afternoon.
14. Mike (work) _____ late.
15. He (sleep) _____ late, too.
16. Lee (correct) _____ his work.
17. They (work) _____ for the same newspaper.
18. Mike and Lee (read) _____ a lot of other newspapers.
19. They (talk) _____ on the phone a lot.
20. They (drink) _____ a lot of coffee, too.
21. Mike and Lee (not, agree) _____ all the time.
22. Lee (not, like) _____ Mike's work all the time.

2 Your Turn

Think of five activities that a friend does. Tell your partner.

**Examples:**
My sister teaches art to children.
She drives to work.
She helps the children.
She likes her job.

4
Unit I

❖ **Writing assignments** build composition skills, such as narrating and describing, through real-life, step-by-step tasks.

## WRITING: Describe a Person

Write a paragraph about your partner.

**Step 1.** Ask and answer the questions with a partner. Record the answers by checking "Yes" or "No." Write additional information under "Other Information."

|  | | Yes | No | Other Information |
|---|---|---|---|---|
| 1. | live/in (city) | _____ | _____ | _____ |
| 2. | work | _____ | _____ | _____ |
| 3. | like/tennis | _____ | _____ | _____ |
| 4. | listen/pop music | _____ | _____ | _____ |
| 5. | have/car | _____ | _____ | _____ |
| 6. | go/movies on weekends | _____ | _____ | _____ |
| 7. | speak/(language) | _____ | _____ | _____ |
| 8. | play/the piano | _____ | _____ | _____ |
| 9. | go on vacation/in the summer | _____ | _____ | _____ |
| 10. | have/brothers and sisters | _____ | _____ | _____ |

**Step 2.** Write sentences about your partner from your notes.

**Example:**

## SELF-TEST

❖ **Self-Tests** at the end of each unit allow students to evaluate their mastery of the grammar while providing informal practice of standardized test taking.

**A** Choose the best answer, A, B, C, or D, to complete the sentence. Mark your answer by darkening the oval with the same letter.

1. Many animals _____ their young in the spring.

   A. are having    Ⓐ Ⓑ Ⓒ Ⓓ
   B. have
   C. has
   D. is have

2. Every year, the Earth _____ around the Sun one time.

   A. travels    Ⓐ Ⓑ Ⓒ Ⓓ
   B. travel
   C. is traveling

6. At the moment, everybody _____ the football game on television.

   A. is seeing    Ⓐ Ⓑ Ⓒ Ⓓ
   B. is watching
   C. is looking at
   D. does watch

7. We _____ vitamins for good health.

   A. are needing    Ⓐ Ⓑ Ⓒ Ⓓ
   B. need have
   C. have need
   D. need

**B** Find the underlined word or phrase, A, B, C, or D, that is incorrect. Mark your answer by darkening the oval with the same letter.

1. Italians usually eats pasta every day
          A    B       C
   of the week.
   D

   Ⓐ Ⓑ Ⓒ Ⓓ

2. How many hours does a baby sleeps?
      A     B        C     D

   Ⓐ Ⓑ Ⓒ Ⓓ

3. People catch sometimes colds in the winter.

6. In India, the cow gives milk and
                 A    B    C
   is working on the farm.
   D

   Ⓐ Ⓑ Ⓒ Ⓓ

7. Camels do not drink often water for days
           A    B    C
   when they travel.
            D

   Ⓐ Ⓑ Ⓒ Ⓓ

# To the Teacher

*Grammar Form and Function* is a three-level series designed to ensure students' success in learning grammar. The series features interesting photos to help students accurately recall grammar points, meaningful contexts, and a clear, easy-to-understand format that integrates practice of the rules of essential English grammar (form) with information about when to apply them and what they mean (function).

## Features

❖ **Flexible approach to grammar instruction** integrates study of new structures (form) with information on how to use them and what they mean (function).
❖ **High-interest photos** contextualize new grammar and vocabulary.
❖ **Comprehensive grammar coverage** targets all basic structures.
❖ **Extensive practice** ensures accurate production and fluent use of grammar.
❖ **Your Turn activities** guide students to practice grammar in personally meaningful conversations.
❖ **Writing assignments** build composition skills like narrating and describing through step-by-step tasks.
❖ **Self-Tests and Unit Quizzes** offer multiple assessment tools for student and teacher use, in print and Web formats.
❖ **Companion Website activities** develop real-world listening and reading skills.

## Components

❖ **Student Book** has 14 units with abundant practice in both form and function of each grammar structure. Each unit also features communicative *Your Turn* activities, a step-by-step *Writing* assignment, and a *Self-Test*.
❖ **Teacher's Manual** provides the following:
   ◆ Teaching tips and techniques
   ◆ Overview of each unit
   ◆ Answer keys for the Student Book and Workbook
   ◆ Expansion activities
   ◆ Culture, usage, and vocabulary notes
   ◆ Answers to frequently asked questions about the grammar structures
   ◆ Unit quizzes in a standardized test format and answer keys for each unit.
❖ **Workbook** features additional exercises for each grammar structure, plus an extra student Self-Test at the end of each unit.
❖ **Website** provides further practice, as well as additional assessments.

# Overview of the Series

## Pedagogical Approach

### What is *form*?

*Form* is the structure of a grammar point and what it looks like. Practice of the form builds students' accuracy and helps them recognize the grammar point in authentic situations, so they are better prepared to understand what they are reading or what other people are saying.

### What is *function*?

*Function* is when and how we use a grammar point. Practice of the function builds students' fluency and helps them apply the grammar point in their real lives.

### Why does **Grammar Form and Function** incorporate both form and function into its approach to teaching grammar?

Mastery of grammar relies on students knowing the rules of English (form) and correctly understanding how to apply them (function). Providing abundant practice in both form and function is key to student success.

### How does **Grammar Form and Function** incorporate form and function into its approach to teaching grammar?

For each grammar point, the text follows a consistent format:

- ❖ **Presentation of Form.** The text presents the complete form, or formal rule, along with several examples for students to clearly see the model. There are also relevant photos to help illustrate the grammar point.
- ❖ **Presentation of Function.** The text explains the function of the grammar point, or how it is used, along with additional examples for reinforcement.
- ❖ **Practice.** Diverse exercises practice the form and function together. Practice moves logically from more controlled to less controlled activities.
- ❖ **Application.** Students apply the grammar point in open-ended communicative activities. **Your Turn** requires students to draw from and speak about personal experiences, and **Writing** provides a variety of writing assignments that rely on communicative group and pair discussions. **Expansion** activities in the Teacher's Manual provide additional creative, fun practice for students.

## What is the purpose of the photos in the book?

Most people have a visual memory. When you see a photo aligned with a grammar point, the photo helps you remember and contextualize the grammar. The photo reinforces the learning and retention. If there were no visual image, you'd be more likely to forget the grammar point. For example, let's say you are learning the present progressive. You read the example "She is drinking a glass of water." At the same time, you are shown a photo of a girl drinking a glass of water. Later, you are more likely to recall the form of the present progressive because your mind has made a mental picture that helps you remember.

# Practice

## How were the grammar points selected?

We did a comprehensive review of courses at this level to ensure that all of the grammar points taught were included.

## Does **Grammar Form and Function** have controlled or communicative practice?

It has both. Students practice each grammar point through controlled exercises and then move on to tackle open-ended communicative activities.

## Do students have a chance to personalize the grammar?

Yes. There are opportunities to personalize the grammar in **Your Turn** and **Writing**. **Your Turn** requires students to draw from and speak about personal experiences, and **Writing** provides a variety of writing assignments that rely on communicative group and pair discussions.

## Does **Grammar Form and Function** help students work toward fluency or accuracy?

Both. The exercises are purposefully designed to increase students' accuracy and enhance their fluency by practicing both form and function. Students' confidence in their accuracy helps boost their fluency.

## Why does the text feature writing practice?

Grammar and writing are linked in a natural way. Specific grammar structures lend themselves to specific writing genres. In *Grammar Form and Function*, carefully devised practice helps students keep these structures in mind as they are writing.

## In addition to the grammar charts, what other learning aids are in the book?

The book includes 11 pages of appendices that are designed to help the students as they complete the exercises. In addition to grammar resources such as lists of irregular verbs and spelling rules for endings, the appendices also feature useful and interesting information, including grammar terms, rules for capitalization and punctuation, writing basics, and even maps. In effect, the appendices constitute a handbook that students can use not only in grammar class, but in other classes as well.

## Are there any additional practice opportunities?

Yes, there are additional exercises in the Workbook and on the Website. There are also **Expansion** activities in the Teacher's Manual that provide more open-ended (and fun!) practice for students.

# Assessment

## What is the role of student self-assessment in **Grammar Form and Function?**

Every opportunity for student self-assessment is valuable! *Grammar Form and Function* provides two Self-Tests for each unit – one at the end of each Student Book unit and another at the end of each Workbook unit. The Self-Tests build student confidence, encourage student independence as learners, and increase student competence in following standardized test formats. In addition, the Self-Tests serve as important tools for the teacher in measuring student mastery of grammar structures.

## Does **Grammar Form and Function** offer students practice in standardized test formats?

Yes, the two Self-Tests and the Unit Quiz for each unit all utilize standardized test formats. Teachers may use the three tests in the way that best meets student, teacher, and institutional needs. For example, teachers may first assign the Self-Test in the Workbook as an untimed practice test to be taken at home. Then in the classroom, teachers may administer the Self-Test in the Student Book for a more realistic, but still informal, test-taking experience. Finally, teachers may administer the Unit Quiz from the Teacher's Manual as a more standardized timed test.

## How long should each Self-Test or Unit Quiz take?

Since there is flexibility in implementing the Self-Tests and Unit Quizzes, there is also flexibility in the timing of the tests. When used for informal test-taking practice at home or in class, they may be administered as untimed tests. When administered as timed tests in class, they should take no more than 20 minutes.

## How can I be sure students have mastered the grammar?

*Grammar Form and Function* provides a variety of tools to evaluate student mastery of the grammar. Traditional evaluation tools include the practice exercises, Self-Tests, and Unit Quizzes. To present a more complete picture of student mastery, the series also includes **Your Turn** activities and **Writing**, which illustrate how well students have internalized the grammar structures and are able to apply them in realistic tasks. Teachers can use these activities to monitor and assess students' ability to incorporate new grammatical structures into their spoken and written discourse.

# Unit Format

## What is the unit structure of **Grammar Form and Function**?

Consult the guide to *Grammar Form and Function* on pages IX-XI. This walkthrough provides a visual tour of a Student Book unit.

## How many hours of instruction are in **Grammar Form and Function 2**?

The key to *Grammar Form and Function* is flexibility! The grammar structures in the Student Book may be taught in order, or teachers may rearrange units into an order that best meets their students' needs. To shorten the number of hours of instruction, teachers may choose not to teach all of the grammar structures, or use all of the exercises provided. On the other hand, teachers may add additional hours by assigning exercises in the Workbook or on the Website. In addition, the Teacher's Manual provides teaching suggestions and expansion activities that would add extra hours of instruction.

# Ancillary Components

## What can I find in the Teacher's Manual?

❖   Teaching tips and techniques
❖   Overview of each unit
❖   Answer keys for the Student Book and Workbook
❖   Expansion activities
❖   Culture, usage, and vocabulary notes
❖   Answers to frequently asked questions about the grammar structures
❖   Unit quizzes in a standardized test format and quiz answer keys.

## How do I supplement classroom instruction with the Workbook?

The Workbook exercises can be used to add instructional hours to the course, to provide homework practice, and to reinforce and refresh the skills of students who have mastered the grammar structures. It also provides additional standardized test-taking practice.

## What can students find on the Website?

Students and teachers will find a wealth of engaging listening and reading activities on the *Grammar Form and Function* Website. These listening segments introduce students to the aural dimension of key grammar points. As with the Workbook, the Website exercises can be used to add instructional hours to the course, to provide homework practice, and to reinforce and refresh the skills of students who have mastered the grammar structures.

# UNIT 1

## THE PRESENT TENSES

# 1a The Simple Present Tense: Statements

## Form

Mike and Lee **work** in the same office. They **read** all the newspapers every morning. Mike is a writer. He **writes** about movies for a newspaper. Lee **checks** his work.

1. To form the simple present tense, use the base form of the verb for most forms. Add –s or –es to third person singular subjects (*he, she, it,* or singular nouns).

2. In negative statements, we use *do not (don't)* or *does not (doesn't)* plus the base verb.

| AFFIRMATIVE STATEMENTS | | NEGATIVE STATEMENTS | | |
|---|---|---|---|---|
| Subject | Verb | Subject | *Do/Does Not* | Base Verb |
| I | | I | | |
| You | | You | | |
| We | **work.** | We | **do not**<br>**don't** | |
| They | | They | | **work.** |
| The computers | | The computers | | |
| He/She/It | **works.** | He/She/It | **does not**<br>**doesn't** | |
| The computer | | The computer | | |

3. When we add –s to base verbs, we change the spelling for some verbs.

| Singular | Examples | | |
|---|---|---|---|
| 1. Add –s to most verbs. | walk–walk**s** | get–get**s** | sing–sing**s** |
| | leave–leave**s** | like–like**s** | run–run**s** |
| 2. Add –es to verbs that end in *sh, ch, ss, x,* or *o.* | finish–finish**es** | catch–catch**es** | go–go**es** |
| | cross–cross**es** | relax–relax**es** | do–do**es** |
| 3. If a verb ends in a consonant + *y,* change the *y* to *i* and add –es. | try–tr**ies** | worry–worr**ies** | study–stud**ies** |
| 4. If a verb ends in a vowel + *y,* add –s. | pay–pay**s** | play–play**s** | buy–buy**s** |

4. Two verbs are irregular in the simple present tense, *be* and *have*. Also, *be* forms its negative differently from other verbs.

| | AFFIRMATIVE STATEMENTS | | | NEGATIVE STATEMENTS | | |
| | Subject | Verb | | Subject | Negative Verb | |
| --- | --- | --- | --- | --- | --- | --- |
| **Be** | I | **am** | late. | I | **am not**<br>**'m not** | late. |
| | You<br>We<br>They | **are** | | You<br>We<br>They | **are not**<br>**'re not**<br>**aren't** | |
| | He/She/It | **is** | | He/She/It | **is not**<br>**'s not**<br>**isn't** | |
| **Have** | I<br>You<br>We<br>They | **have** | a problem. | I<br>You<br>We<br>They | **don't have** | a problem. |
| | He/She/It | **has** | | He/She/It | **doesn't have** | |

## Function

1. We use the simple present tense when we talk about habitual actions and for things that happen all the time or are always true.

   > Mike **talks** on the phone a lot.
   > He **writes** movie reviews on his computer every day.

2. We use the negative contracted forms *don't* and *doesn't* in speech and informal writing. We use the full forms *do not* and *does not* in formal writing and in speech when we want to emphasize the negative.

   > INFORMAL: I'm sorry. I **don't** have time to help you now.
   > FORMAL OR EMPHATIC: The president **does not** want this report to be late.

## 1 Practice

**Complete the sentences with the correct form of the verb in parentheses. Make the verb negative if the word *not* is in the parentheses.**

1. Mike (live) _____*lives*_____ in New York City.
2. He (have) _____ an apartment near the office.
3. He (not, take) _____ the bus to work.
4. He (walk) _____ to work.
5. Mike (like) _____ his job.
6. He (not, be) _____ an office worker.
7. He (be) _____ a writer.
8. He (write) _____ about movies.
9. He (go) _____ to the movies every day.
10. He (see) _____ new movies.
11. He (have) _____ a small computer.
12. He (take) _____ his computer with him to the movies.
13. He (not, go) _____ home at 5:00 in the afternoon.
14. Mike (work) _____ late.
15. He (sleep) _____ late, too.
16. Lee (correct) _____ his work.
17. They (work) _____ for the same newspaper.
18. Mike and Lee (read) _____ a lot of other newspapers.
19. They (talk) _____ on the phone a lot.
20. They (drink) _____ a lot of coffee, too.
21. Mike and Lee (not, agree) _____ all the time.
22. Lee (not, like) _____ Mike's work all the time.

## 2 Your Turn

**Think of five activities that a friend does. Tell your partner.**

**Example:**
My sister teaches art to children.
She drives to work.
She helps the children.
She likes her job.
She sees a movie every weekend.

Your Turn

Think of four things you do every day and four things you don't do every day. List them here, and then talk about them with a partner.

**Examples:**
I exercise every day.
I don't cook every day.

Things I do every day:

1. _____

2. _____

3. _____

4. _____

Things I don't do every day:

5. _____

6. _____

7. _____

8. _____

4  Practice

Complete the sentences with the *–s* or *–es* spelling of the verb in parentheses.

1. John (get up) _____*gets up*_____ at noon.

2. He (eat) _____ breakfast.

3. He (watch) _____ television.

4. He (meet) _____ his friends.

5. He (eat) _____ lunch.

6. He (try) _____ to find a job.

7. He (listen) _____ to music with his friends.

8. In the evening, he (eat) _____ dinner in a restaurant.

9. He (go out) _____ with his friends.

10. John (come) _____ home at four o'clock in the morning.

11. On Sundays, he (stay) _____ home.

12. He (wash) _____ his clothes.

13. He (clean) _____ his apartment.

**14.** He (fix) _____ things in the apartment.

**15.** He (relax) _____ .

**16.** He (call) _____ his mother.

**17.** His mother (worry) _____ about him.

5 ## What Do You Think?

**Why does John's mother worry about him?**

6 ## Practice

**Work with a partner. Tell your partner what each of the people below do.**

**Example:**
A mechanic fixes cars.

| doctor | mechanic | teacher | painter | chef |

# 1b Adverbs of Frequency

**Form**

This is Ann Philips.
She's a host on morning television.
We **often** see her on "Good Morning."
She **always** gets up early on workdays.
She **usually** arrives at the studio at 4:30 in the morning.

*Never, rarely, seldom, sometimes, often, usually,* and *always* are adverbs of frequency. They come between the subject and the simple present verb.

| 0% | | | | | 100% |
|---|---|---|---|---|---|
| never | rarely | sometimes | often | usually | always |
| | seldom | | | | |

| Subject | Adverb of Frequency | Simple Present Tense | |
|---------|---------------------|---------------------|---|
| I | **never** | **eat** | Chinese food. |
| You | **rarely** | **go** | to the theater. |
| He | **seldom** | **sees** | friends. |
| She | **sometimes** | **drinks** | tea. |
| It | **often** | **snows** | in winter. |
| We | **usually** | **get up** | early. |
| They | **always** | **have** | breakfast. |

## Function

Adverbs of frequency tell us how often something happens.

Ann **always** starts the show at 7:00 in the morning.
She **never** gets angry on the show.
She **usually** smiles a lot on the show.

## 7  Practice

**Rewrite the sentences and put the adverbs in the correct position.**

1. On workdays, I get up at 3:30 in the morning.

    (always) *From Monday to Friday, I always get up at 3:30 in the morning.*

2. I take a shower.

    (always) _____

3. I leave the house at 4:15.

    (usually) _____

4. I get to the studio at 4:30.

    (usually) _____

5. "Good Morning" starts at 7:00.

    (always) _____

6. I leave the studio at 10:00.

    (usually) _____

7. I go to the gym after work.

    (usually) _____

8. I go shopping after the gym.

    (sometimes) _____

**9.** My husband comes home at 7:30 in the evening.

(usually) _____

**10.** We stay home in the evening.

(always) _____

**11.** We go out on weekdays.

(sometimes) _____

**12.** We watch television.

(often) _____

**13.** I go to bed at 9:00.

(usually) _____

**14.** On weekends, I get up before 10:00 in the morning.

(rarely) _____

**15.** We see friends.

(often) _____

**16.** We go to the movies.

(never) _____

**17.** I get up early on Monday.

(always) _____

## 8  Practice

**Work with a partner. Talk about Ann's life.**

**Example:**
Ann always gets up early on weekdays.

## 9  Your Turn

**Which of these do you always do, sometimes do, or never do during the week?**

**Example:**
I always cook dinner, and I usually do my homework.

| | | | |
|---|---|---|---|
| cook dinner | go to school | have lunch | see friends |
| do my homework | go to the movies | play football | watch television |

# 1c   The Present Progressive Tense: Statements

People **are walking** to their gates.
They **are carrying** suitcases.

1. We form the present progressive tense with a present form of *be* (*am, is,* or *are*) + the *–ing* form of a verb.

| AFFIRMATIVE AND NEGATIVE STATEMENTS | | | |
|---|---|---|---|
| Subject | Form of *Be* | *(Not)* | Verb + *–ing* |
| I | **am** | | |
| You | **are** | | |
| He/She/it | **is** | **(not)** | **working.** |
| We | **are** | | |
| They | | | |

| FULL FORMS | CONTRACTIONS | |
|---|---|---|
| Full Form | Subject + Form of *Be* | Form of *Be* + *Not* |
| I am (not) | I'm (not) | * |
| You are (not) | You're (not) | You aren't |
| He/She/ It is (not) | He's (not) | He isn't |
| | She's (not) | She isn't |
| | It's (not) | It isn't |
| We are (not) | We're (not) | We aren't |
| They are (not) | They're (not) | They aren't |

*There is no contraction for *am not*.

2. When we add –ing to a base verb, we change the spelling for some verbs.

| Base Verb Ending | Rule | Example | |
|---|---|---|---|
| For most verb endings | Add –ing | start | start**ing** |
| | | play | play**ing** |
| | | study | study**ing** |
| The verb ends in a consonant + e. | Drop e, add –ing. | live | liv**ing** |
| | | move | mov**ing** |
| | | decide | decid**ing** |
| The verb ends in a single vowel + a consonant. | Double the consonant, add –ing. | stop | stop**ping** |
| | | plan | plan**ning** |
| | | prefer | prefer**ring** |
| **Exceptions:** Do not double w or x. | | fix | fix**ing** |
| | | show | show**ing** |
| If a verb has two or more syllables and the stress is not on the last syllable, do not double the consonant. | | open | open**ing** |
| | | travel | travel**ing** |
| | | exit | exit**ing** |
| The verb ends in ie. | Change ie to y and add –ing. | tie | tying |
| | | die | dying |

## Function

A man **is standing** next to a bench.
He **is wearing** a coat.
They are waiting at the airport.

1. We use the present progressive to talk about what is happening *now*.

2. We use contractions in speech and in informal writing. We use full forms in formal writing and when we want to give emphasis to what we are saying.

## 10 Practice

**Write the _-ing_ forms of the verbs.**

| Base Verb | Verb + _-ing_ |
|---|---|
| **1.** listen | _listening_ |
| **2.** wait | _____ |
| **3.** study | _____ |
| **4.** die | _____ |
| **5.** stay | _____ |
| **6.** admit | _____ |
| **7.** swim | _____ |
| **8.** choose | _____ |
| **9.** write | _____ |
| **10.** cut | _____ |
| **11.** sleep | _____ |
| **12.** rain | _____ |
| **13.** start | _____ |
| **14.** hit | _____ |
| **15.** happen | _____ |
| **16.** begin | _____ |
| **17.** win | _____ |
| **18.** tie | _____ |
| **19.** open | _____ |
| **20.** hope | _____ |

## 11 Practice

**Complete the sentences with the present progressive tense of the verb in parentheses.**

I love airports. At the moment, I (wait) _____ _am waiting_ _____ for my plane.
1

I have three hours. So what am I doing? I (not, sleep) _____!
2

I (watch) _____ people. Look at that man. He's outside the
3

bookstore. He (carry) _____ a big black bag. He
4

(look) _____ around. He (walk) _____
5                                              6

away now. He (not, smile) _____. He looks worried. Now he
7

(go) _____ to the departure gate. Here comes a woman. She
                    8

(not, walk) _____. She (run) _____
                       9                                      10

after the man. She (hold) _____ a passport in her hand.
                                    11

She (shout) _____ something. The man
                      12

(turn) _____, and now he (smile) _____.
                  13                                           14

The woman (wave) _____ her hand with the passport. He
                              15

(put) _____ his arm around her now. They look happy.
                 16

## 12 Practice

**Test your memory. Work with a partner. Make three true statements and three false statements about the photo on page 9. Your partner tells you if they are true or false without looking at the photo.**

**Example:**
You:             The people are sitting down.
Your partner: That's false.

## 13 Your Turn

**Describe two of the people in the photo on page 10. Write three sentences about what they are wearing and what they are doing.**

**Example:**
The man on the right is sitting down.

**Person 1**

1. _____

   _____

2. _____

   _____

3. _____

   _____

**Person 2**

1. _____

   _____

2. _____

   _____

3. _____

   _____

## 1d The Simple Present Tense OR The Present Progressive Tense

Charlie always **starts** work at nine.
Charlie **loves** his job.

Today, Charlie **isn't working**.
Charlie **is staying** in bed.

| We use the simple present tense for: | We use the present progressive tense for: |
|---|---|
| 1. Repeated actions or habits.<br><br>Charlie **gets up** at 7:00 every day. | 1. Things that are happening now.<br><br>He **is trying** to sleep. |
| 2. Things that happen all the time or are always true.<br><br>He always **stays** home when he's sick.<br>He **gets** tired when he works too much. | |

## 14 Practice

**Complete the conversation with the correct form of the present progressive or the simple present of the verb in parentheses.**

*Detective Roberts is watching a house. He's talking to Detective Jason on his cell phone.*

Detective Roberts:  An old woman (come) _____*is coming*_____ out of the
                    ‾‾‾‾‾‾‾‾‾‾‾‾‾‾1

                    house.

Detective Jason:    That's Mrs. Johnson. She (live) _____
                    ‾‾‾‾‾‾‾‾‾‾‾‾‾‾‾‾‾2

                    there. She's the housekeeper. It's 8:00 o'clock. She usually

(leave) _____ the house at 8:00. She
                3

(go) _____ to the store to do the grocery
              4

shopping. She usually (come) _____ back
                                        5

around 9:30.

Detective Roberts:    Wait! A car (stop) _____ in front of the house.
                                              6

A man (get) _____ out. He is tall and thin
                  7

and has gray hair. He (wear) _____ a uniform.
                                      8

Detective Jason:      I know he (not, live) _____ there.
                                                  9

Detective Roberts:    He (ring) _____ the doorbell.
                                    10

Nobody (answer) _____. He
                          11

(wait) _____ now. He
              12

(look) _____ at the house carefully. He
              13

(go) _____ to the back of the house. He
            14

(jump) _____ over the wall.
              15

Detective Jason:      Go get him, Roberts!

*Detective Roberts runs after the man and then returns to his car.*

Detective Roberts:    No luck. He says he (look) _____ for the gas
                                                      16

meter. He is from the gas company. He has a badge.

## 15 Practice

**Solve the riddles. Complete the sentences with the correct form of the verb in parentheses.
At the end of each paragraph, identify the thing that the paragraph describes.**

**A.**

I usually (stand) _____*stand*_____ in the kitchen. I
                          1

(have) _____ a door. People (open) _____
              2                                            3

the door and (put) _____ things inside me. Part of me
                          4

(freeze) _____ things for people. Right now, a woman
                5

(take) _____ out a bottle of cold water.
            6

What am I? _____.
                  7

**B.**

You (find) _____ me in the kitchen or bathroom.
                              1
You probably (use) _____ me every day. You
                                      2
(use) _____ me to clean things. Right now, I am in
            3
the kitchen sink. Someone (rub) _____ me all over a pot.
                                        4
What am I? _____ .
                  5

**C.**

I (have) _____ six legs. I (fly) _____
                1                                      2
around in rooms. I (live) _____ in warm weather. Some people
                                3
(not, like) _____ me. Right now, I
                  4
(sit) _____ on a window. I (try) _____
            5                                        6
to get out. A man (come) _____ toward me. He has a rolled up
                                7
newspaper in his hand.

What am I? _____ .
                  8

## 1e  Nonprogressive Verbs

Timmy **wants** a cookie.
He **loves** chocolate cookies.
Right now, he**'s thinking** about eating one.

1.  We do not usually use some verbs in the present progressive tense. We call these *nonprogressive verbs.*

    CORRECT:      That cake **tastes** good.
    INCORRECT:   That cake ~~is tasting~~ good.

    CORRECT:      Shirley **wants** a sandwich.
    INCORRECT:   Shirley ~~is wanting~~ a sandwich.

| Common Nonprogressive Verbs | | | |
|---|---|---|---|
| be | hate | love | smell |
| believe | have | need | taste |
| enjoy | hear | prefer | think |
| feel | know | remember | understand |
| forget | like | see | want |

2.  Sometimes we use the verbs *have* and *think* in the present progressive tense.

| Verb | Example | Explanation |
|---|---|---|
| **Think** | He **thinks** it is a good idea. | *Thinks* means *believes.* |
| | He **is thinking** about eating a cookie. | *Is thinking* refers to the thoughts going through his mind. |
| **Have** | Shirley **has** a cell phone. | *Have* means *possess.* |
| | She**'s having** a good time. | You can use *have* in the present progressive in certain idiomatic expressions: **have a good/bad time** **have problems/difficulty** **have breakfast/lunch/dinner** You can also use the simple present with these expressions. Compare: She always **has** a good time at parties. Look at her dance! She**'s having** a good time. |

## 16   Practice

**Complete the letter with the simple present or the present progressive of the verbs in parentheses.**

Dear Pete,

    I (write) _____*am writing*_____ to you from Sandy Beach, California. I am here
                    1

with Kate and Sally. We (stay) _____ at my friend Brenda's house.
                                              2

She (have) _____ 3 _____ a beautiful house by the beach here. She

(come) _____ 4 _____ here every summer.

We (have) _____ 5 _____ a good time. Every morning, we

(go) _____ 6 _____ to the beach, and we (swim) _____ 7 _____.

At noon, we (come) _____ 8 _____ back to the house and

(have) _____ 9 _____ lunch. We (rest) _____ 10 _____

in the afternoon, and then we (go) _____ 11 _____ into town. We

(sit) _____ 12 _____ in a café or (eat) _____ 13 _____ dinner

in a restaurant.

Today, it (rain) _____ 14 _____. We (stay) _____ 15 _____

at home. I (not, like) _____ 16 _____ this weather. Kate and Sally

(watch) _____ 17 _____ videos. Brenda (cook) _____ 18 _____

lunch for us. It (smell) _____ 19 _____ good.

I hope to see you soon.

Love,
Annie

## 1f  *See, Look At, Watch, Hear, and Listen To*

She **is listening to** music.

The children **are watching** television.

One man **is looking at** his watch.

1. We use several verbs to express the senses of seeing and hearing. They are different from each other in meaning and in the tenses that we use with them.

| VERBS OF SEEING | | | |
|---|---|---|---|
| | Verb | Meaning | Example |
| **Action Verbs** | watch | We *watch* something or someone that is moving. We usually *watch* something that we are paying attention to. | Charles **is watching** television.<br><br>He **watches** television every evening. |
| | look at | We *look at* something or someone for a reason. | Susan **is looking at** a painting. She is an art student.<br><br>She **looks at** paintings carefully. |
| **Nonaction Verb** | see | We *see* things because our eyes are open. | I **see** the blackboard at the front of the room. |

| VERBS OF HEARING | | | |
|---|---|---|---|
| | Verb | Meaning | Example |
| **Action Verb** | listen to | We *listen to* something or someone for a reason. | They **are listening to** music.<br><br>They **listen to** music often. |
| **Nonaction Verb** | hear | When we *hear,* we receive sounds with our ears. | I **hear** the music coming from the other room. (I may not be paying attention to it.) |

2. We can use action verbs either with the simple present tense or with the present progressive tense. But we do not usually use nonaction verbs with the present progressive tense.

## 17 Practice

**Complete the sentences with the correct verb. Use the simple present or the present progressive tense.**

1. Right now the students (listen to/hear) ___*are listening to*___ the teacher. She is teaching the present progressive.

2. Tommy (watch/look at) _____ a football game on television right now.

3. Susan (watch/look at) _____ her watch. She wants to know what time it is.

4. The teacher (look at/see) _____ Bob. She is waiting for an answer to her question.

5. I am studying in my room, but I (hear/listen to) _____ the television in the next room.

6. I (look at/see) _____ the teacher so I can understand better.

7. Tony (listen to/hear) _____ Susan carefully. She is giving him directions to the bank.

8. Dick turns on the television and (watch/see) _____ the news every morning at 7:00.

9. It is 11:00 at night. Tim is in bed. He (hear/listen to) _____ a noise in his apartment. He gets up. He (see/look at) _____ his cat on the kitchen table.

10. Mary is eating soup in a restaurant. She looks down and (see/look at) _____ a hair in the soup. She calls the waiter.

11. (hear/listen to) _____ that sound! I think someone is trying to get in!

12. Brenda is only four years old. She likes magazines. She can't read, but she (look at/see) _____ the photos.

## 18  Your Turn

**Ask and answer the questions with a partner.**

**Example:**
You:          What are you looking at right now? What do you see?
Your partner:   I'm looking out the window. I see buildings and students.

1. What are you looking at right now? What do you see?
2. What are you listening to right now? What do you hear?
3. What do you like to watch on television?

## 1g   Yes/No Questions and Short Answers; Wh- Questions

| | |
|---|---|
| Woman: | **Are you waiting** for the flight to London at 10:00? |
| Man: | **Yes, I am.** Do you live in London? |
| Woman: | **No, I don't.** I live in Montreal. **Where do** you **live**? |
| Man: | I live in Singapore. |

1. Yes/No questions are questions that we can answer with the words *yes* or *no.*

2. Wh- questions begin with a question word like *who* or *what*. We call them wh- questions because all except one begin with the letters *wh-*. The question words are *who, whom, what, where, when, why, which,* and *how.*

| | YES/NO QUESTIONS | | | SHORT ANSWERS |
|---|---|---|---|---|
| | *Do/Does* | Subject | Base Verb | |
| **Simple Present** | Do | I | **need** a haircut? | Yes, you **do.** <br> No, you **don't.** |
| | | you | | Yes, I/we **do.** <br> No, I/we **don't.** |
| | | we | | Yes, you **do.** <br> No, you **don't.** |
| | | they | | Yes, they **do.** <br> No, they **don't.** |
| | Does | he/she/it | | Yes, he/she/it **does.** <br> No, he/she/it **doesn't.** |

| YES/NO QUESTIONS | | | SHORT ANSWERS |
|---|---|---|---|
| *Am/Is/Are* | Subject | Verb + *–ing* | |

| | *Am/Is/Are* | Subject | Verb + *–ing* | SHORT ANSWERS |
|---|---|---|---|---|
| **Present Progressive** | **Am** | I | | Yes, you **are.** <br> No, you **aren't.** <br> OR No, you**'re not.** |
| | **Are** | you | | Yes, I **am.** <br> No, I**'m not.*** |
| | **Is** | he/she/it | | Yes, he/she/it **is.** <br> No, he/she/it **isn't.** <br> OR No, he/she/it**'s not.** |
| | **Are** | you | **leaving** now? | Yes, we **are.** <br> No, we **aren't.** <br> OR No, we**'re not.** |
| | | we | | Yes, you **are.** <br> No, you **aren't.** <br> OR No, you**'re not.** |
| | | they | | Yes, they **are.** <br> No, they **aren't.** <br> OR No, they**'re not.** |

*There is no contraction for *am not*.

3.  We do not contract *am*, *is*, and *are* in short answers.

CORRECT:      Yes, I am. Yes, she is. Yes, they are.
INCORRECT:    Yes, ~~I'm.~~  Yes, ~~she's.~~  Yes, ~~they're.~~

| WH– QUESTIONS | | | | |
|---|---|---|---|---|
| | Wh– Word | *Do/Does* | Subject | Base Verb | |
| **Simple Present** | **What** | **do** | I | **need?** | |
| | **Where** | | you | **live?** | |
| | **Why** | | we | **study** | so hard? |
| | **When** | | they | **have** | lunch? |
| | **Who**** | | you | **like?** | |
| | **Which** | **does** | he/she/it | **prefer?** | |
| | **How** | | | **make** | that soup? |

| | Wh– Word | *Am/Is/Are* | Subject | Verb + *–ing* | |
|---|---|---|---|---|---|
| **Present Progressive** | **Why** | **am** | I | **doing** | your homework? |
| | **Which** book | **are** | they | **reading?** | |
| | **How** | | you | **doing** | that? |
| | **What** | | we | **working** | on? |
| | **Who**** | | they | **visiting?** | |
| | **Where** | **is** | he/she/it | **going?** | |
| | **When** | | | **leaving?** | |

**In formal written English, the wh- word would be *whom*.

## 19 Practice

**Complete the conversation with the simple present or the present progressive of the verbs in parentheses. You sometimes need to use short answers.**

Woman: Excuse me, (wait) ____are____ you ___waiting___ for the flight to London
                               **1**               **2**

            at 10:00?

Man:    Yes, I _____ .
                      **3**

Woman: Is this the right gate?

Man:    Yes, it is. (live) _____ you _____ in London?
                            **4**                  **5**

Woman: No, I _____. At the moment, I
                        **6**

        (study) _____ at Cambridge University.
                     **7**

Man:    Oh! What (study) _____ you _____?
                        **8**          **9**

Woman: I (work) _____ on a degree in business management.
                     **10**

Man:    Why (do) _____ you _____ it at Cambridge?
                **11**          **12**

Woman: It's a famous university, and my parents (think) _____ it's
                                       **13**

        the best. What about you? (go) _____ you often _____ to
                                 **14**                 **15**

        London?

Man:    Yes, I (go) _____ there on business. I
                       **16**

        (have) _____ a meeting there tomorrow.
                    **17**

Woman: Oh. What kind of work (do) _____ you _____?
                             **18**          **19**

Man:    I (work) _____ for the marketing department of a company.
                     **20**

        I often (travel) _____ to different countries around the
                        **21**

        world.

Woman: What (do) _____ your company _____?
                **22**                  **23**

Man:    It publishes dictionaries.

Woman: Look! They (board) _____ passengers now. We should
                       **24**

        get in line.

## 20 Practice

**Complete the sentences with the simple present or the present progressive of the verb in parentheses.**

Kenny Lemkin (work) _____ *works* _____ at a bank. He
                                        1

(go) _____ to work every day. He never
                    2

(arrive) _____ late and he rarely (take) _____
                    3                                                              4

a day off. But Kenny (not, be) _____ at work this morning.
                                        5

Right now, he (pack) _____ a suitcase, and he
                                6

(sing) _____. He (look) _____ for his
                    7                                            8

passport. "Where is it? Oh, I (know) _____ where it is," he thinks.
                                                9

It's in his pocket. Now Kenny (sit) _____ in a taxi. He
                                                    10

(smile) _____. Now he's on an airplane. It is
                    11

(fly) _____ to Rio. Kenny (look) _____
                12                                                    13

very happy.

## 21 Practice

**Ask and answer these questions about Kenny with a partner.**

**Example:**
Kenny/work/at a restaurant
You:            Does Kenny work at a restaurant?
Your partner:   No, he doesn't. He works at a bank.

1. Kenny/usually/go/to work every day
2. Kenny/arrive/late
3. Kenny/pack/a suitcase/right now
4. Kenny/look for/his passport
5. Kenny's taxi/go/to the bank
6. Kenny/go/Tokyo

## 22 What Do You Think?

**Do you think Kenny is going on a business trip or on a vacation? Is he going alone? What will he do in Rio?**

**Read the postcard. Then answer the questions with complete sentences.**

Dear Uncle Joe,

    We are on one of the Greek islands. It's called Mykonos. We are staying in a hotel by the beach. We are having a wonderful time. I'm writing this postcard from the hotel. Richard is lying on the beach right now, and Lenny and Linda are swimming in the sea.

      See you soon,
    Laura, Richard, and the kids

Mr. Joseph Kelly
851 W. 37th St.
New York, NY 10006

**1.** Who is writing the postcard?

   *Laura is writing the postcard.*

**2.** Who is she writing to?

_____

**3.** Where are Laura and her family staying?

_____

**4.** Where is she writing from?

_____

**5.** Are they having a good time?

_____

**6.** What are Lenny and Linda doing?

_____

# WRITING: Describe a Person

**Write a paragraph about your partner.**

**Step 1. Ask and answer the questions with a partner. Record the answers by checking "Yes" or "No." Write additional information under "Other Information."**

| | Yes | No | Other Information |
|---|---|---|---|
| **1.** live/in (city) | _____ | _____ | _____ |
| **2.** work | _____ | _____ | _____ |
| **3.** like/tennis | _____ | _____ | _____ |
| **4.** listen/pop music | _____ | _____ | _____ |
| **5.** have/car | _____ | _____ | _____ |
| **6.** go/movies on weekends | _____ | _____ | _____ |
| **7.** speak/(language) | _____ | _____ | _____ |
| **8.** play/the piano | _____ | _____ | _____ |
| **9.** go on vacation/in the summer | _____ | _____ | _____ |
| **10.** have/brothers and sisters | _____ | _____ | _____ |

**Step 2. Write sentences about your partner from your notes.**

**Example:**
Kumiko lives in Tokyo.
She doesn't work.
She goes to school.

**Step 3. Rewrite the sentences in the form of a paragraph. Write a title (your partner's name). For more writing guidelines, see pages 407–411.**

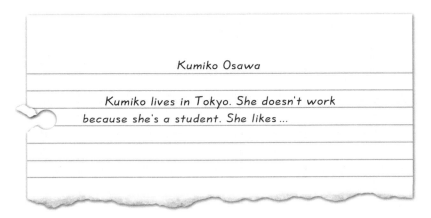

Kumiko Osawa

Kumiko lives in Tokyo. She doesn't work because she's a student. She likes ...

**Step 4. Evaluate your paragraph.**

**Checklist**
_____ Did you indent the first line?
_____ Did you give the paragraph a title?
_____ Did you write the title with a capital letter for each word?

**Step 5. Edit your work. Work with a partner or your teacher to edit your sentences. Correct spelling, punctuation, vocabulary, and grammar.**

**Step 6. Write your final copy.**

# SELF-TEST

**A**   **Choose the best answer, A, B, C, or D, to complete the sentence. Mark your answer by darkening the oval with the same letter.**

1. Many animals _____ their young in the spring.

   A. are having   Ⓐ Ⓑ Ⓒ Ⓓ
   B. have
   C. has
   D. is have

2. Every year, the Earth _____ around the Sun one time.

   A. travels   Ⓐ Ⓑ Ⓒ Ⓓ
   B. travel
   C. is traveling
   D. does traveling

3. Snow _____ in the Sahara Desert.

   A. sometimes falls   Ⓐ Ⓑ Ⓒ Ⓓ
   B. sometimes is falling
   C. falls sometimes
   D. is falling sometimes

4. Sharks _____ bones.

   A. do not have   Ⓐ Ⓑ Ⓒ Ⓓ
   B. are not having
   C. have not
   D. doesn't have

5. Pandas _____ to eat bamboo.

   A. are preferring   Ⓐ Ⓑ Ⓒ Ⓓ
   B. is preferring
   C. prefer
   D. are prefer

6. At the moment, everybody _____ the football game on television.

   A. is seeing   Ⓐ Ⓑ Ⓒ Ⓓ
   B. is watching
   C. is looking at
   D. does watch

7. We _____ vitamins for good health.

   A. are needing   Ⓐ Ⓑ Ⓒ Ⓓ
   B. need have
   C. have need
   D. need

8. Young children _____ the pictures in books.

   A. always look at   Ⓐ Ⓑ Ⓒ Ⓓ
   B. always see
   C. look at always
   D. always watch

9. When _____ breakfast?

   A. you usually have   Ⓐ Ⓑ Ⓒ Ⓓ
   B. usually have you
   C. do you usually have
   D. you are usually having

10. _____ French?

    A. All Canadians speak   Ⓐ Ⓑ Ⓒ Ⓓ
    B. All Canadians are speaking
    C. Are all Canadians speaking
    D. Do all Canadians speak

**B Find the underlined word or phrase, A, B, C, or D, that is incorrect. Mark your answer by darkening the oval with the same letter.**

1. Italians <u>usually</u> <u>eats</u> pasta <u>every day</u>
           A      B           C
   <u>of the week</u>.
     D

   Ⓐ Ⓑ Ⓒ Ⓓ

2. <u>How many</u> <u>hours</u> does <u>a baby</u> <u>sleeps</u>?
      A        B          C    D

   Ⓐ Ⓑ Ⓒ Ⓓ

3. <u>People</u> catch <u>sometimes</u> <u>colds</u> <u>in the</u> winter.
     A            B      C    D

   Ⓐ Ⓑ Ⓒ Ⓓ

4. <u>Do</u> bears <u>eat</u> only meat, or <u>they do</u> <u>eat</u>
    A        B              C    D
   plants, too?

   Ⓐ Ⓑ Ⓒ Ⓓ

5. <u>Why</u> <u>are</u> kangaroos only <u>live</u> <u>in Australia</u>?
    A   B               C    D

   Ⓐ Ⓑ Ⓒ Ⓓ

6. In India, the cow <u>gives</u> <u>milk</u> <u>and</u>
                     A    B    C
   <u>is working</u> on the farm.
     D

   Ⓐ Ⓑ Ⓒ Ⓓ

7. Camels <u>do not</u> <u>drink</u> <u>often</u> water for days
             A      B    C
   when they <u>travel</u>.
             D

   Ⓐ Ⓑ Ⓒ Ⓓ

8. When <u>do</u> people <u>use</u> computers, they
        A         B
   <u>often</u> <u>use</u> the Internet to get information.
     C     D

   Ⓐ Ⓑ Ⓒ Ⓓ

9. <u>Men and women</u> in Iceland <u>have</u> long lives
           A                  B
   because the air <u>has</u> clean and they <u>have</u>
                 C                 D
   good health care.

   Ⓐ Ⓑ Ⓒ Ⓓ

10. People in Thailand <u>not</u> <u>use</u> chopsticks.
                      A   B
    <u>They</u> use <u>spoons</u>.
      C      D

    Ⓐ Ⓑ Ⓒ Ⓓ

# UNIT 2

## THE PAST TENSES

## 2a   The Simple Past Tense

Pablo Picasso **lived** in France.
He **worked** a lot and **painted** many pictures.

1. To form the simple past tense of regular verbs in affirmative statements, add *–ed* to the base verb.

2. In negative statements, use *did not* + a base verb.

3. In questions, use *did* + a base verb + the subject.

| AFFIRMATIVE STATEMENTS | | NEGATIVE STATEMENTS | | |
|---|---|---|---|---|
| Subject | Past Tense Verb | Subject | *Did Not/Didn't* | Base Verb |
| I | | I | | |
| You | | You | | |
| He/She/It | worked. | He/She/It | did not<br>didn't | work. |
| We | | We | | |
| They | | They | | |

| YES/NO QUESTIONS | | | SHORT ANSWERS | |
|---|---|---|---|---|
| *Did* | Subject | Base Verb | Yes, | No, |
| | I | | you **did.** | you **didn't.** |
| | you | | I/we **did.** | I/we **didn't.** |
| **Did** | he/she/it | **work?** | he/she/it **did.** | he/she/it **didn't.** |
| | we | | you **did.** | you **didn't.** |
| | they | | they **did.** | they **didn't.** |

2. We change the spelling of some regular verbs before adding *–ed*.

| Base Verb Ending | Rule | Example | |
|---|---|---|---|
| Most verbs | Add *–ed*. | start | start**ed** |
| | | obey | obey**ed** |
| | | predict | predict**ed** |
| The verb ends in a consonant + *e*. | Add *–d*. | live | live**d** |
| | | move | move**d** |
| | | decide | decide**d** |
| The verb ends in a single vowel + a single consonant. | Double the consonant, add *–ed*. | stop | stop**ped** |
| | | plan | plan**ned** |
| | | prefer | prefer**red** |
| **Exceptions:** Do not double *w* or *x*. | | fix | fix**ed** |
| | | show | show**ed** |
| If a verb has two or more syllables and the stress is not on the last syllable, do not double the consonant. | | open | open**ed** |
| | | travel | travel**ed** |
| | | exit | exit**ed** |
| | | color | color**ed** |
| The verb ends in a consonant + *y*. | Change *y* to *i* and add *–ed*. | worry | worr**ied** |
| | | study | stud**ied** |
| The verb ends in *ie*. | Add *–d*. | tie | tie**d** |
| | | die | die**d** |

## Function

**Did** Picasso **paint** pictures of his wives?
Yes, he did. He **painted** a lot of them.

We use the simple past tense to talk about actions and situations completed in the past. We often say when the situation or action happened (for example, *yesterday, last night*).

# 1 Practice

**Write the -ed forms of the verbs.**

| Base Verb | -ed Form |
|-----------|----------|
| 1. listen | _listened_ |
| 2. wait | _____ |
| 3. study | _____ |
| 4. die | _____ |
| 5. stay | _____ |
| 6. admit | _____ |
| 7. rain | _____ |
| 8. start | _____ |
| 9. happen | _____ |
| 10. tie | _____ |
| 11. open | _____ |
| 12. hope | _____ |

# 2 Practice

**Complete the sentences. Use the simple past tense of the verbs in parentheses.**

Pablo Picasso was born in Malaga, Spain in 1881. His first word was "lápiz"

(Spanish for pencil), and he (learn) _____learned_____ to draw before he

(talk) _____. He (hate) _____ school. He
         2                              3

(like) _____ to paint pictures instead. His father was an artist.
         4

Pablo often (watch) _____ him paint pictures. One day, he
                          5

(finish) _____ one of his father's paintings. When his father
              6

(return) _____, he (not, believe) _____ it. It was
              7                                        8

wonderful! His father never (paint) _____ again. Pablo was only 13.
                                          9

Picasso (travel) _____ to Paris. He (live) _____ in
                      10                                      11

a small room. He sometimes (work) _____ by the light of a candle. Many
                                        12

people (realize) _____ that he was a genius.
                      13

One day, a French minister (visit) _____ Picasso. Some paint
                                        14

(spill) _____ on the minister's trousers by accident. Picasso
             15

(apologize) _____ and (want) _____ to pay to clean
                    16                                    17
them. The minister said, "No, please, Monsieur Picasso, just sign my trousers." His

paintings (change) _____ people's ideas about art. Picasso
                          18
(love) _____ to paint. He (not, stop) _____. He
              19                                          20
(continue) _____ to paint until the end. He (die) _____
                  21                                                      22
at the age of 91.

## 3 | Practice

**Write a question using the prompts. Then write a negative statement. Finally, write a correct sentence using words from the list.**

| | | |
|---|---|---|
| France | Paris | the United States |
| Juliet | radium | Thomas Edison |
| Mount Everest | slower | |

1. Pablo Picasso/live/in London

   _Did Pablo Picasso live in London?_

   _No, he didn't live in London._

   _He lived in Paris._

2. Charlie Chaplin/invent/the light bulb

   _____

   _____

   _____

3. Marie and Pierre Curie/discover/penicillin

   _____

   _____

   _____

4. Marilyn Monroe/come/from France

   _____

   _____

   _____

5. engineers/construct/the Statue of Liberty/in the United States

   _____

   _____

   _____

**6.** trains/travel/faster/50 years ago

_____

_____

**7.** Romeo/love/Cleopatra

_____

_____

**8.** Sir Edmund Hillary and Tenzing Norgay/climb/Mount Fuji

_____

_____

# 2b Irregular Verbs

Marie Curie **was** a famous scientist.
Marie **went** to Paris to study.
There, she **met** Pierre Curie.

Many common verbs do not end in _–ed_ for the simple past. They are irregular. Here is the past form of the verb _go_.

| AFFIRMATIVE STATEMENTS | | NEGATIVE STATEMENTS | | |
|---|---|---|---|---|
| Subject | Past Tense Verb | Subject | _Did Not/Didn't_ | Base Verb |
| I | | I | | |
| You | | You | | |
| He/She/It | **went** to Paris. | He/She/It | **did not**<br>**didn't** | **go** to Paris. |
| We | | We | | |
| They | | They | | |

| YES/NO QUESTIONS | | | SHORT ANSWERS | |
|---|---|---|---|---|
| *Did* | Subject | Base Verb | Yes, | No, |
| **Did** | I | **go** to Paris? | you **did.** | you **didn't.** |
| | you | | I/we **did.** | I/we **didn't.** |
| | he/she/it | | he/she/it **did.** | he/she/it **didn't.** |
| | we | | you **did.** | you **didn't.** |
| | they | | they **did.** | they **didn't.** |

| WH– QUESTIONS | | | |
|---|---|---|---|
| Wh– Word | *Did* | Subject | Base Verb |
| When | **did** | I | **go** to Tokyo? |
| Where | | you | **go** last night? |
| Why | | he/she/it | **go** out? |
| Who* | | we | **go** out with last week? |
| How (often) | | they | **go** out last week? |

*In formal written English, the wh- word would be *whom*.

See page 404 for a list of irregular verbs.

## 4 Practice

**Complete the sentences with the simple past tense of the verbs in parentheses. Use the list of irregular verbs on page 404.**

Maria Sklodowska was born in Poland. She (have) _____*had*_____ a sister,
<sub>1</sub>

Bronya. Maria was a good student. She (love) _____ science. She and her
<sub>2</sub>

sister (want) _____ to go to college. In those days, women
<sub>3</sub>

(not, go) _____ to college in Poland. So Maria and Bronya
<sub>4</sub>

(decide) _____ to go to Paris to study. It was expensive for two girls to
<sub>5</sub>

study at one time. Bronya (leave) _____ for Paris first. Maria
<sub>6</sub>

(work) _____ as a teacher in Poland. She (send) _____
<sub>7</sub> <sub>8</sub>

money to Bronya. Bronya (finish) _____ her studies, and then she
<sub>9</sub>

(help) _____ Maria to study.
<sub>10</sub>

Maria (become) _____ a student at the Sorbonne University
<sub>11</sub>

in Paris. In Paris, she (change) _____ her name to Marie. She
<sub>12</sub>

(study) _____ science. She (not, have) _____ much money.
<sub>13</sub> <sub>14</sub>

She (live) _____ in a small room. She (climb) _____ six
                    15                                                16
floors to her room. It (not, have) _____ any electricity or water. She
                                            17
(eat) _____ very little.
              18
    One day, she (meet) _____ Pierre Curie, and her life
                                19
(change) _____. They (marry) _____ one year later.
                20                                       21
Pierre was also a scientist. They (work) _____ together a lot. Together they
                                                22
(discover) _____ radium. They (win) _____ a Nobel Prize
                    23                                          24
for the discovery. Three years later, Pierre (die) _____ in an accident.
                                                            25
Marie was very sad, but she (continue) _____ her work. In 1911, she
                                                26
(get) _____ another Nobel Prize. Marie (give) _____
            27                                                      28
her life to her work. She (die) _____ in 1934 from cancer.
                                        29
    Marie (have) _____ a daughter, Irene. Irene
                        30
(continue) _____ her mother's work. She, too,
                    31
(receive) _____ a Nobel Prize. Irene died of cancer, too.
                    32

## 5 | Practice

**Write questions with the prompts and then answer them with short answers.**

**1.** Marie/study in Poland

   *Did Marie study in Poland?* _____

   *No, she didn't.* _____

**2.** women/go to college in Poland

   _____

   _____

**3.** Marie/send her sister money from Poland

   _____

   _____

**4.** Marie/study at the university in Paris

   _____

   _____

**5.** Marie/have a lot of money

   _____

   _____

**6.** Marie/meet Pierre in Paris

_____

_____

**7.** Marie and Pierre/marry

_____

_____

**8.** Marie and Pierre Curie/win the Nobel Prize

_____

_____

**9.** Pierre/die in an accident

_____

_____

**10.** Marie/have a son

_____

_____

**11.** Irene/become an actress

_____

_____

**12.** Irene/receive a Nobel Prize

_____

_____

## 6 | Your Turn

**Tell your classmates or your partner about your life. Use the simple past tense.**

**Example:**
I was born in Peru. When I was two, we went to live in Mexico City.

## 7 | Practice

**Complete the paragraphs with the simple past tense of the verbs in parentheses.**

**A.**

Elvis Presley was born in 1935 in Mississippi. He (spend) _____*spent*_____ a lot
of time with African-American musicians. He (learn) _____ a lot from them.
In 1953, he (pay) _____ to make a record for his mother's birthday. The

owner of the record company (listen) _____ to it and
4
(like) _____ it. Then, he (offer) _____ Elvis work.
5                              6
His first record, in 1954, was a hit. Teenagers (love) _____ it. They
7
(scream) _____ when they saw Elvis. Elvis (record) _____
8                                                      9
94 gold singles. He (star) _____ in 27 films. Elvis continued to be
10
famous, and he (perform) _____ in many concerts. His life
11
(end) _____ sadly. He (die) _____ at the age of 42. Radio
12                                13
stations (play) _____ his songs, and his fans (cry) _____.
14                                                      15

**B.**

James Dean was born in 1931. His mother (die) _____ when he was
1
young. He (live) _____ with his uncle and aunt on their farm. Later, he
2
(study) _____ acting for two years. Then he (start) _____
3                                                      4
to work in theater and the movies. He also (appear) _____ in a TV
5
commercial. In 1954, he (act) _____ in a play. Some important people from
6
Hollywood (like) _____ him in the play. They (offer) _____
7                                                      8
him a movie contract. James Dean (star) _____ in only three films, but
9
he (become) _____ popular. He (die) _____ in a car crash
10                                11
in 1955.

## 2c The Past Progressive Tense

We **were playing** outside.
The sky **was getting** darker.
Then we saw it. A tornado!
It **was coming** this way!

1. We form the past progressive tense with a past form of *be* (*was* or *were*) and verb + *–ing*.

2. See page 406 for spelling rules for *–ing* verb forms.

## AFFIRMATIVE AND NEGATIVE STATEMENTS

| Subject | *Was/Were (Not)* | Verb + *–ing* |
|---------|------------------|---------------|
| I | was<br>was not<br>wasn't | |
| You | were<br>were not<br>weren't | |
| He/She/It | was<br>was not<br>wasn't | **working.** |
| We | were<br>were not<br>weren't | |
| They | were<br>were not<br>weren't | |

## YES/NO QUESTIONS · SHORT ANSWERS

| *Was/Were* | Subject | Verb + *–ing* | Yes, | No, |
|------------|---------|---------------|------|-----|
| **Was** | I | | you **were.** | you **weren't.** |
| **Were** | you | | I **was.** | I **wasn't.** |
| **Was** | he/she/it | **working?** | he/she/it **was.** | he/she/it **wasn't.** |
| | we | | you **were.** | you **weren't.** |
| **Were** | you | | we **were.** | we **weren't.** |
| | they | | they **were.** | they **weren't.** |

## WH– QUESTIONS

| Wh– Word | *Was/Were* | Subject | Verb + *–ing* |
|----------|-----------|---------|---------------|
| **How** (fast) | | the tornado | **moving?** |
| **What** | **was** | I | **saying?** |
| **Who*** | | she | **calling?** |
| **Where** | | you | **going** yesterday? |
| **Why** | **were** | they | **studying** at midnight? |
| **Why** | | they | **sleeping** in class? |

*In formal written English, the wh– word would be *whom*.

We use the past progressive tense to describe an action in progress at a particular time in the past.

We were watching the news on television at 6:00 last night.

**8** Practice

**Complete the sentences with the past progressive tense of the verbs in parentheses.**

1. Last night, television and radio stations (warn) _____ *were warning* _____ people about the tornado.

2. It (get) _____ closer.

3. People (run) _____ for shelter.

4. The tornado (destroy) _____ everything in its way.

5. We (not, watch) _____ television.

6. We (study) _____ in the library.

7. Suddenly the librarian started shouting. She (tell) _____ us to run to the basement.

**9** Practice

**Complete the sentences with the past progressive of the verbs in parentheses.**

Amanda Ferguson (drive) _____ *was driving* _____ to her mother's house. She
                                    1
(not, listen) _____ to the radio. She didn't know that a tornado
                        2
(come) _____ toward her.
                  3
    The sky (get) _____ darker and darker, but she thought
                                  4
it was just an ordinary storm. Suddenly, there was a big noise. It was as dark as

night, and the wind (blow) _____ very hard. Pieces of houses
                                              5
and trees (fly) _____ everywhere. Then she knew what
                        6
(happen) _____. She was inside a tornado!
                    7
    Amanda screamed. Then she saw her mother's house. But she

(look) _____ down at it from 25 feet in the air! Amanda was
                  8
lucky! The tornado dropped the car in her mother's back yard. She lived to tell the story.

## 10 | Practice

**Read the paragraph. Then write wh- questions for the answers. Use the wh- word in parentheses and the past progressive tense.**

> Susan was walking on the beach. She noticed that the wind was blowing very hard. The waves were crashing on the sand. Black clouds were coming toward the land very fast. When she got back to the house, her husband was covering the windows with wood. A hurricane was coming!

1. (where) _Where was Susan walking?_

   Answer: She was walking on the beach.

2. (how hard) _____

   Answer: It was blowing very hard.

3. (where) _____

   Answer: On the sand.

4. (how fast) _____

   Answer: They were coming very fast.

5. (when) _____

   Answer: When she got home.

## 11 | Your Turn

**Say four things that were happening last night at 8:00.**

**Example:**
I was sitting on the sofa in my apartment. My brother was watching television.

## 2d  The Simple Past Tense OR The Past Progressive Tense

Ken Johnson **was riding** his bicycle when a tornado **lifted** him into the air. While he **was flying** through the sky, he **saw** a horse right next to him! The boy **was crying** when the tornado **put** him down safely in a field.

1. We often use the past progressive and simple past tenses together in a sentence. The past progressive describes the longer action that was in progress in the past; the simple past describes the shorter action that happened in the middle of the longer action.

   I **was working** when I **heard** the tornado.

2. We use the simple past, not the past progressive, to show that one action followed another.

   I **picked up** my baby when I **heard** the tornado.
   (First she heard the tornado. Then she picked up her baby.)

3. When one action interrupts another, we use *when* before the simple past action or *while* before the past progressive action.

   I was hiding in the basement **when** the tornado passed over my house.
   **While** I was hiding in the basement, the tornado passed over my house.

4. We can change the order of the parts of a sentence with *when* or *while*.

   **When** the tornado passed over my house, I was hiding in the basement.
   The tornado passed over my house **while** I was hiding in the basement.

   When we begin a sentence with *when* or *while* plus a subject and a verb, we put a comma between the two parts.

5. We use the past progressive with two actions that continued at the same time in the past. We use *while* to show the actions were happening at the same time.

    **While** I was hiding in the basement, my husband was looking for me.

6. Remember, we do not usually use the present progressive tense with nonprogressive verbs. (See page 15.) The same is true for the past progressive tense.

    CORRECT:     We saw the tornado.
    INCORRECT:  We ~~were seeing~~ the tornado.

---

**12** Practice

**Complete the sentences with the simple past or past progressive of the verbs in parentheses.**

It (rain) _____*was raining*_____ very hard when the bus

(leave) _____ the school. When we

(get) _____ home, my Aunt Millie and Uncle Ben

(wait) _____ for us. They (tell) _____

us to run into their storm cellar underground. When I (look) _____

up the road, I (see) _____ that a tornado (come)

_____ toward our house. We all (run) _____

toward the shelter. But it was too late. The tornado (pass) _____

over us while we (try) _____ to get down the stairs.

We (close) _____ the door when the wind suddenly

(pull) _____ it off. The noise was as loud as a train, and

it was very dark. My uncle (hold) _____ me down when suddenly

the tornado (lift) _____ him and threw him against a wall.

Everyone (scream) _____ for help while the tornado

(throw) _____ things on top of us. Suddenly the wind

(stop) _____. It (become) _____ very

quiet. My uncle and sister were hurt, but we all (survive) _____.

Your Turn

One of your classmates did not come to school yesterday. He/she had a cold.
Imagine what he/she was doing while you were studying at school.

**Example:**
While we were doing exercises in our English class, my classmate was resting in bed.

## 2e Past Time Clauses

### Form / Function

**When young Mozart played,**
everyone listened.

1. A clause is a group of words with a subject and a verb. Some clauses are main clauses. A main clause can stand alone as a complete sentence. This sentence is a main clause.

   Mozart played for the queen.

2. Time clauses start with words like *when, while, before,* or *after.* Time clauses are dependent clauses. We must use dependent clauses with a main clause.

| Main Clause | Time Clause |
|---|---|
| Everyone listened | **when he played.** |

3. We can put a time clause at the beginning or the end of a sentence. If the time clause comes first, we use a comma after it.

**While he was speaking,** he stood up.
He stood up **while he was speaking.**

**Before he took the money,** he counted it.
He counted the money **before he took it.**

4. In a sentence with a clause starting with *when,* both verbs can be in the simple past tense.

**When** they **asked,** he **sang.**
(First they asked. Then he sang.)

## |14| Practice

**Complete the sentences with the correct form of the verbs in parentheses.**

Mozart was born in Austria in 1756. When he (be) _____ *was* _____
                                                              **1**
four years old, he (start) _____ to play the piano. His father
                                    **2**
(teach) _____ him. Before he (be) _____
              **3**                                              **4**
five, he (begin) _____ to write music. When he
                          **5**
(be) _____ six, he (give) _____ concerts all
          **6**                                      **7**
over Europe. He (play) _____ for important people like kings and
                                **8**
queens. They (pay) _____ a lot of money to hear him. Mozart's
                            **9**
family (need) _____ the money to live. Once, he
                      **10**
(go) _____ to Vienna and (play) _____
          **11**                                          **12**
for the Empress Maria Theresa. She (love) _____ Mozart's playing.
                                                      **13**
When he (finish) _____, he (climb) _____
                          **14**                                        **15**
up on her knee and (give) _____ her a kiss.
                                    **16**
        When he (be) _____ 11, he
                              **17**
(write) _____ an opera. One time, when
                **18**
he (be) _____ 14 years old, he
                  **19**
(hear) _____ music in the Sistine Chapel in Rome. When
              **20**

he (get) _____ home, he (remember) _____

everything and (write) _____ it down exactly.

Mozart (marry) _____ Constanze Weber. They

(be) _____ happy together and (have) _____

six children. Mozart (work) _____ hard because he always

(have) _____ money problems. He

(begin) _____ to work in the evening and often

(work) _____ all night. He (like) _____

to write while he (stand) _____ up. He

(sleep) _____ very little. Mozart (die) _____

at the age of 35. No one (go) _____ to his funeral.

## 15 Your Turn

**Say four things you did after you went home yesterday.**

**Example:**
After I went home yesterday, I changed my clothes.

# 2f  Used To

Three hundred years ago, life in North America was very different. People **used to carry** lanterns for light. They **didn't use to have** electricity.

*Used to* + base verb takes the same form in all persons.

| AFFIRMATIVE STATEMENTS | | NEGATIVE STATEMENTS | |
|---|---|---|---|
| Subject | *Used To* + Base Verb | Subject | *Didn't Use To* + Base Verb |
| I | | I | |
| You | | You | |
| He/She/It | **used to work** hard. | He/She/It | **didn't use to work** hard. |
| We | | We | |
| They | | They | |

| YES/NO QUESTIONS | | | SHORT ANSWERS | |
|---|---|---|---|---|
| *Did* | Subject | *Use To* + Base Verb | Yes, | No, |
| | I | | you **did.** | you **didn't.** |
| | you | | I/we **did.** | I/we **didn't.** |
| **Did** | he/she/it | **use to work** hard? | he/she/it **did.** | he/she/it **didn't.** |
| | we | | you **did.** | you **didn't.** |
| | they | | they **did.** | they **didn't.** |

## Function

We use *used to* when we want to emphasize the fact that a habit or situation no longer exists.

> Most people **used to walk** or ride horses. Today they drive cars.
> They **used to wash** clothes by hand. Today they have washing machines.
> They **didn't use to drink** water because it often wasn't clean. Today people can drink water because it is clean.

## 16 Practice

**Rewrite the sentences using *used to* or *did/didn't use to*.**

1. Did people wash a lot?

   *Did people use to wash a lot?*

2. No, people didn't wash very often.

   *No, people didn't use to wash very often.*

3. Why didn't they wash often?

   *Why didn't they use to wash often?*

4. They didn't have water inside the house.

   _____

**5.** Did people live for a long time?

_____

**6.** No, most people lived a short life.

_____

**7.** They didn't have many doctors.

_____

**8.** A doctor visited a town a few times a year.

_____

**9.** Mothers made medicines for the family from plants.

_____

**10.** Most of the medicines tasted bad.

_____

**11.** Some of these medicines killed people.

_____

## 17 Practice

**Rewrite the sentences using _used to_ or _did/didn't use to._**

Life was very different in the early English colonies in North America from the way it is today.

**1.** How did people eat?

_How did people use to eat?_

**2.** Did people eat with their fingers?

_____

**3.** Yes, they did. It was good manners to eat with your fingers.

_____

**4.** In many homes, there was one big pot on the table.

_____

**5.** People put their fingers into the pot to take out food.

_____

**6.** People didn't have plates.

_____

**7.** They used a wooden board.

_____

**8.** Did children eat with the father and mother?

_____

**9.** Yes, they did. But children didn't talk at the table. They didn't even sit down.

_____

_____

**10.** Did they stand up through the whole meal?

_____

**11.** Yes, children stood up through the whole meal.

_____

**12.** What did people do when they had a toothache?

_____

**13.** People went to the barber when they had a toothache. Barbers pulled teeth.

_____

_____

**14.** What furniture did they have then?

_____

**15.** They didn't have much furniture in the 1600s.

_____

**16.** Many families had only one chair.

_____

**17.** Where did the father sit?

_____

**18.** The father always sat in the chair.

_____

|18| Practice

**Find and correct the errors in the underlined parts of the sentences. Some sentences have no errors. Tommy's grandparents live on a farm far away. He is going to visit them for the first time. He is asking his mother questions.**

Tommy:     How do they cook their food? Do they use wood?

                         _used to burn_
Mother:     No. They ~~used burn~~ wood in the stove, but now they have electricity.
                   1

Tommy:      <u>Did they used to buy</u> their wood?
            **2**

Mother:     No, they didn't. They <u>used to cut</u> it themselves.
                                        **3**

Tommy:      <u>Used they to grow</u> their own food?
            **4**

Mother:     Yes, they did. They <u>use to grow</u> almost everything. But now they buy many
                                        **5**

            things at the store.

Tommy:      Where do they get their water?

Mother:     Well, they <u>use get</u> it from a stream, but now they have a well.
                            **6**

Tommy:      Do they have lots of animals?

Mother:     Only a few. They <u>used to have</u> lots of animals.
                                **7**

Tommy:      <u>What animals used they have?</u>
                            **8**

Mother:     They <u>use to have</u> lots of chickens, cows, and goats.
                        **9**

Tommy:      What <u>did you used do</u> for fun when you were little?
                        **10**

Mother:     Oh, we <u>used to sing,</u> play games, read, and listen to the radio.
                        **11**

Tommy:      Will I be able to watch television?

Mother:     Of course. They <u>didn't used to have</u> television, but they do now.
                                **12**

**Your Turn**

**A. Write four things you used to do as a child that you do not do now.**

**Example:**
When I was a child, I used to cry a lot. Now I don't.

1. _____

2. _____

3. _____

4. _____

**B. Share your sentences with a partner. Then write four things that your partner said.**

**Example:**
When she was a child, she used to climb trees.

1. _____

2. _____

3. _____

4. _____

# WRITING: Describe a Time in the Past

Write a description of life in your country 100 years ago.

**Step 1. Work with a partner. Ask and answer questions about life 100 years ago. The prompts below will help you, or you can use your own ideas.**

**Example:**
go out at night a lot
You:          Did people use to go out at night a lot?
Your partner: No, they didn't. They sometimes used to go to concerts or the theater.

1. go out at night a lot
2. cook on a stove that burns wood
3. go to the movies together
4. eat at home
5. watch television

6. listen to the radio
7. read magazines
8. play games at home
9. wear different clothes

**Step 2. Write the answers to the questions. Then rewrite the answers in paragraph form. Write a title in a few words (Life One Hundred Years Ago). For more writing guidelines, see pages 407–411.**

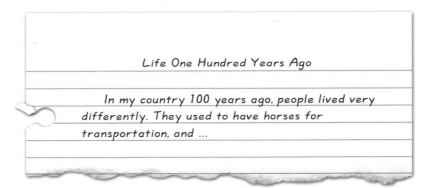

*Life One Hundred Years Ago*

*In my country 100 years ago, people lived very differently. They used to have horses for transportation, and ...*

**Step 3. Evaluate your paragraph.**

**Checklist**

_____ Did you indent the first line?

_____ Did you give your paragraph a title?

_____ Did you put the title in the center of the page?

**Step 4. Edit your work. Work with your partner or your teacher to edit your sentences. Correct spelling, punctuation, vocabulary, and grammar.**

**Step 5. Write your final copy.**

# SELF-TEST

**A**  **Choose the best answer, A, B, C, or D, to complete the sentence. Mark your answer by darkening the oval with the same letter.**

1. Ken _____ in a rock group, but now he doesn't.

   **A.** sang          Ⓐ Ⓑ Ⓒ Ⓓ
   **B.** sung
   **C.** used to sing
   **D.** was singing

2. When the earthquake struck, people _____.

   **A.** slept          Ⓐ Ⓑ Ⓒ Ⓓ
   **B.** used to sleep
   **C.** are sleeping
   **D.** were sleeping

3. Alexander Graham Bell _____ the telephone in 1876.

   **A.** invent         Ⓐ Ⓑ Ⓒ Ⓓ
   **B.** invented
   **C.** used to invent
   **D.** were inventing

4. It _____ while people were waiting for the bus.

   **A.** is raining      Ⓐ Ⓑ Ⓒ Ⓓ
   **B.** rains
   **C.** used to rain
   **D.** was raining

5. Early colonists _____ to wash a lot.

   **A.** did not use     Ⓐ Ⓑ Ⓒ Ⓓ
   **B.** did not used
   **C.** used not
   **D.** did use not

6. Why _____ young?

   **A.** people died     Ⓐ Ⓑ Ⓒ Ⓓ
   **B.** died people
   **C.** did people die
   **D.** people did die

7. _____ have doctors in 1800?

   **A.** Used they to    Ⓐ Ⓑ Ⓒ Ⓓ
   **B.** Did they use to
   **C.** Did they used to
   **D.** Did use to they

8. The students were taking the test when they _____ the noise.

   **A.** were hearing    Ⓐ Ⓑ Ⓒ Ⓓ
   **B.** were heard
   **C.** hear
   **D.** heard

9. What _____ last night?

   **A.** you did         Ⓐ Ⓑ Ⓒ Ⓓ
   **B.** you did do
   **C.** did you do
   **D.** you do

10. While the spectators _____ the game, part of the stadium collapsed.

    **A.** were watching   Ⓐ Ⓑ Ⓒ Ⓓ
    **B.** watching
    **C.** watched
    **D.** was watching

**B** Find the underlined word or phrase, A, B, C, or D, that is incorrect. Mark your answer by darkening the oval with the same letter.

1. When Van Gogh moved from Holland to
     A           B                  C
   France, he start to paint with bright colors.
           D

   (A) (B) (C) (D)

2. While Marie studying at the university,
     A          B    C
   she married Pierre Curie.
       D

   (A) (B) (C) (D)

3. Harriet Beecher Stowe worked on her
                     A
   book after everyone was going to bed.
        B           C    D

   (A) (B) (C) (D)

4. Charles Lindberg flown alone across the
                 A         B   C
   Atlantic Ocean in 1927.
              D

   (A) (B) (C) (D)

5. Louis Braille invented a system of writing
             A
   for blind people when he was teaching in
    B         C      D
   a school for them.

   (A) (B) (C) (D)

6. When Franklin D. Roosevelt become
     A                    B
   president, the United States was suffering
            C         D
   from hard times.

   (A) (B) (C) (D)

7. When the Englishman Scott reached the
     A                B
   South Pole, he seen the Norwegian flag.
            C     D

   (A) (B) (C) (D)

8. When the German immigrants arrived in
     A                B
   the United States in the 1800s, they
                       C
   were bringing the hamburger steak
       D
   with them.

   (A) (B) (C) (D)

9. While he was hiking in the Alps,
     A     B
   Georges de Mestral was getting the idea
                 C
   for Velcro.®
    D

   (A) (B) (C) (D)

10. In ancient Rome, a wife use to wear her
                  A       B
    gold ring in public, but at home she wore
                    C      D
    a ring made of iron.

    (A) (B) (C) (D)

# UNIT 3

## THE FUTURE TENSES

# 3a  *Be Going To*

The astronauts are in the spacecraft. The engines are making a loud noise. Everyone is counting 10, 9, 8, 7. In a few seconds, the spacecraft **is going to take off.** It **is going to travel** in space for 30 days. The astronauts **are not going to visit** other planets.

| AFFIRMATIVE AND NEGATIVE STATEMENTS, FULL FORMS, AND CONTRACTIONS | | | |
|---|---|---|---|
| Subject | *Am/Is/Are (Not)* | *Going To* | Base Verb |
| I | am<br>'m<br><br>am not<br>'m not | | |
| You | are<br>'re<br><br>are not<br>'re not<br>aren't | | |
| He/She/It | is<br>'s<br><br>is not<br>'s not<br>isn't | going to | leave. |
| We | are<br>'re | | |
| They | are not<br>'re not<br>aren't | | |

| YES/NO QUESTIONS | | | | SHORT ANSWERS | |
|---|---|---|---|---|---|
| *Am/Is/Are* | Subject | *Going To* | Base Verb | Yes, | No, |
| **Am** | I | | | you **are.** | you**'re not.** you **aren't.** |
| **Are** | you | | | I **am.** | I**'m not.** |
| **Is** | he/she/it | **going to** | **leave?** | he/she/it **is.** | he/she/it**'s not.** he/she/it **isn't.** |
| | we | | | you **are.** | you**'re not.** you **aren't.** |
| **Are** | you | | | we **are.** | we**'re not.** we **aren't.** |
| | they | | | they **are.** | they**'re not.** they **aren't.** |

Note: We often pronounce *going to* as "gonna."

## Function

1. We use *be going to* + a base verb to talk about plans for the future.

   The astronaut **is going to do** some experiments in space.
   The spacecraft **is going to travel** in space for 30 days.

2. We use *be going to* + a base verb to talk about something in the future that we can see as a result of something in the present.

   The engines are making a loud noise. In a few seconds, the spacecraft **is going to take** off.

   Be careful! You**'re going to fall!**

## 1 Practice

**Complete the sentences with the *be going to* form of the verb in parentheses.**

In a minute, the astronauts (enter) _____ *are going to enter* _____
                                              1
the spacecraft. The air in the spacecraft is different. The astronauts

(not, have) _____ any weight. They
                        2
(do) _____ everyday things in a different way.
              3
They (not, sleep) _____ in regular beds. They
                              4
(sleep) _____ in hanging beds. They
                  5

(fold) _____ their arms when they sleep. This holds their
                    6

arms in place. It (be) _____ difficult to take a shower.
                              7

It (take) _____ a long time because they need special
                    8

equipment.

## 2 Practice

**What is going to happen in these situations on a spacecraft? Write a question and a negative answer with _be going to_. Use the prompts in parentheses.**

1. One astronaut misses her family. She picks up a special phone.

   (call, her boss) _Is she going to call her boss?_

   _No, she is going to call her family._

2. Today's astronauts have free time. Astronaut Robert Barnes has some music on CDs with him.

   (listen, to a baseball game) _____

   _____

3. Astronaut Nadia Smith likes to look at the Earth from the window. She has some free time in half an hour.

   (watch, television) _____

   _____

4. It's time for lunch. The astronauts have special trays in front of them like airplane food.

   (eat, breakfast) _____

   _____

5. Robert is putting on a special suit. He plans to take a walk in space.

   (take a walk, inside the station) _____

   _____

6. Nadia feels tired. She didn't sleep well.

   (rest, tomorrow) _____

   _____

## 3 Your Turn

**Tell your partner five things you are going to do when you go home today. Then tell the class what your partner is going to do.**

**Example:**
I'm going to relax, and then I'm going to do my homework.

# 3b *Will*

## Form

Scientists want to build colonies in space in the future. The first colony **will be** 240,000 miles from Earth. Thousands of people **will live** and **work** in the colony.

### AFFIRMATIVE AND NEGATIVE STATEMENTS

| Subject | Will (Not) | Base Verb |
|---------|------------|-----------|
| I | **will** | |
| You | **'ll** | |
| He/She/It | | **leave.** |
| We | **will not** | |
| They | **won't** | |

| YES/NO QUESTIONS | | | SHORT ANSWERS | |
|------|---------|-----------|------|------|
| Will | Subject | Base Verb | Yes, | No, |
| | I | | you **will.** | you **won't.** |
| | you | | I/we **will.** | I/we **won't.** |
| **Will** | he/she/it | **leave?** | he/she/it **will.** | he/she/it **won't.** |
| | we | | you **will.** | you **won't.** |
| | they | | they **will.** | they **won't.** |

## Function

1. We use *will* + a base verb to make predictions about the future or what we think will happen.

   People **will live** in space colonies.
   There **won't be** any pollution in space colonies.

2. We use *will* when we decide to do something at the moment of speaking.

> A: We need some help here.
> B: OK. I**'ll be** there in 10 minutes.
>
> A: Which one do you want? The red one or the blue one?
> B: I**'ll take** the red one.

3. We often use *probably* with *will*. *Probably* usually comes between *will* and the base verb.

> I**'ll probably see** you tomorrow.
> Olga **will probably call** us tonight.
> She**'ll probably not call** us tomorrow.
> OR She **probably won't call** us tomorrow.

4. We can use verbs like *intend, hope,* and *plan* to express future events and situations. Use the simple present tense followed by an infinitive (*to* + base verb).

> They **plan** (now) **to build** a colony in space (in the future).

## 4 | Practice

**Complete the sentences with *will* or the simple present of the verbs in parentheses.**

1. Space colonies (be) _____ *will be* _____ islands in space.

2. They (not, be) _____ on planets. They (be) _____
   in space.

3. A space colony (not, have) _____ bad weather.

4. The people (control) _____ the weather in the colony.

5. A space colony (look) _____ like a wheel in space.

6. Scientists (intend) _____ to have more than 10,000 people on
   the colony.

7. They (plan) _____ to have animals on the colony.

8. The colony (not, need) _____ gasoline.

9. Cars (run) _____ on electricity.

10. Scientists think it (take) _____ 25 years to build a space colony.

11. It (cost) _____ hundreds of billions of dollars.

12. They (hope) _____ to build the colony in this century.

Practice

Andy is 16 years old now. What will he be like 10 years from now? Use the prompts and *will* or *won't* to write sentences that Andy could say about himself.

1. I/probably/have a job

   *I'll probably have a job.*

2. I/be married

   _____

3. I/probably/have children

   _____

4. I/not/be/a millionaire

   _____

5. I/not/look the same as I do now

   _____

6. I/probably/have a nice car

   _____

7. I/probably/live in an apartment

   _____

8. I/probably/not/live in the city

   _____

### 6 Your Turn

Say which of the sentences in Practice 5 will be true for you.

**Example:**
I will probably have a job.

### 7 Your Turn

What do you intend to do tonight? What do you hope to do next week? What do you plan to do next summer?

**Example:**
I intend to call my family tonight.

## 3c  *Be Going To* OR *Will*

### Function

"I**'ll take** 10 oranges, please."

"Look! It**'s going to rain.**"

| Will | Be Going To |
|---|---|
| 1. We use *will* for actions that we decide at the moment of speaking. <br><br> A: The tomato sauce splashed all over my shirt. <br> B: Don't worry. I**'ll clean** it for you. | 1. We use *be going to* for actions that we have already decided to do. <br><br> A: Why are you moving the furniture? <br> B: I**'m going to clean** the floor. |
| 2. We use *will* to talk about things that we think or believe will happen in the future. <br><br> A: It's time for the news on television. <br> B: Let's watch it. I think it **will be** interesting. | 2. We use *be going to* to talk about something in the future that will be a result of something in the present. <br><br> A: I want to watch the news. <br> I**'m going to turn** on the television. |

**8** | Practice

**Complete the sentences with *be going to* or *will* and the verbs in parentheses.**

**A.**

A: My father is coming to dinner tonight, so I (make) <u>*am going to make*</u> a
   <sub>1</sub>

   special dessert. Oh no! I don't have any sugar. Can you go to the store for me?

B: Sure, I (go) _____.
   <sub>2</sub>

A: Take an umbrella with you. Look at the sky! It (rain) _____.
   <sub>3</sub>

B: This umbrella is broken. I (take) _____ your umbrella, OK?
   <sub>4</sub>

**B.**

A: I (go) _____ to the new mall tomorrow.
   <sub>1</sub>

B: Oh, what (get) _____ you _____?
   <sub>2</sub>                    <sub>3</sub>

A: I (look) _____ for a pair of brown shoes.
   <sub>4</sub>

B: I'm free tomorrow. I (go) _____ with you.
   <sub>5</sub>

**C.**

A: We (have) _____ a meeting at 5:00 tomorrow.
   <sub>1</sub>

B: OK. I (see) _____ you there.
   <sub>2</sub>

**D.**

A: What (do) _____ you _____ for your vacation this summer?
   <sub>1</sub>                    <sub>2</sub>

B: I don't know. I (probably, spend) _____ my vacation with
   <sub>3</sub>

   my parents. They (rent) _____ a small house by the beach
   <sub>4</sub>

   for a month.

**E.**

A: I (leave) _____ at 4:30. The traffic is really bad on Friday
   <sub>1</sub>

   evenings.

B: You're right. I think I (do) _____ the same.
   <sub>2</sub>

**Complete the sentences with *will* or *be going to* and the verbs in parentheses.**

1.  Thanks for lending me this book. I (give) _____'ll give_____ it back to you

    when I see you again.

2.  A:  I have a terrible headache.

    B:  Wait. I (get) _____ an aspirin for you.

3.  Don't make so much noise. You (wake) _____ everybody up.

4.  This plant is not growing. It does not look good. I think it (die)

    _____.

5.  This food looks terrible. I (not, eat) _____ it.

6.  Look at that smoke! That battery (blow up) _____!

7.  Don't worry about the mess. I (clean) _____ it up.

# 3d  The Present Progressive Tense to Express Future Time

John is in a hurry. He**'s giving** a presentation to his boss in fifteen minutes, and at 12:00 he**'s leaving** for Texas.

We can use the present progressive to talk about future plans.

## 10 Practice

**Look at Janet's schedule for next week. Then use the present progressive tense to complete the sentences about her plans.**

## Schedule

| | | |
|---|---|---|
| Monday: | | Have lunch with John at 1:00. Go to gym after work. |
| Tuesday: | | Attend meetings from 8:00 to 4:00. |
| Wednesday: | | Go to the doctor at 1:30. |
| Thursday: | | Pick up photos at 6:00. |
| Friday: | | Meet Pamela outside the movie theater at 7:00. |
| Saturday: | | Go to Ken and Stella's house for dinner at 7:30. |
| Sunday: | | Play tennis with Mary at 10:00. |

1. _She's having lunch with John_ _____ at 1:00.

2. _____ after work on Monday.

3. _____ from 8:00 to 4:00 on Tuesday.

4. _____ at 1:30 on Wednesday.

5. _____ at 6:00 on Thursday.

6. _____ outside the movie theater at 7:00 on Friday.

7. _____ for dinner at 7:30 on Saturday.

8. _____ at 10:00 on Sunday.

## II Practice

Look at Jim's schedule for tomorrow. Then complete the conversation about his plans with the present progressive of the verbs in parentheses.

### Schedule

| | |
|---|---|
| 8:00 | Leave the house for the airport |
| 9:30 | Catch the plane to San Francisco |
| 12:00 | Have lunch with Carlos at the Blue Moon Restaurant |
| 2:00 | Go to the San Francisco office and work until 5:00 |
| 6:00 | Meet Judy in the office lobby |
| 6:30 | Have dinner with Judy and Dave at the Prado restaurant |
| 9:30 | Catch the plane back home |

Ken: What (do) _____are_____ you _____doing_____
                         **1**                     **2**
      tomorrow Jim?

Jim: I (go) _____ to San Francisco.
                         **3**

Ken: What time (leave) _____ you _____?
                       **4**                     **5**

Jim: I (leave) _____ home at 8:00 in the morning.
                       **6**

Ken: What time (fly) _____ you _____?
                   **7**                  **8**

Jim: At 9:30. I (have) _____ lunch with Carlos at 12:00 in San
                           **9**
      Francisco.

Ken: Where (eat) _____ you _____?
                 **10**                **11**

Jim: At the Blue Moon restaurant. Then I (go) _____ to the
                                     **12**
      office. I (work) _____ at the office until 5:00. Then I
                       **13**
      (meet) _____ Judy at 6:00.
                     **14**

Ken: Where (go) _____ you _____?
           15                              16

Jim: We (have) _____ dinner at the Prado restaurant. Dave
                        17

(come) _____, too.
              18

Ken: That's a busy day. When (come) _____ you
                                          19

_____ back?
          20

Jim: I (catch) _____ a flight at 9:30.
                        21

## 12 Your Turn

**Work with a partner. Ask and answer questions about today and tomorrow.**

**Example:**
You:            Where are you going after class?
Your partner: I'm going to the library.

1. Where are you going after class?
2. How are you getting there?
3. What time are you leaving home tomorrow?
4. Are you meeting anyone today or tomorrow?
5. What are you doing this evening?

# 3e  The Simple Present Tense to Express Future Time

**Function**

School **starts** on January 8th.
The semester **ends** on June 5th.

We use the simple present for the future when it is part of a timetable or planned on a calendar.

The flight **arrives** at 10:30 tomorrow.
The train from the airport **leaves** at 11:00.

## 13 Practice

**Look at today's program for a school group's trip to Disney World. Use the verbs from the list to write about their day. Use the verb *have* two times. Use the simple present tense.**

arrive      depart      have      leave      return      take

Dear Parents:
　　Here is the schedule for your child's trip to Disney World on Saturday, May 1.

| | |
|---|---|
| **8:00** | Take the bus to Disney World |
| **11:30** | Arrive at Disney World |
| **12:00** | Lunch |
| **1:00** | Tour of Disney World |
| **5:30** | Depart for home |
| **6:00** | Sandwiches and drinks on the bus |
| **9:00** | Arrive at school |

_____          _____
Date　　　　　　　　　　　　　　　　　　　　　Signature

1. *The children leave for Disney World* _____ at 8:00.

2. *They* _____ at 11:30.

3. _____ at 12:00.

4. _____ from 1:00 to 5:00.

5. _____ at 5:30.

6. _____ at 6:00.

7. _____ at 9:00.

## 14 Practice

**Complete the sentences with the simple present or the present progressive of the verbs in parentheses.**

1. This afternoon, I (watch) _____*am watching*_____ television. The big game
   $_{1}$

   (start) _____ at noon. Then my favorite quiz show
   $_{2}$

   (begin) _____ at 4:00.
   $_{3}$

2. The final exam (start) _____ at 10:00 tomorrow and
   $_{4}$

   (end) _____ at 12:00.
   $_{5}$

3. My flight (arrive) _____ at 3:30 tomorrow, and then I
   $_{6}$

   (take) _____ a taxi to the hotel.
   $_{7}$

**4.** The bank (open) _____ at 9:00 in the morning and
8

(close) _____ at 5:00 in the afternoon.
9

**5.** I (have) _____ dinner with Ben tonight. We
10

(meet) _____ after work.
11

**6.** Jenny (leave) _____ her job at the end of the week. She
12

(take) _____ a vacation before she looks for another one.
13

**7.** I (buy) _____ a new car this week. Then I
14

(drive) _____ to Canada for my vacation.
15

**8.** Do you remember that I (give) _____ a birthday party for
16

Sandy? (come) _____ you _____?
17              18

# 3f   The Future Conditional

**Form / Function**

If I **go** to the library, **I'll study.**
If I **study** hard, **I'll pass** the test.

1. A conditional sentence has a main clause and a dependent clause that starts with *if*. The *if* clause expresses a condition. The main clause gives the result. Conditional sentences about future events or situations use the simple present tense in the *if* clause and the future tense in the main clause.

| *If* Clause—Present Tense | Main Clause—Future Tense |
| --- | --- |
| If I **study** hard, | I **will pass** the test. |
| If you **don't study,** | you **will fail.** |
| If he **fails,** | his parents **won't give** him any money. |
| If we **don't go** out, | we**'ll have** more time to study. |
| If they **don't pass,** | they**'ll repeat** the class. |

2. An *if* clause can come before or after the main clause. The meaning is the same. When the *if* clause comes first, we put a comma (,) after it.

    **If you don't study,** you will fail.
    You will fail **if you don't study.**

3. We use future conditional sentences to talk about events or situations that can possibly happen in the future.

    If I see Yuko tomorrow, I'll borrow her notes.
    If she gets an A, she'll be very happy.

## 15 Practice

**Write sentences about what Katerina and Paolo hope will happen in the future. Use the result of one sentence as the condition of the next. Use results from the lists that make sense.**

### Katerina

| | |
|---|---|
| become a dentist | pass her high school exams |
| earn a lot of money | study dentistry |
| go to the university | study more |

| Condition | Result |
|---|---|
| **1.** If she doesn't go out before the test, | *she'll study more.* |
| **2.** *If she studies more,* | *she'll* |
| **3.** | |
| **4.** | |
| **5.** | |
| **6.** | |

### Paolo

| | |
|---|---|
| buy other businesses | retire when he's thirty-five |
| get a job | save money |
| make a lot of money | start his own business |

| Condition | Result |
|---|---|
| **1.** If he graduates this year, | *he'll get a job.* |
| **2.** | |
| **3.** | |
| **4.** | |
| **5.** | |
| **6.** | |

## 16 Practice

**Work with a partner. Ask and answer questions about Katerina and Paolo.**

**Example:**
You:            What will Katerina do if she goes to the university?
Your partner:  She'll study dentistry.

## 3g  Future Time Clauses

We'll walk on Tower Bridge
**before we go to Big Ben.**

**After we walk on Tower Bridge,**
we'll go to Big Ben.

1. A future time clause can begin with conjunctions such as *before, after, as soon as,* or *when*. We usually use the simple present, not *will* or *going to*, in the time clause.

| FUTURE TIME CLAUSE | | | MAIN CLAUSE | |
|---|---|---|---|---|
| Conjunction | Subject | Simple Present Tense Verb | Subject | Future Tense Verb |
| Before | I | **go** to London, | I | **will get** some British money. |
| When | she | **goes** to London, | she | **will spend** a lot. |
| After | they | **visit** the sights, | they | **will go** shopping. |
| As soon as | we | **arrive,** | we | **will call** you. |

2. A future time clause is a dependent clause. It must be used with a main clause.

   CORRECT:    When I get there, I will call you.
   INCORRECT: ~~When I get there.~~

3. We can put the time clause before or after the main clause. They both have the same meaning. When the time clause comes first, we put a comma after it.

   **As soon as we arrive**, we'll call you.
   We'll call you **as soon as we arrive.**

## 17 Practice

**Anne and Paul are planning a trip to London. Complete the sentences with the correct form of the verbs in parentheses.**

1. They (get) _____*will get*_____ some traveler's checks before they
   (leave) _____*leave*_____.

2. Anne (make) _____ a list of all the interesting places to
   visit before they (go) _____.

3. When they (get) _____ to London, they
   (stay) _____ at the Clifton Hotel. It's a small hotel in
   the center of London.

4. As soon as they (arrive) _____ at the hotel, they
   (call) _____ us.

5. When they (be) _____ in London, they
   (not, go) _____ to other towns.

6. They (not, have) _____ time to see everything before
   they (leave) _____.

7. After they (visit) _____ the sites, they
   (go) _____ shopping.

8. When they (walk) _____ around London, they
   (take) _____ photos.

9. They (take) _____ the subway or the bus when they
   (visit) _____ places.

10. When they (get) _____ tired, they
    (take) _____ a taxi.

11. After they (walk) _____ on Tower Bridge, they
    (go) _____ to see Big Ben, the clock.

12. When they (be) _____ hungry, they
    (eat) _____ some fish and chips.

**13.** If it (rain) _____ hard, they

(visit) _____ the British Museum.

**14.** When they (leave) _____ the hotel in the morning,

they (take) _____ their umbrellas with them.

**15.** After they (see) _____ Big Ben, they

(buy) _____ tickets to see a play.

**16.** If they (not, get) _____ tickets to the theater, they

(go) _____ to the ballet.

**17.** If they (have) _____ any time left, they

(take) _____ a ride on a boat on the river.

**18.** When Anne (go) _____ shopping, she

(spend) _____ a lot of money.

**19.** She (buy) _____ an English teapot when she

(see) _____ one.

**20.** They (get) _____ lots of souvenirs before they

(leave) _____ .

## 18 Practice

**Find the errors in the sentences and rewrite them correctly. If a sentences has no errors, write *No change*.**

**1.** If I get some time off this winter, I go to Arizona for a vacation.

*If I get some time off this winter, I will go to Arizona*

*for a vacation.*

**2.** It will be warm, when I get to Phoenix.

_____

**3.** As soon as I will arrive, I will put on light clothes and walk in the sun.

_____

**4.** After I visit the sights in Phoenix I will rent a car and drive to the Grand Canyon.

_____

**5.** I take a lot of pictures as soon as I will get there.

_____

**6.** I will hike to the bottom of the canyon if I have time.

_____

**7.** When I get back to Phoenix I will play golf for a day or two.

_____

**8.** Before I will leave, I visit the Heard Museum.

_____

**9.** When I get on the airplane to go home, I will think, "It's going to be cold in Chicago!"

_____

## 19 Your Turn

**Make predictions for the next five years about a famous person or yourself.**

**Example:**
Madonna will have another baby.

## 20 Your Turn

**Tell your partner three things that you think will happen in your future. Use sentences with future time clauses.**

**Example:**
After I finish this course, I'll look for a good job.

## 21 Your Turn

**Work with a partner. Think of three superstitions. Tell them to the class using _if_ and the future tense.**

**Example:**
In my country, if you see a black cat, you will have bad luck.

# WRITING: Describe a Future City

Write a paragraph about the city of the future.

**Step 1. Work with a partner. Ask and answer questions about the city of the future. Write the answers. These prompts may help you.**

1.  What kind of buildings will it have?
2.  What kind of transportation will people use?
3.  What kind of weather will it have?
4.  What kind of places for sports will it have?
5.  How will they control crime?
6.  Will there be animals?
7.  Will people live and work in the same city?
8.  Will there be stores?
9.  Will people go to restaurants?
10. Will people go to movies?
11. How clean will the city be?
12. What kind of people will live in this city?

**Step 2. Rewrite your answers in paragraph form. Write a title in a few words (The City of the Future). For more writing guidelines, see pages 407–411.**

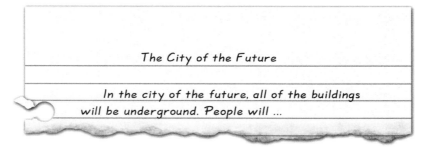

The City of the Future

In the city of the future, all of the buildings
will be underground. People will ...

**Step 3. Evaluate your paragraph.**

**Checklist**

_____ Did you indent the first line?

_____ Did you give your paragraph a title?

_____ Did you put the title in the middle of the page?

_____ Did you capitalize the title correctly?

**Step 4. Edit your work. Work with a partner or your teacher to edit your sentences. Correct spelling, punctuation, vocabulary, and grammar.**

**Step 5. Write your final copy.**

# SELF-TEST

A   Choose the best answer, A, B, C, or D, to complete the sentence. Mark your answer by darkening the oval with the same letter.

1. I _____ with the administrator at 3:00 this afternoon.

   A. will going to meet   Ⓐ Ⓑ Ⓒ Ⓓ
   B. going meet
   C. am going to meet
   D. will to meet

2. They _____ to finish the construction next year.

   A. intend   Ⓐ Ⓑ Ⓒ Ⓓ
   B. are going to intend
   C. will intend
   D. intending

3. She'll call me when she _____ at the airport.

   A. will arrive   Ⓐ Ⓑ Ⓒ Ⓓ
   B. is arriving
   C. is going to arrive
   D. arrives

4. People _____ gasoline cars in the future.

   A. won't drive probably   Ⓐ Ⓑ Ⓒ Ⓓ
   B. are going to probably not drive
   C. probably won't drive
   D. are not driving probably

5. The bank _____ at ten o'clock.

   A. will to open   Ⓐ Ⓑ Ⓒ Ⓓ
   B. open
   C. going to open
   D. opens

6. Before I take the test tomorrow, I _____ my notes.

   A. review   Ⓐ Ⓑ Ⓒ Ⓓ
   B. do reviewing
   C. will review
   D. will to review

7. If it snows tomorrow, we _____ problems.

   A. are having   Ⓐ Ⓑ Ⓒ Ⓓ
   B. had
   C. have
   D. will have

8. I leave for Bangkok tomorrow. The conference _____ on Monday.

   A. starts   Ⓐ Ⓑ Ⓒ Ⓓ
   B. going to start
   C. will start
   D. starting

9. In the future, people _____ in underground cities.

   A. will live   Ⓐ Ⓑ Ⓒ Ⓓ
   B. live
   C. are living
   D. going to live

10. Architects _____ the plan will not have any problems.

   A. will hope   Ⓐ Ⓑ Ⓒ Ⓓ
   B. hoping
   C. are hope
   D. hope

**B** Find the underlined word or phrase, A, B, C, or D, that is incorrect. Mark your answer by darkening the oval with the same letter.

1. NASA <u>be</u> <u>planning</u> <u>to send</u> astronauts
        A     B     C
   <u>to</u> Mars in this century.
   D

   Ⓐ Ⓑ Ⓒ Ⓓ

2. <u>The scientists</u> <u>will</u> <u>hope</u> <u>to build</u> a space
        A      B    C    D
   station to orbit the earth in the future.

   Ⓐ Ⓑ Ⓒ Ⓓ

3. If <u>the United States</u> <u>will build</u> the space
          A        B
   station, <u>it</u> <u>will be</u> called *The Eagle*.
          C   D

   Ⓐ Ⓑ Ⓒ Ⓓ

4. You <u>won't</u> <u>be able</u> to vote <u>if</u> you <u>will</u> not
        A    B       C     D
   register by tomorrow.

   Ⓐ Ⓑ Ⓒ Ⓓ

5. <u>Scientists</u> <u>are</u> <u>probably</u> be able to predict
       A     B    C
   <u>earthquakes</u> in the future.
       D

   Ⓐ Ⓑ Ⓒ Ⓓ

6. <u>In the future</u>, people <u>are going</u> to the
       A             B
   moon <u>for</u> <u>their</u> vacations.
       C    D

   Ⓐ Ⓑ Ⓒ Ⓓ

7. He <u>is going to</u> celebrate <u>after</u> he <u>will get</u>
       A            B     C
   a good score <u>on</u> the test.
          D

   Ⓐ Ⓑ Ⓒ Ⓓ

8. Scientists <u>think</u> <u>transportation</u> <u>is</u> much
          A     B     C
   faster <u>in the future</u>.
       D

   Ⓐ Ⓑ Ⓒ Ⓓ

9. In the future, <u>people</u> <u>are driving</u> <u>electric</u>
               A     B    C
   <u>cars</u>.
    D

   Ⓐ Ⓑ Ⓒ Ⓓ

10. The store <u>is opening</u> <u>at</u> 10:00 every
           A     B
    <u>morning</u> except <u>on</u> Sundays.
       C        D

    Ⓐ Ⓑ Ⓒ Ⓓ

# UNIT 4

# NOUNS, ARTICLES, AND QUANTITY

# 4a  Singular and Plural Nouns

Ben works on **a farm.** He has
**a dog** and **a horse.** He takes
care of the **cows, chickens,**
and **sheep.**

1. Nouns name people, places, and things.

2. Singular nouns refer to one thing. Plural nouns refer to two or more things. All
   nouns have a singular form. Many nouns also have plural forms, but some do not.

**SINGULAR NOUNS**

3. We often use the articles *a* or *an* in front of a singular noun. We use *a* with nouns
   that start with a consonant sound. Some consonant sounds are spelled with the
   letters *b, c, d, f, g, h, j, k, l, m, n, p, q, r, s, t, v, w, x, y,* and *z.*

   **a** hat          **a** dog          **a** farmer          **a** neighborhood

   **a** university (the *u* in university starts with a *y* sound)

   We use *an* when a word begins with a vowel sound. Some vowel sounds are
   spelled with the letters *a, e, i, o,* and *u.*

   **an** animal       **an** eye          **an** ice cream

   **an** uncle        **an** hour (the *h* in *hour* is silent)

4. *A* and *an* have the same meaning. They mean "one."

**PLURAL NOUNS**

5. Many nouns have plural forms. We do not use the articles *a* and *an* before plural
   nouns.

6. We form the plural of most nouns by adding –*s* to the singular form. Sometimes
   there are other spelling changes.

## REGULAR PLURAL NOUNS

| Rule | Singular Noun | Plural Noun |
|---|---|---|
| Add −s to most nouns. | horse | horse**s** |
| Add −es to nouns ending in s, ss, sh, ch, and x. | bus | bus**es** |
| | glass | glass**es** |
| | dish | dish**es** |
| | watch | watch**es** |
| | box | box**es** |
| Nouns ending in a consonant + y: change y to i and add −es. | country | countr**ies** |
| | party | part**ies** |
| Nouns ending in a vowel + y: add −s. | boy | boy**s** |
| | key | key**s** |
| Nouns ending in f or fe: change f or fe to −ves. | life | li**ves** |
| | leaf | lea**ves** |
| **Exceptions:** | belief | belief**s** |
| | chief | chief**s** |
| | roof | roof**s** |
| Nouns ending in o: Some add −es. | echo | echo**es** |
| | hero | hero**es** |
| | potato | potato**es** |
| | tomato | tomato**es** |
| Some add −s. | piano | piano**s** |
| | photo | photo**s** |
| | radio | radio**s** |
| | zoo | zoo**s** |
| Some can add either −s or −es. | zero | zero**s**/zero**es** |
| | volcano | volcano**s**/volcano**es** |
| | tornado | tornado**s**/tornado**es** |

7. Some nouns have irregular plural forms.

## IRREGULAR PLURAL NOUNS

| Singular | Plural |
|---|---|
| man | **men** |
| woman | **women** |
| child | **children** |
| tooth | **teeth** |
| foot | **feet** |
| mouse | **mice** |
| goose | **geese** |
| fish | **fish** |
| sheep | **sheep** |
| deer | **deer** |
| species | **species** |
| ox | **oxen** |

## 1 Practice

**Complete the sentences with *a* or *an*.**

1. I took my nephew to _____*a*_____ zoo last weekend.

2. We saw _____ elephant and her baby.

3. There were _____ zebra and _____ antelope.

4. We spent almost _____ hour watching the monkeys.

5. We saw _____ hippopotamus in _____ lake.

6. It was _____ huge animal!

7. There was _____ exhibit of snakes, and my nephew loved it.

8 We met _____ guide there. He learned about snakes at _____ university in Florida.

9. My nephew wanted to hold _____ snake, and the guide said yes.

10. I let him do it. I'm _____ good uncle, aren't I?

11. We had _____ ice cream cone before we left.

## 2 Practice

**Underline the nouns in the sentences. Write *S* if a noun is singular. Write *P* if it is plural.**

                *P*     *P*        *P*        *S*
1. There were a lot of <u>men</u>, <u>women</u>, and <u>children</u> in the <u>park</u>.

2. It was beautiful. The leaves were changing color.

3. There were geese on the lake.

4. A man and a woman were in a boat on the lake.

5. They were paddling the boat with their feet.

6. I could see many fish in the lake.

7. Some kids were listening to their radio and dancing.

8. Others were riding their bicycles.

9. It was a beautiful day for a walk in the park.

## 3 Practice

**Write the plurals of the following words under the correct headings.**

| baby | child | fox | lady | photo | sandwich | tomato |
|------|-------|-----|------|-------|----------|--------|
| bird | city | half | leaf | piano | sheep | toy |
| bush | dress | hero | mouse | potato | table | wolf |
| category | fish | key | ox | radio | tax | zoo |
| cherry | foot | knife | peach | roof | thief | |

| -s | -es | -ies | -os | -oes | -ves | Irregular |
|-----|------|------|-----|------|------|-----------|
| birds | bushes | babies | _____ | _____ | _____ | _____ |
| _____ | _____ | _____ | _____ | _____ | _____ | _____ |
| _____ | _____ | _____ | _____ | _____ | _____ | _____ |
| _____ | _____ | _____ | _____ | _____ | _____ | _____ |
| _____ | _____ | _____ | | | _____ | _____ |
| | _____ | | | | | _____ |

## 4 Practice

**Complete the sentences with the plural form of the nouns in parentheses.**

Don: Did you go shopping yesterday?

Carla: Yes, I did. I bought a lot of things because they were on sale.

Don: Oh, what did you buy?

Carla: I bought two (dress) _dresses_ , two (shirt) _____ ,
$\quad$ 1 $\qquad$ 2

$\quad$ three (scarf) _____ , and two (tie) _____ for you.
$\qquad$ 3 $\qquad$ 4

Don: Did you buy anything for the house?

Carla: Yes, I bought two beautiful (dish) _____ , six (knife) _____ ,
$\qquad$ 5 $\qquad$ 6

$\quad$ six (fork) _____ , and six (glass) _____ .
$\qquad$ 7 $\qquad$ 8

Don: Wow! You sure bought a lot of things!

## 5 Your Turn

**Look around the classroom. Write the plural names of things you see. Who found the most things?**

| chairs | _____ | _____ | _____ |
|--------|-----------|-----------|-----------|
| _____ | _____ | _____ | _____ |
| _____ | _____ | _____ | _____ |

# 4b Nouns as Subjects, Objects, and Objects of Prepositions

## Form / Function

**Sheep** eat **grass.**
**Lambs** are baby sheep.
The **lambs** are lying on the **grass.**

1. A noun can be the subject of a sentence. The subject names the thing or person that does the action in a sentence.

2. A noun can be the object of a verb. The object names the thing or person that receives the action of the verb.

3. A noun can be the object of a preposition. The object of a preposition is a noun or pronoun that follows a preposition. A preposition and the words following it are a prepositional phrase.

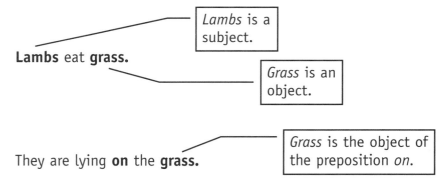

**Lambs** eat **grass.**

> *Lambs* is a subject.

> *Grass* is an object.

They are lying **on** the **grass.**

> *Grass* is the object of the preposition *on.*

| Some Prepositions | | | | |
|---|---|---|---|---|
| about | before | down | off | toward |
| above | behind | during | on | under |
| across | below | for | out | until |
| after | beside | from | over | up |
| against | besides | in | since | upon |
| among | between | into | through | with |
| around | beyond | near | throughout | within |
| at | by | of | to | without |

## 6 | Practice

**Underline and label the subject (S), verb (V), and object (O) of each sentence.**

        *S  V  O*
1. The <u>farm</u> <u>has</u> <u>cows.</u>

2. The cows give milk.

3. The family drinks the milk.

4. The farm has chickens.

5. Don feeds the chickens.

6. The chickens lay eggs.

7. Don has a dog.

8. The dog follows Don.

9. His brother has a cat.

10. The cat hates the dog.

11. The cat chases the chickens.

## 7 | Practice

**Label the subject (S), verb (V), preposition (P), and the object of the preposition (OP).**

     *S  V  P  OP*
1. <u>Ben</u> <u>lives</u> <u>on</u> a <u>farm.</u>

2. Ben wears a hat on the farm.

3. Ben works on the farm with his brother and father.

4. His mother cooks the food for the family.

5. His mother grows vegetables in a garden behind the farmhouse.

6. The family eats the vegetables from the garden.

7. The family drinks milk from the cows on the farm.

8. The family eats eggs from the chickens in the yard.

9. Ben drives his truck to the town on Saturdays.

10. Ben buys groceries from the store in town.

11. Ben takes his dog with him on the truck.

12. Ben and his dog come back to the farm for lunch.

13. His mother prepares lunch with fresh bread.

14. His mother makes the bread at home for the family.

# 4c   Count Nouns and Noncount Nouns

Fresh **air** is good for your **health.**
Fresh **air** has a lot of **oxygen.**

1. Count nouns are nouns that we can count (one book, two books, three books, etc.). They can be singular or plural (a chair, two chairs).

2. We put *a* or *an* before singular nouns.

3. We cannot count noncount nouns. They have no plural.

4. We do not use the articles *a* or *an* with noncount nouns.

5. Some nouns that are usually noncount can also be count nouns, but the meaning is different.

NONCOUNT NOUN:  She makes salad dressing with olive **oil.**
COUNT NOUN:      She uses several **oils** in her cooking. (*Oils* = kinds of oil)

NONCOUNT NOUN:  Brazil produces a lot of **coffee.**
COUNT NOUN:      Can I buy you **a coffee?** (*A coffee* = a cup of coffee)

Here are some common noncount nouns in categories.

| Categories | Examples of Noncount Nouns | | |
|---|---|---|---|
| Solids | beef | glass | pasta |
| | bread | gold | plastic |
| | butter | ham | pork |
| | chalk | ice-cream | silk |
| | cheese | iron | soap |
| | chicken | margarine | steel |
| | coal | meat | wood |
| | cotton | nylon | wool |
| | fish | paper | yogurt |
| Liquids | beer | juice | soup |
| | blood | milk | tea |
| | coffee | oil | vinegar |
| | gasoline | shampoo | water |
| | honey | soda | wine |
| Powders and Grains | cereal | flour | salt |
| | corn | pepper | sand |
| | dust | rice | sugar |
| Gases | air | oxygen | smog |
| | fog | pollution | smoke |
| | hydrogen | smell | steam |
| Names of Categories | clothing | fruit | mail |
| | email | furniture | money |
| | food | jewelry | traffic |
| School Subjects and Languages | biology | Korean | music |
| | Chinese | literature | science |
| | history | math | Spanish |
| Weather | darkness | light | sunshine |
| | frost | rain | thunder |
| | hail | sleet | weather |
| | ice | snow | wind |
| Physical Forces | electricity | light | speed |
| | gravity | magnetism | weight |

| Categories | Examples of Noncount Nouns | | |
|---|---|---|---|
| Abstract Nouns (things we cannot touch) | advice | health | love |
| | beauty | help | luck |
| | crime | homework | peace |
| | education | information | poverty |
| | fun | innocence | progress |
| | guilt | insurance | time |
| | happiness | kindness | wealth |
| | hate | knowledge | work |

## 8 Practice

**Complete the paragraph with the singular or plural form of the nouns in parentheses. Use the singular form if the noun is a noncount noun. Use the plural form if the noun is a count noun.**

When I go to the supermarket, I read all of the (label) ___*labels*___ . That
                                                                1

takes a lot of (time) _____ . I don't eat frozen (food) _____ .
                            2                                                      3

I prefer fresh (fruit) _____ and (vegetable) _____ .
                            4                                      5

I like (apple) _____ , (banana) _____ , and
                      6                              7

(strawberry) _____ . But the (vegetable) _____ are always
                      8                                          9

the same. There are always (potato) _____ , (tomato) _____ ,
                                              10                            11

and (carrot) _____ . I also get (milk) _____ ,
                      12                                        13

(butter) _____ , (cheese) _____ , and
                  14                              15

(egg) _____ . And (ice cream) _____ , of course!
              16                                    17

## 9 Your Turn

**Agree or disagree with the statements below.**

**Examples:**
Meat is good for you.
I agree. Meat is good for you.
I disagree. Meat is bad for you.

**1.** Meat is good for you.

**2.** Eggs are bad for you.

**3.** Sugar is good for you.

**4.** Coffee is bad for you.

**5.** Water is bad for you.

## 10  Your Turn

**Write about what you eat.**

**Example:**
For breakfast, I eat bread and jam. For lunch, I eat a sandwich and some fruit, and for dinner, I eat fish or chicken and some vegetables. I drink a lot of coffee and tea, but I never drink any soda.

## 11  Practice

**Complete the sentences with the singular or plural of the nouns in parentheses.**

**A.**

Today cars run on (gasoline) _____*gasoline*_____, but one day they will
                                        1

run on (electricity) _____. Then there will be no more
                            2

(pollution) _____. The (air) _____ will be clean. There
                  3                              4

won't be (smog) _____ or (smoke) _____ from
                        5                                6

(car) _____ and other (traffic) _____.
            7                                      8

**B.**

My new living room looks nice. There are no (rug) _____ on
                                                          1

the floor. The floor is made of (wood) _____. There is a lot of
                                              2

(light) _____ in the room from the two big (window) _____.
              3                                                          4

I have two big (armchair) _____. They are covered in blue
                                5

(cotton) _____. The (furniture) _____ is all
                6                                    7

new and modern. I have two small (table) _____ made of
                                                  8

(steel) _____ and (glass) _____, and there are two big
              9                            10

(lamp) _____.
              11

**C.**

I need to get some (information) _____ about my
1

(class) _____ next semester. I want to take (science) _____
2 3

subjects like (biology) _____, (chemistry) _____, and
4 5

(physics) _____. Ben has a lot of (knowledge) _____ about
6 7

these things. He took these (course) _____ here last semester. He can give
8

me (help) _____ and some good (advice) _____, I'm sure.
9 10

## 12 Practice

**Work with a partner. Write as many nouns as you can for the categories below. The pair with the most correct is the winner.**

**1.** Things you see on a farm

_animals_     _fences_     _____     _____

**2.** Things you wear

_____     _____     _____     _____

**3.** What things are made of

_____     _____     _____     _____

# 4d  A, An, and *Some*

**Function**

There is **a** vase with **some** flowers in it, **a** wallet, **some** keys on **a** key chain, **a** pair of sunglasses, and **some** mail.

1. We use *a* or *an* in front of singular count nouns.

   **a** book     **an** orange

2. We use *some* in front of noncount nouns. We don't use *a* or *an* in front of noncount nouns.

   CORRECT:     I need **some** milk to make this cake.
   INCORRECT:   I need ~~a milk~~* to make this cake.

3. We also use *some* with plural count nouns.

   **a** book     **some** books

*It is possible to say "a milk," but the meaning is "a serving of milk."

## 13  Practice

**What does Pete carry with him? Complete the sentences with *a, an,* or *some*.**

I have _____*a*_____ wallet. In the wallet, there is _____ money, and there
        1                                                    2
are _____ business cards. I also have _____ identification card,
        3                                          4
_____ check book, and _____ credit cards. In my pocket, I have
    5                              6
_____ pen, _____ keys, _____ cell phone, and _____
    7                8                  9                              10
address book.

## 14  Practice

**Nancy always carries a lot of things in her bag. Complete the sentence with *a, an,*
or *some*.**

She has _____*a*_____ hairbrush, _____ make-up bag, _____ coin
        1                              2                        3
purse, _____ wallet, _____ pack of tissues, _____ bottle of water,
        4                5                              6
_____ pens, _____ apple, _____ umbrella, _____
    7                8                  9                        10
notepad, _____ paperclips, _____ calendar, _____ rubber bands,
            11                        12                    13
_____ jewelry, and _____ letters.
    14                        15

**Your Turn**

Someone takes you to a restaurant. You can eat whatever you want. Don't think about diet or the price. Tell the class what you want to eat and drink.

**Example:**
I want a big steak with some French fries. I want some hot bread with some cheese. Then I'll have some ice cream with some strawberries and cream.

## 4e  *Some, Any, Much, Many, A Little, A Few,* and *A Lot Of*

### Form / Function

A: Did you see **any** crocodiles at the zoo?
B: Yes, we saw **a few.**

|  | Affirmative | Negative |
|---|---|---|
| **Count Nouns** | There are **many** kangaroos. | There aren't **many** kangaroos. |
|  | There are **a lot of** snakes. | There aren't **a lot of** snakes. |
|  | There are **some** big towns. | There aren't **any** big towns. |
|  | There are **a few** trees. | There aren't **many** trees. |
| **Noncount Nouns** | There is **a lot of** sunshine. | There isn't **much** sunshine. |
|  | There is **some** rain. | There isn't **any** rain. |
|  | There is **a little** snow. | There isn't **much** snow. |

16 **Practice**

**Ted and Julia went to Australia. Their friend is asking questions about their vacation. Circle the correct expression in parentheses.**

Mary:  Did you see a lot of wild animals? How about koala bears?

Ted:  No, we didn't see ((any) / some) koala bears, but we saw (a little / a lot of)
                              1                                              2
kangaroos. They were everywhere in the countryside.

Mary: Did you stay in the cities or did you go to the countryside?

Ted:  We didn't spend (a few / any) time in the city. We drove into a desert area called the
      3
      outback. You don't see (any / a few) people for hours, and of course there isn't
      4
      (a few / any) traffic. There is (a lot of / any) sunshine, and there aren't
      5                              6
      (a few / any) trees. You see, there isn't (much / a few) water in this area. I'm
      7                                          8
      glad we took (much / a lot of) water with us in bottles. There are (much / a few)
      9                                                                   10
      farms. We met (any / a few) nice people, and someone took us to a river where there
      11
      are (a lot of / much) crocodiles. We saw (a few / any) crocodiles after ten minutes.
      12                                        13
      I was really scared! Julia wanted to stay longer, but we didn't have (a lot of / a few)
      14
      time and had to get back to the city and the airport. I have (any / a lot of) photos
      15
      to show you.

## 17  Practice

**Complete the sentences with *many, much, a few,* or *a little*. Some sentences have more than one correct answer.**

I live in a small town in Australia. There aren't _____*many*_____ houses there.
                                                        1
There are _____ stores in the town, but they don't sell
                  2
_____ products. There aren't _____ things to see
        3                                          4
in the town, and there isn't _____ entertainment. There aren't
                                    5
_____ young people, and they go to the city on weekends to have
        6
_____ fun. The city is only _____ hours drive from the
        7                                        8
town, and there isn't _____ traffic on the way.
                              9

## 18  Your Turn

**What do you do on Saturdays? Talk about your free time activities, the things you buy, etc. Make five sentences. Use *much, many, a lot of, a little,* and *a few*.**

**Example:**
I have a lot of free time on Saturdays. I go out with a few friends. I do a little homework.

## 4f  Few, A Few, Little, and A Little

He has **a few** cookies.

She has **few** cookies.

1. We use *few* and *a few* with plural count nouns (*books, tables,* etc.).

   *A few* means not many, but enough. It has a positive meaning.

   > I have **a few** apples. I can make an apple pie.

   *Few* means almost none. It has a negative meaning.

   > There are **few** apples. We must get some more.

2. We use *little* and *a little* with noncount nouns (*milk, time,* etc.).

   *A little* means not much, but enough.

   > I have **a little** time. I can finish this exercise.

   *Little* means almost none. It has a negative meaning.

   > I have **little** time. I must hurry.

## 19 Practice

**Complete the sentences with *a few*, *few*, *a little*, or *little*.**

1. Stella knew _____*little*_____ English before she took _____*a few*_____ courses.

2. I like to listen to _____ music when I drive, especially _____ old Beatles songs.

**3.** There is _____ time before the train leaves, so we can buy

_____ magazines and things from the store.

**4.** There's _____ food left in the refrigerator. I'll go to the supermarket

and get _____ things.

**5.** A: Do you need _____ help?

B: Yes, please. There are _____ questions I can't answer.

**6.** He's a strange man. I think he has _____ secrets.

_____ people understand him.

**7.** I have _____ free time now. I'm very busy with my job, but there are

_____ days when I don't have to work.

**8.** My mother sent me _____ money, so I am going to buy

_____ things I need.

**9.** I bought _____ books. They were on sale. Everybody was buying them.

There will be _____ books left now.

**10.** He knows _____ English, so he's going to take _____

English classes.

**11.** Can you put _____ milk and _____ spoons of sugar

on my cereal?

**12.** _____ students did not pass the test; they said they had

_____ time.

**13.** I live _____ blocks from the train station, so there is

_____ noise from the trains. Sometimes it wakes me up.

**14.** There are many pieces of furniture left on sale, but _____ are nice.

**15.** I have _____ problems. I need _____ advice.

**16.** I'd like _____ vegetables and _____ chicken, please.

**17.** We took _____ summer clothes with us, but we had

_____ days of warm weather.

**18.** She's having a party and invited _____ friends over.

**19.** Are you hungry? There's _____ milk and _____ cookies.

**20.** She lost _____ points on the test because she was

_____ minutes late.

# 4g Units of Measure with Nouns

A: What's in the grocery bags?
B: There's **a bag of** potato chips, **a loaf of** bread, **a bunch of** celery, and many other things.

1. We use units of measure such as *a cup of coffee* or *a glass of water* to express quantities of noncount nouns and count nouns.

2. Count nouns following the units of measure are plural.

3. Here are some units of measure.

| | | |
|---|---|---|
| a bag of chips | a head of lettuce | a sheet of paper |
| a bar of soap | a jar of jam | a slice of cake |
| a bottle of water | a loaf of bread | a tube of toothpaste |
| a box of chocolates | a package of spaghetti | two pounds of apples/cheese |
| a bunch of bananas | a piece of fruit | ten gallons of gasoline |
| a can of tomatoes/soup | a piece of information | two cartons of milk |
| a carton of milk/juice | a roll of toilet paper | two cups of tea |

## 20 Practice

**Pam wrote a note for Pete. Complete the note with the following quantity words.**

a bag of          a tube of
a bar of          bottles of
a bunch of        cartons of
a can of          pounds of
a loaf of         sheets of
a pound of

### Shopping List

Pete,

I'll be home late. Can you go to the store for me? Here's a list.

2   _cartons of_  milk
    _a loaf of_  bread
    _____  cheese
3   _____  water
    _____  toothpaste
2   _____  red apples
    _____  bananas
    _____  vegetable soup
    _____  potato chips
    _____  soap
100 _____  paper for my computer

## 21 Your Turn

**Work with a partner. Look at the following shopping list. Ask questions with *how much* or *how many* for each item. Answer with quantity expressions such as numbers, *some, a lot of, a few,* and *a little*.**

**Example:**
soap
A: How much soap do you need?
B: Not much. Just two bars.

### Shopping List

apples          margarine

bread           oranges

chips           potatoes

honey           rice

juice           soap

lettuce         vitamin C

light bulbs     yogurt

# 4h  Possessive Nouns

My uncle's name is Jim.
He's in the photo, and
that's Jim's son, Tommy.

1.  We use 's (apostrophe + s) or ' (apostrophe) to talk about things that belong to people.

| Singular Possessive Noun | Plural Possessive Noun |
| --- | --- |
| My uncle's name is Jim.<br>(one uncle) | My uncles' names are Jim and Ken.<br>(more than one uncle) |
| It's the boy's bag. (one boy) | They are the boys' bags. (more than one boy) |
| This is the girl's room. (one girl) | This is the girls' room. (more than one girl) |

2.  We add 's or just ' for names and nouns that end in –s.

> This is James's friend. OR This is James' friend.
> That is the boss's car. OR That is the boss' car.

3.  We use 's with irregular plurals.

> These are the children's books.
> They sell women's clothes.
> That's a men's store.

## 22  Practice

**Add 's or ' to the underlined nouns to show possession.**

Rita:   Where did you take this photo?

Laura:  At my  <u>friend's</u>  house. My  <u>friend</u>  name is Carla. That day was the
              <sub>1</sub>                            <sub>2</sub>

<u>twins</u>  birthday party. This is Cindy, my  <u>brother</u>  wife. And that is
  <sub>3</sub>                                              <sub>4</sub>

<u>Cindy</u>  sister.
  <sub>5</sub>

Rita: Who are the two boys?

Laura: The __boys__ names are Ken and Dave. They are __Cindy__ sons. And that's the
        **6**                                           **7**
        __boys__ teacher, Mrs. Parkinson.
        **8**

## 23 Practice

**Rewrite these questions using possessive nouns.**

1. What's the first name of your father?

   *What's your father's first name?* _____

2. What are the names of your friends?

   _____

3. What's the name of your mother?

   _____

4. What are the colors of the shirts of the women in class?

   _____

5. What are some of the favorite movies of your classmates?

   _____

6. What's the telephone number of your doctor?

   _____

7. What are the colors of the shoes of the men in class?

   _____

## 24 Your Turn

**Write answers to the questions in Practice 23.**

1. My *father's first name is Frank.* _____
2. My _____
3. My _____
4. In class, the _____
5. My _____
6. My _____
7. In class, the _____

# 4i  *A, An,* or *The*

There is **a** woman outside. She is sitting on **a** truck. **The** truck is big and old. **The** woman is young.

1.  We use *a* or *an* when we talk about a person or a thing (singular count noun) for the first time. We use *the* when we talk about it for the second time.

    There is **a** woman outside. **The** woman is sitting on **a** truck.

2.  We use *a* or *an* when we talk about a general, not a specific, person or thing.

    I spent **a** year in Mexico City.

3.  We use *the* when the person we are speaking to knows which person or thing we are talking about.

    Ted:    Where's Bill?
    Annie:  He's in **the** house.
    (Both Ted and Annie know which house they are talking about.)

4.  We use *the* with count nouns (singular and plural) and noncount nouns.

    She has a truck. **The** truck is old. (singular count noun)
    I ate two cookies. **The** cookies were delicious. (plural count noun)
    We had some coffee. **The** coffee was good. (noncount noun)

## 25 | Practice

**Complete the sentences with *a, an,* or *the*.**

**A.**

Kelly had ___a___ pain in her back, so she went to _____ doctor that her friend
         **1**                                **2**
recommended. _____ doctor gave her _____ tablet to take every day. After _____ few
              **3**                **4**                  **5**
days, _____ pain went away.
     **6**

**B.**

I gave Lucy _____ gift for her ninth birthday. It was _____ box of paints. Now she
             **1**                         **2**
spends _____ hour or more every day painting. She wants to be _____ artist one day.
        **3**                               **4**
Yesterday, she painted _____ picture of _____ woman. _____ painting is very good. She
                    **5**          **6**        **7**
is going to give it to _____ friend.
            **8**

**C.**

I live in _____ apartment in Boston. It is _____ old apartment building in _____
        **1**                   **2**               **3**
center of _____ city. There is _____ elevator and _____ doorman at _____ entrance of
      **4**             **5**           **6**         **7**
the building. I have _____ view from my kitchen window. _____ apartment is nice, but
                **8**                    **9**
it is hot in _____ summer.
       **10**

**D.**

Yesterday was _____ very bad day. I had a lot of work at _____ office. On the way
             **1**                       **2**
back, I missed my train and took _____ taxi. When I arrived home, there was _____
                        **3**                    **4**
message from _____ friend on my answering machine. She told me to meet her at _____
           **5**                             **6**
restaurant at seven. She gave me _____ name of the restaurant and its address. I went
                          **7**
to _____ restaurant, but she wasn't there. I waited for _____ hour and came back home.
    **8**                                 **9**
I was hungry, tired, and in _____ bad mood.
                   **10**

# 4j ◆ Generalizations

**Giraffes** live in Africa.
**Giraffes** are tall.
**Giraffes** have long necks.
**Giraffes** eat leaves.

1. We do not use *the* when we talk about something in general.

   **Giraffes** are tall.
   **Diamonds** are expensive.
   I love **fish.**

2. We use *the* when we talk about specific things.

   **The** giraffes that we saw at the zoo were beautiful.
   **The** diamond in your ring is beautiful.
   **The fish** that you made last night was delicious.

## 26 Practice

**Complete the sentences with *the* or *X* (no article).**

1. Drinkable __X__ water is more expensive than __X__ salt in some parts of the world.

2. _____ water that we drink in this city is not good. Many people buy _____ water in bottles.

3. She loves _____ coffee. She drank all _____ coffee in the pot.

4. Which is more important for you, _____ love or _____ money?

5. I love _____ photographs, and I really like _____ photographs you took of Rome.

6. You know, _____ cars can't run without _____ gas.

7. Although _____ formal education is important, _____ education you get at home is just as important.

8. I think that _____ money is important. Where is _____ money I gave you yesterday?

9. Did you know that _____ oranges have Vitamin C? _____ oranges we had this morning were very sweet.

10. Do you know that _____ glass is made from _____ sand?

11. They say that _____ time is _____ money. I will never forget _____ time I spent in Singapore with you.

12. We studied _____ French at school, but _____ French we studied was not very natural.

13. I think that _____ watches are not so expensive today. Most watches today work on _____ batteries.

14. In this city, _____ museums are closed on Mondays, but _____ Museum of Science is open this Monday for a special exhibit.

15. I learned that _____ land animals don't live in Antarctica. Only _____ seals and _____ penguins can live there.

16. It's true that _____ life is very difficult without _____ electricity.

17. It's a fact that _____ doctors make more money than _____ teachers.

18. I like working with _____ people, and _____ people in this department are wonderful.

19. We all have _____ problems. Helen told me about _____ problems she has at work.

20. Don is a vegetarian. He doesn't eat _____ meat, but he eats _____ eggs and _____ cheese.

## 27 Practice

**Complete the sentences with *the, a, an,* or *X* (no article).**

John gave Linda __X__ flowers for her birthday. It was _____ hot day, and _____
                  1                                    2                  3

flowers looked terrible by the time he gave them to her. He also bought _____ chocolates
                                                                                4

for her. He put _____ chocolates in _____ car, and when she opened _____ box, they
                 5                       6                          7

were warm and soft. Then he took her to _____ movie. _____ movie was a horror film.
                                            8          9

John forgot Linda didn't like _____ horror movies. _____ movie was frightening. At the
                                    10                11

end of _____ movie, John heard _____ scream. He thought it was _____ woman in
          12                    13                      14

_____ movie, but it was Linda.
  15

## 28 Your Turn

**Say five things you like and five things you don't like. Use the ideas from the list or your own.**

**Example:**
I like cats, but I don't like their hair.

soccer                      classical music          modern art
chocolates              horror movies           rock music

# WRITING: Write a Friendly Letter

**Complete a letter to a friend about a vacation.**

**Step 1. Work with a partner. Think of a famous vacation place. It may be anywhere in the world. Ask and answer questions about this place. Write your answers. Answer the questions using** *some, any, a lot of, much, many, a,* **and** *the.*

**Ask questions like these:**
What kinds of things did you see?
What photos did you take?
What kinds of things did you eat?
What gifts or souvenirs did you buy?

**Step 2. Rewrite your answers as a paragraph to complete a letter like this one. For more writing guidelines, see pages 407–411.**

> August 18, 20XX
>
> Dear Hamid,
>     You were right. Alex and I had a fantastic time at the pyramids in Egypt. Everyone should go there at least once.
>
>     When we were there, we saw _____
> _____
> _____
> _____
> _____
>
>     Thanks again for your advice. I'm telling all of my friends that they must visit the Egyptian pyramids. It was the best vacation I've ever had.
>
>     Your friend,
>     Julio

**Step 3. Evaluate your paragraph.**

**Checklist**

_____ Did you indent the first line?

_____ Did you describe your experiences on your vacation?

_____ Did you use articles and quantifying words like *many, much, some, any, a, an,* and *the?*

**Step 4. Edit your work. Work with a partner to edit your sentences. Correct spelling, punctuation, vocabulary, and grammar.**

**Step 5. Write your final copy.**

# SELF-TEST

A   Choose the best answer, A, B, C, or D, to complete the sentence. Mark your answer by darkening the oval with the same letter.

1.  There is _____ at this time.

    A. many traffic       Ⓐ Ⓑ Ⓒ Ⓓ
    B. a lot of traffic
    C. lot of traffic
    D. traffics

2.  Did you see _____ kangaroos in Australia?

    A. much               Ⓐ Ⓑ Ⓒ Ⓓ
    B. a
    C. a little
    D. any

3.  We need _____ from the supermarket.

    A. a loaf of bread    Ⓐ Ⓑ Ⓒ Ⓓ
    B. a piece of bread
    C. a bread
    D. a packet of bread

4.  There are _____ tourists in small towns.

    A. few                Ⓐ Ⓑ Ⓒ Ⓓ
    B. any
    C. little
    D. much

5.  The price of a _____ of lettuce is going up again.

    A. piece              Ⓐ Ⓑ Ⓒ Ⓓ
    B. bar
    C. bunch
    D. head

6.  It's bedtime. Can you turn off _____?

    A. a light            Ⓐ Ⓑ Ⓒ Ⓓ
    B. the light
    C. light
    D. lights

7.  I have _____ on me.

    A. a money            Ⓐ Ⓑ Ⓒ Ⓓ
    B. few money
    C. a little money
    D. a few money

8.  These are _____ toys.

    A. the children's     Ⓐ Ⓑ Ⓒ Ⓓ
    B. the children
    C. the childrens'
    D. the childrens

9.  In this town, there is _____.

    A. an university      Ⓐ Ⓑ Ⓒ Ⓓ
    B. a university
    C. the university
    D. university

10. In _____, the police don't carry guns.

    A. some country       Ⓐ Ⓑ Ⓒ Ⓓ
    B. some countries
    C. some country's
    D. some countries'

**B** **Find the underlined word or phrase, A, B, C, or D, that is incorrect. Mark your answer by darkening the oval with the same letter.**

1. Everyday <u>life</u> is <u>difficult</u> without <u>an</u>
   A       B         C

   <u>electricity</u>.
   D

   Ⓐ Ⓑ Ⓒ Ⓓ

2. There <u>are</u> <u>a lot of</u> <u>sheeps</u> <u>in</u> New Zealand.
        A     B      C    D

   Ⓐ Ⓑ Ⓒ Ⓓ

3. Could <u>you</u> please <u>give</u> me <u>some</u> <u>advices</u>?
         A        B      C     D

   Ⓐ Ⓑ Ⓒ Ⓓ

4. He needs <u>any</u> <u>help with</u> <u>his</u> <u>homework</u>.
         A     B     C     D

   Ⓐ Ⓑ Ⓒ Ⓓ

5. <u>The grass</u> looks <u>green</u> today because
      A          B

   <u>we got</u> <u>any</u> rain this week.
     C     D

   Ⓐ Ⓑ Ⓒ Ⓓ

6. <u>A pollution</u> is <u>a</u> problem in many large
     A        B

   <u>cities</u> <u>in the United States</u>.
     C       D

   Ⓐ Ⓑ Ⓒ Ⓓ

7. <u>Some</u> people <u>say</u> that <u>the money</u> cannot
     A        B      C

   buy <u>happiness</u>.
      D

   Ⓐ Ⓑ Ⓒ Ⓓ

8. California has <u>a good weather</u>, but
             A

   <u>there are</u> <u>a lot of</u> <u>earthquakes</u>.
     B      C      D

   Ⓐ Ⓑ Ⓒ Ⓓ

9. <u>Vegetarians</u> don't eat <u>meats</u>, and some
     A          B

   don't eat <u>eggs</u> or <u>cheese</u>.
        C     D

   Ⓐ Ⓑ Ⓒ Ⓓ

10. Could I have <u>some</u> <u>informations</u> about
           A     B

    <u>the courses</u> <u>for next semester</u>?
      C       D

    Ⓐ Ⓑ Ⓒ Ⓓ

Nouns, Articles, and Quantity

# UNIT 5

## PRONOUNS

# 5a  Subject and Object Pronouns

At the moment, **he** doesn't like **her,** and **she** doesn't like **him. They** are angry.

1. Many sentences in English have a subject, a verb, and an object. The subject and the object can be nouns.

| Subject (Noun) | Verb | Object (Noun) |
|---|---|---|
| **Mike** | plays | **football** very well. |
| **Helena and Joe** | love | **their children.** |

2. We can replace nouns with pronouns.

| Subject (Pronoun) | Verb | Object (Pronoun) |
|---|---|---|
| **He** | plays | **it** very well. |
| **They** | love | **them.** |

3. Pronouns used as subjects are sometimes different from pronouns used as objects.

| Subject Pronouns | Object Pronouns |
|---|---|
| I | me |
| you | you |
| he | him |
| she | her |
| it | it |
| we | us |
| they | them |

4. A pronoun can refer to a noun or to a noun phrase (a noun + a group of words related to the noun).

| Subject (Noun) | Verb | Object (Noun Phrase) | Subject (Pronoun) | Verb | Object (Pronoun) | |
|---|---|---|---|---|---|---|
| Lisa | drives | **an old black car.** | **She** | bought | **it** | last year. |

5. We use object pronouns after prepositions.

| Subject | Verb | Prepositional Phrase (Noun Phrase Object) | Subject (Pronoun) | Verb | Prepositional Phrase (Pronoun Object) |
|---|---|---|---|---|---|
| We | listened | to **the math teacher.** | **We** | listened | **to him.** |

6. Remember to use the correct pronoun forms.

CORRECT:    My friends and I went to the mall.
INCORRECT:  My friends and ~~me~~ went to the mall.

CORRECT:    Sam saw my friends and me at the mall.
INCORRECT:  Sam saw my friends and ~~I~~ at the mall.

CORRECT:    I went to the mall with you and him.
INCORRECT:  I went to the mall with you and ~~he.~~

---

### 1 | Practice

**Complete the sentences with a subject or an object pronoun.**

1. Eddy likes football, but I don't like _____*it*_____.

2. As for me, _____ like tennis, but Eddy doesn't like _____.

3. Eddy's favorite movie star is Arnold Schwarzenegger, but I don't like _____ very much.

4. He also likes Britney Spears, but I don't like _____.

5. My favorite movie stars are Jodie Foster and Mel Gibson, but Eddy doesn't like _____.

6. My friends and _____ are going shopping, but Eddy doesn't want to come with _____.

7. Eddy likes _____, but I don't like him.

8. Why do I talk about _____ so much?

## 2 Practice

**Complete the sentences with subject and object pronouns.**

**A.**

I am a student at a university. I am studying computer science. ____It____ is a
                                                                  1
good subject. My friend, Tom, is taking the same courses with _____.
                                                                    2
_____ do our homework together in the library. I like the library. _____ is
      3                                                                        4
a quiet place. Tom and _____ have our final examinations next week. I want to
                            5
pass _____. Then my parents will buy a motorcycle for _____.
          6                                                        7

**B.**

I work for Mr. Kim on Saturdays. I help _____ in his store and he pays
                                              1
_____ money. I am saving _____ to buy my mother a necklace.
      2                              3
_____ is going to be very happy. _____ is going to be a surprise
      4                                      5
for _____.
          6

**C.**

My mother can't find her glasses. _____ is looking for _____ all over
                                        1                          2
the house. She says she put _____ on the table in the kitchen, and now
                                  3
_____ are not there. She says she can't drive without _____. My father
      4                                                            5
has to drive _____ to work tomorrow.
                  6

**D.**

Mike: Is Maria coming to the party?

Ken:   I invited _____, but I don't know if _____ will come. Her
                      1                                  2
       parents are visiting, and she may take _____ somewhere.
                                                    3

Mike: What about Bill? Did you invite _____ when you saw him yesterday?
                                            4

Ken:   Yes, he is coming with Janet. _____ will both come.
                                          5

Mike: Oh no! Not Janet! I really don't want to see _____.
                                                          6

**3** Your Turn

**Talk or write about two gifts you gave or received recently.**

**Example:**
My father gave me a computer for my birthday last year. I love it.

## 5b   Possessive Adjectives and Possessive Pronouns

### Form / Function

A: Is this **your** key?
B: No, it isn't **mine.**

| Possessive Adjectives | Possessive Pronouns |
|:---:|:---:|
| my | mine |
| your | yours |
| his | his |
| her | hers |
| its | its* |
| our | ours |
| their | theirs |

*We rarely need to use the possessive pronoun *its*.

1.  We put a possessive adjective before a noun. We use a possessive pronoun alone.
    There is no noun after it.

    This is **my** key. It's **mine.**
    That is **their** car. It's **theirs.**
    **Their** car is blue. **Mine** is red.

2. We use possessive adjectives and possessive pronouns to show that something belongs to somebody.

    Excuse me, is this **your** pen? OR Excuse me, is this pen **yours?**

3. Be careful when using *its/it's* and *their/they're*. They are pronounced the same but their meanings are different.

| Word | Meaning | Example |
|------|---------|---------|
| its | Possessive form of *it*. | It's a great car, but I don't like **its** color. |
| it's | Contraction of *it is*. | Where's the car? <br> **It's** in the garage. |
| their | Possessive adjective of *they*. | **Their** car has a flat tire. |
| they're | Contraction of *they are*. | **They're** getting it fixed now. |
| there | Shows location | The car is in the garage. It's safe **there.** |
| | Shows existence | **There** is a problem with my car. |

## 4 Practice

**Underline the correct word.**

**A.**

Paolo:    Is this (<u>your</u>/yours) wallet?
                           1

Lillian:  No, it's not (mine/my). I thought it was (your/yours).
                         2                            3

Paolo:    No, I have (my/mine) in my pocket. Maybe (its/it's) Ingrid's.
                       4                          5

Lillian:  If it is (her/hers), she will be very worried. She went to the airport with
                    6

          (her/hers) husband. He came to pick (her/she) up in (his/him) car. They
            7                                  8                9

          went to meet (her/hers) parents. (They're/Their) coming from Canada to stay
                        10                    11

          with (them/they) for the holidays.
               12

**B.**

        (Our/Ours) television is not working. (Our/Ours) neighbors have an extra
           1                                     2

television, and (they're/there) going to give (it/its) to (us/we). We have to fix
                3                              4         5

(our/ours) or get a new one. (They're/Their) expensive, you know. Our neighbors don't
  6                            7

mind, so we may watch (theirs/their) for a long time.
                       8

**C.**

The Parkers are (our/ours) neighbors. (They're/Their) very rich. They have two cars in
<br>**1** **2**

(theirs/their) garage, and the Porsche parked in front of (our/ours) house is (their/theirs),
<br>**3** **4** **5**

too. Everybody thinks (its/it's) (our/ours), but (our/ours) is an old Honda. We park it in
<br>**6** **7** **8**

front of (our/ours) other neighbor's house. We like to leave it (their/there).
<br>**9** **10**

## 5c Reflexive Pronouns

**Form**

She's looking at **herself** in the mirror.

| Subject Pronouns | Reflexive Pronouns |
|---|---|
| I | myself |
| you (singular) | yourself |
| he | himself |
| she | herself |
| it | itself |
| we | ourselves |
| you (plural) | yourselves |
| they | themselves |

1. We use reflexive pronouns as objects when the subject and the object of the verb or preposition refer to the same person or thing.

| Subject | Verb | Object |
|---|---|---|
| **She** | hurt | **herself.** |
| **The machine** | can't work | by **itself.** |

2. Reflexive pronouns often come after these verbs and phrases.

| | | |
|---|---|---|
| be proud of | enjoy | take care of |
| behave | help* | talk to |
| burn | hurt | teach |
| cut | introduce | work for |

*If you *help yourself to something*, it means "serve yourself something."
For example, "Help yourself to the potatoes."

I **cut myself** while I was shaving.
Did you **enjoy yourself** at the party?
Sue **taught herself** how to cook.

3. We use the reflexive pronoun with the preposition *by* when we mean "alone" or "without any help."

Lillian painted the bathroom **by herself.**
He sits **by himself** for hours.

4. We do not usually use reflexive pronouns with verbs such as *dress, wash,* and *shave.* But we can use these verbs with a reflexive pronoun if we want to show someone did something unusual or with a lot of effort.

I got up, **dressed,** and went to work.
Timmy is only three years old, but he can **dress himself.**

---

**6** Practice

**Complete the sentences with the correct reflexive pronoun.**

1. A:  What a beautiful dress! Where did you buy it?

   B:  I made it _____ *myself.* _____

2. A:  Do you want me to go shopping with you?

   B:  No, I prefer to go by _____

3. A:  Who painted your house?

   B:  We painted it _____

**4.** A: Could you wash this shirt for me?

   B: No, you'll have to wash it _____

**5.** A: Did Paolo get some help with his homework?

   B: No, he did it by _____

**6.** A: Did Helen buy that birthday cake?

   B: No, she made it _____

**7.** A: Timmy is big for a three-year-old.

   B: Yes, and he can dress _____

**8.** A: Tom and I are going to Min's party.

   B: OK. Enjoy _____

**9.** A: Emily is good with computers.

   B: Yes, she taught _____

**10.** A: Do you want me to turn off the iron?

   B: No, it will turn _____ off automatically.

## 7 Practice

**Johnnie is five and Jenny is seven. They are alone in the kitchen. Complete the sentences with the correct reflexive pronoun.**

1. Johnnie and Jenny are trying to make breakfast by _themselves._

2. Johnnie got the box of cereal from the shelf by _____

3. He helped _____ to the cereal and the milk.

4. He taught _____ how to make cereal when he was four.

5. Jenny was trying to cut a bagel and cut _____

6. Then she tried to toast the bagel and burned _____

7. In the end, Johnnie and Jenny made and ate breakfast by _____

## 8 Your Turn

**Talk about your family or friends. Say ten things they do themselves. Use *himself, herself, ourselves,* and *themselves.* You may use ideas from the list or your own.**

**Example:**
choose (one's) clothes
My little sister chooses her clothes herself.

| | | |
|---|---|---|
| choose (one's) clothes | do the laundry | make the bed |
| clean the windows | fix the car | paint the house |
| cook the meals | make (one's) clothes | wash the car |

# 5d  *Another, The Other, Other, Others, and The Others*

These cookies are good.
Can I have **another**?

1. We use *another* and *the other* as adjectives before nouns.

|  | Adjective | Noun |
|---|---|---|
| Jenny ate | **another** | cookie. |
| Melanie ate | **the other** | cookie. |

2. We use *another* and *the other* as pronouns.

|  | Pronoun |
|---|---|
| Jorge ate | **another.** |
| Toshi ate | **the other.** |

3. We use the adjective *other* (with no –*s*) with a plural noun.

|  | Adjective | Noun |
|---|---|---|
| There are | **other** | **cookies** in the box. |
| I like | | **kinds** of cookies. |

4. We use the pronoun *others* (with –*s*) when there is no noun that follows.

|  | Adjective , |  |
|---|---|---|
| There are | **others** | on the plate. |

*Others = other cookies*

1. *Another* means one more of the same thing (or the same group) we had before.

    These cookies are good. Can I have **another?** (one more of the same cookies)

2. *The other* means the one that is left of the same thing.

    There are two pieces of chocolate left. I'll take one and you take **the other.**

3. *Other* and *others* mean several more of the same group. *The others* means the ones left of the same group.

    There are **other** cookies in the box.
    There are **others** in the box.
    These cookies have nuts in them. **The others** have coconut.

## 9 Practice

**Complete the sentences with *another* or *the other*.**

1. One country in Europe is France. _Another_ is Italy.

2. There are two countries I want to visit. One is France, and _____ is Italy.

3. Paris is a city in Europe. Rome is _____ city in Europe.

4. In France, people speak French. Belgium is _____ country where people speak French.

5. There are three European countries where people speak French. One is France, _____ is Belgium, and _____ is Switzerland.

6. Paris is a beautiful city in Europe. Prague is _____ beautiful city in Europe.

7. A popular fruit in the United States is the banana. The orange is _____.

8. There are two popular fruits in my home. One is the banana, and _____ is the apple.

9. The potato is a popular vegetable. The carrot is _____.

10. People usually eat three meals. Breakfast is one meal, lunch is _____, and dinner is _____.

11. There are many popular flavors of ice cream. One is vanilla; _____ is strawberry.

12. We buy two flavors of ice cream. One is vanilla, and _____ is chocolate.

## 10 Practice

**Complete the sentences with *other, others,* or *the others*.**

1. Baseball is a popular sport. _____Others_____ are basketball and football.

2. There are three popular team sports at this school. One is baseball. _____ are basketball and football.

3. Some sports are team sports like football. _____, like tennis, are not team sports.

4. There are many kinds of water on the Earth. Oceans are one kind. Some _____ are seas, lakes, and rivers.

5. There are four oceans. The Pacific and the Atlantic are two. _____ are the Indian and the Arctic Oceans.

6. Only one student was late for the test. _____ were on time.

7. Some students live with their parents. _____ live on campus. The rest of the students live in apartments in the city.

8. Some universities give computers to their students. _____ universities don't.

## 11 Practice

**Complete the sentences with *another, other, the other, others,* or *the others*.**

1. Our teacher was absent today, so _____ teacher came in her place.

2. I wasn't happy because I like our usual teacher, but all of _____ students in my class were happy.

3. Our usual teacher always gives us homework, but _____ teacher didn't.

4. Some students talk a lot in class. _____ don't, and a few rarely talk.

5. After we finished our exercises in class, she gave us a few _____ to do for homework.

6. Some teachers give a lot of homework. Some _____ teachers don't.

7. A few of us understood the lesson, but some _____ didn't.

8. Some students always ask the teacher questions. All of _____ students keep quiet.

9. There are usually four choices in a multiple choice question. One is correct, and _____ are not correct.

**10.** Most teachers tell students to write their essays on the computer.

_____ teachers want hand-written essays. Some teachers will accept both.

**11.** Some teachers give high grades most of the time. Some _____ always

give low grades.

**12.** We have a lot of tests. For example, we have a test today, and we will have

_____ test tomorrow.

## 5e   *One* and *Ones*

Man:     Do you like the red tie?
Woman:  No, I like this **one.**

1. We use the pronoun *one* in the singular and *ones* in the plural so that we do not repeat the noun.

    Do you like the red tie?
    No, I like the blue **one** (tie).
    I never wear brown shoes. I always wear black **ones** (shoes).

2. *One/ones* and *some/any* are indefinite (like the article *a*). *It* and *they/them* refer to something definite (like the article *the*).

    I don't have a passport. I need **one.**
    I don't have any envelopes. I need **some.**

    I have my passport. I received **it** yesterday.
    I have envelopes. I bought **them** yesterday.

## 12 Practice

**Complete the sentences with *one* or *ones*.**

1. A: Which is your car?

   B: The black _one_ .

2. A: Can I borrow your dictionary?

   B: Sorry, I don't have _____.

3. A: I need a ticket.

   B: I have _____.

4. A: Which phone did you use?

   B: The _____ on your desk.

5. A: I like your shoes.

   B: Oh, thanks. They are the _____ I bought yesterday.

6. A. Which pants fit you better?

   B: The black _____.

7. A: Hand me the glass, please.

   B: Which _____?

8. A: Which scarves do you like best?

   B: The expensive _____.

## 13 Practice

**Complete the sentences with *one, ones, some, it,* or *them*.**

1. I'm sorry, but I broke this glass. I dropped _____ _it._ _____

2. I'm making a sandwich. Would you like _____, too?

3. If you need change for the parking meter, I have _____

4. She bought some cookies and ate all of _____

5. My computer broke down, so I bought a new _____ this week.

6. Where are my glasses? Do you see _____

7. I am throwing away the old magazines and keeping the new _____

8. I bought some greeting cards. I got funny _____ this year.

9. A: Where's your car?

   B: I parked _____ in the parking lot behind the building.

10. I don't have any stamps, but Lin has _____

11. We need to call a taxi. I'll call for _____

12. I don't like the white roses. I prefer the red _____

## 5f Indefinite Pronouns (*Something, Somebody, Anything, Anybody, Everything, Everybody, Nothing, and Nobody*)

This is strange. There's **something** wrong. The door is open.

I don't hear **anything,** and there isn't **anybody** in the house.

|  | Affirmative Sentences | Negative Sentences | Questions |
|---|---|---|---|
| **People** | someone/somebody | anyone/anybody | anyone/anybody |
|  | no one/nobody |  | no one/nobody |
|  | everyone/everybody |  | everyone/everybody |
| **Things** | something | anything | anything/something |
|  | nothing |  | nothing |
|  | everything |  | everything |
| **Places** | somewhere | anywhere | anywhere/somewhere |
|  | everywhere |  | everywhere |

1. We use *someone/somebody* (a person), *something* (a thing), and *somewhere* (a place) in affirmative statements.

   I can see **somebody** in the store.
   He lives **somewhere** near the airport.

2. We use *anyone/anybody, anything,* and *anywhere* for questions and negative statements.

   I can't hear **anything.**
   Is there **anybody** here?

3. We can use *no one/nobody, nothing,* and *nowhere* in place of *not anyone/anybody, not anything,* and *not anywhere.*

   There isn't **anybody** in the house.
   There is **nobody** in the house.

4. We use the adjective *every* with singular count nouns.

   **Every** student must take the test. (*Every* student means "all the students.")

5. We use the pronouns *everyone/everybody, everything,* and the adverb *everywhere* in affirmative statements and questions. We use a singular verb with these pronouns.

   **Is everybody** here?
   Yes, **everybody is** here, but **everything is not** ready for the party.

## Function

1. Unlike other pronouns, indefinite pronouns do not take the place of a noun or a noun phrase.

2. We use indefinite pronouns with *some* and *any* to talk about an unknown person, place, or thing.

   I saw **someone** take your jacket. (I don't know who took it.)
   I put my glasses **somewhere,** and now I can't find them.
   (I don't know where I put them.)
   Did you find **anything** to eat? (I don't know if you found some food or not.)

3. We use indefinite pronouns with *every* to talk about all people, places, or things that we are talking about.

   We invited **everyone** to the party.
   Did they go **everywhere** in New York?
   They didn't buy **everything** they wanted.

## 14 Practice

**Underline the correct word in parentheses.**

**A.**

Ben:  I lost my grammar book yesterday. I left it (<u>somewhere</u>/anywhere).
                                                         1

Lee:  Did you look in the classroom?

Ben: Yes, I did. It wasn't there. It isn't (everywhere/anywhere).
                                                        2

Lee: Did you ask (anyone/nobody)?
                        3

Ben: Yes, I asked my teacher, and I asked (everyone/anyone) in my class.
                                                      4

Lee: Don't worry. You can share a book with (someone/no one) in class tomorrow.
                                                              5

Ben: But I don't want to share a book with (anyone/someone). I want my book. I have
                                                        6

all the answers in it.

**B.**

Nancy: I have (nothing/anything) to do this afternoon. Let's go (somewhere/anywhere).
                          1                                                  2

I have my mother's car so we can go (anywhere/nowhere) we like.
                                              3

Tina: Well, I don't want to go (somewhere/anywhere) special because I'm not wearing
                                          4

dressy clothes.

Nancy: OK. Then, let's get (something/anything) to eat and go (somewhere/anywhere)
                                  5                                        6

nice and quiet where (nobody/somebody) can disturb us.
                              7

Tina: That's a great idea. I haven't done (something/anything) like this for a long time.
                                                    8

**C.**

Claudia is going to a party on Saturday, but she has (anything/nothing) to wear.
                                                                  1

She went to the big department store near her home yesterday but didn't find

(something/anything) nice. This morning she went (somewhere/anywhere) else, but
          2                                                    3

(everything/anything) was expensive. At another store, (everything/anything) was nice,
          4                                                          5

but (nothing/anything) would fit her. There's (nowhere/everywhere) else to go. Claudia is
          6                                              7

going to look in her closet and find (something/anything) to wear to the party.
                                              8

| 15 | **Your Turn** |

**Work in pairs. Make up six song titles with the pronouns from the list.**

**Example:**
"Everybody Needs Someone to Love"

somewhere        something
someone          anything
nothing          everywhere

# WRITING: Write a Personal Description

Write a description of your best friend.

**Step 1. Think about your best friend. Write the answers to the following questions. Then think of other things to say about your friend.**

1. What is your friend's name?
2. Does your friend have any brothers or sisters?
3. What does your friend do?
4. What does your friend like?
5. What does your friend dislike?
6. What do you do together?
7. Why do you like your friend?

**Step 2. Rewrite your answers in paragraph form. Write a title in a few words (My Best Friend). For more writing guidelines, see pages 410–411.**

**Step 3. Evaluate your paragraph.**

**Checklist**

_____ Did you indent the first line?

_____ Did you give your paragraph a title?

_____ Did you put the title at the top center of the page?

**Step 4. Edit your work. Work with a partner to edit your sentences. Correct spelling, punctuation, vocabulary, and grammar.**

**Step 5. Write your final copy.**

# SELF-TEST

**A** Choose the best answer, A, B, C, or D, to complete the sentence. Mark your answer by darkening the oval with the same letter.

1. Is this _____ suitcase?

   **A.** hers    Ⓐ Ⓑ Ⓒ Ⓓ
   **B.** her
   **C.** her's
   **D.** she's

2. Oh no! Our teacher is giving us _____ test this week.

   **A.** other    Ⓐ Ⓑ Ⓒ Ⓓ
   **B.** the another
   **C.** another
   **D.** another one

3. Sue: I like your shoes.
   Pam: These are _____ I bought in Italy.

   **A.** the one    Ⓐ Ⓑ Ⓒ Ⓓ
   **B.** the ones
   **C.** others
   **D.** ones

4. There isn't a drugstore _____!

   **A.** anywhere    Ⓐ Ⓑ Ⓒ Ⓓ
   **B.** anything
   **C.** nothing
   **D.** somewhere

5. I don't have my credit card. I left _____ at the store.

   **A.** one    Ⓐ Ⓑ Ⓒ Ⓓ
   **B.** them
   **C.** it
   **D.** some

6. I left _____ homework at home.

   **A.** mine    Ⓐ Ⓑ Ⓒ Ⓓ
   **B.** my
   **C.** myself
   **D.** me

7. The children enjoyed _____ at Disneyland, but their parents didn't.

   **A.** theirselves    Ⓐ Ⓑ Ⓒ Ⓓ
   **B.** theyselves
   **C.** them
   **D.** themselves

8. There _____ to park on this street.

   **A.** is anywhere    Ⓐ Ⓑ Ⓒ Ⓓ
   **B.** isn't somewhere
   **C.** isn't nowhere
   **D.** isn't anywhere

9. I need a quarter. Do you have _____?

   **A.** one    Ⓐ Ⓑ Ⓒ Ⓓ
   **B.** quarter
   **C.** it
   **D.** a

10. That is _____.

   **A.** ours car    Ⓐ Ⓑ Ⓒ Ⓓ
   **B.** our car
   **C.** car ours
   **D.** ourselves car

**B** **Find the underlined word or phrase, A, B, C, or D, that is incorrect. Mark your answer by darkening the oval with the same letter.**

1. <u>Some</u> teachers can remember all <u>the</u>
   A                                              B
   <u>student</u> <u>names</u>.
   C           D

   Ⓐ Ⓑ Ⓒ Ⓓ

2. If you don't like <u>your</u> job, <u>you can</u> look
                      A              B
   for <u>other</u> <u>one</u>.
       C        D

   Ⓐ Ⓑ Ⓒ Ⓓ

3. <u>Nobody</u> mentioned <u>the</u> problem <u>to</u>
   A                       B              C
   <u>ourselves</u>.
   D

   Ⓐ Ⓑ Ⓒ Ⓓ

4. We took <u>our</u> little sister with <u>us</u> because
           A                            B
   she doesn't like to stay home <u>by</u> <u>ourself</u>.
                                  C    D

   Ⓐ Ⓑ Ⓒ Ⓓ

5. I didn't buy <u>the</u> shirt because I have <u>one</u>
                A                                B
   just like <u>her</u> in <u>another</u> color.
             C          D

   Ⓐ Ⓑ Ⓒ Ⓓ

6. Only two of the <u>questions</u> on <u>the</u> exam
                    A                  B
   were easy.  <u>Others</u> were <u>difficult</u>.
               C                  D

   Ⓐ Ⓑ Ⓒ Ⓓ

7. There are two very popular <u>cities</u>
                               A
   <u>in the United States</u>. <u>One</u> is New York,
    B                          C
   and <u>another</u> is San Francisco.
       D

   Ⓐ Ⓑ Ⓒ Ⓓ

8. In a multiple choice question, <u>one</u> of the
                                   A
   <u>choices</u> is correct, and <u>others</u> <u>are</u> incorrect.
    B                            C         D

   Ⓐ Ⓑ Ⓒ Ⓓ

9. We looked at <u>my</u> old <u>videos</u> last night,
                A            B
   and we enjoyed <u>themselves</u> <u>a lot</u>.
                  C            D

   Ⓐ Ⓑ Ⓒ Ⓓ

10. <u>Our friend</u> is in the hospital because he
    A
    burned <u>himself</u> by accident, so <u>we</u> visited
           B                             C
    <u>himself</u> last night.
    D

    Ⓐ Ⓑ Ⓒ Ⓓ

# UNIT 6

## THE PERFECT TENSES

# 6a  The Present Perfect Tense

Claudia and Kenny are in New York.
They **have visited** many places.
They **have seen** the Statue of Liberty.
They **have gone** up to the top of the
Empire State Building, and **they've been**
to Central Park.

1. We use the past participle verb form in the present perfect tense. The past participle form of regular verbs is the same as the simple past tense form.

| Simple Past Tense Form | Part Participle |
| --- | --- |
| washed | **washed** |
| finished | **finished** |

2. The past participle of irregular verbs is often different from the simple past form. See page 404 for a list of irregular verbs.

| Simple Past Tense Form | Part Participle |
| --- | --- |
| ate | **eaten** |
| came | **come** |
| did | **done** |
| drank | **drunk** |
| knew | **known** |
| saw | **seen** |
| spoke | **spoken** |
| took | **taken** |
| was | **been** |
| went | **gone** |

3. We form the present perfect tense with *have* or *has* + the past participle of the verb.

| AFFIRMATIVE AND NEGATIVE STATEMENTS | | |
| --- | --- | --- |
| Subject | *Have/Has (Not)* | Past Participle |
| I<br>You | **have**<br>**'ve**<br><br>**have not**<br>**'ve not**<br>**haven't** | |
| He/She/It | **has**<br>**'s**<br><br>**has not**<br>**'s not**<br>**hasn't** | **arrived.** |
| We<br>They | **have**<br>**'ve**<br><br>**have not**<br>**'ve not**<br>**haven't** | |

| YES/NO QUESTIONS | | | SHORT ANSWERS | |
| --- | --- | --- | --- | --- |
| *Have/Has* | Subject | Past Participle | Yes, | No, |
| **Have** | I | | you **have.** | you **haven't.** |
| | you | | I/we **have.** | I/we **haven't.** |
| **Has** | he/she/it | **arrived?** | he/she/it **has.** | he/she/it **hasn't.** |
| **Have** | we | | you **have.** | you **haven't.** |
| | they | | they **have.** | they **haven't.** |

| WH– QUESTIONS | | | | |
| --- | --- | --- | --- | --- |
| Wh– Word | *Have/Has* | Subject | Past Participle | |
| **Where** | **have** | they | **been?** | |
| **What** | **have** | you | **made** | for lunch? |
| **Why** | **has** | the music | **stopped?** | |
| **Who*** | **has** | she | **spoken** | to? |
| **How many** (movies) | **have** | we | **seen** | this year? |
| **How long** | **have** | you | **been** | ill? |

*In formal written English, the wh- word would be *whom*.

1. We use the present perfect tense for an action or situation that happened at some unspecified time in the past. The exact time is not important. The action or situation has importance in the present.

> They**'ve been** to New York. (We're talking about their experiences as of *now*.)
> I**'ve washed** the car. (It's clean *now*.)
> He **hasn't done** his homework. (We're talking about his situation *now*.)

2. We can also use the present perfect to talk about actions that were repeated in the past. The exact time is not stated or important.

> We**'ve taken** two tests this month.
> I**'ve been** to New York three times.

3. We often use the present perfect with the time expressions *for, since, just, already, yet, recently,* and *how long*.

> Lin **has lived** here **since** 1999.
> I **have known** you **for** three years.

## 1 Practice

**Complete the postcard that Kenny wrote to his friend Brian. Use the present perfect tense of the verbs in parentheses.**

Dear Brian,

We (be) ___*have been*___ in New York
            1
for four days, and we have enjoyed it very much. We

(go) _____ to the Empire State
            2
Building, we (see) _____ the Statue
            3
of Liberty, and we (walk) _____ in
            4
Central Park. We (eat) _____ great
            5
food every day, and we (buy) _____
            6
tickets for a Broadway show. We still (not, visit)

_____ the Metropolitan Museum
            7
of Art, but we are going there tomorrow. Claudia

(come) _____ back from
            8
shopping, so I'll close now.

Kenny

Mr. Brian Shih
4125 E. 25th Rd.
Phoenix, AZ 86000

Practice

**Work with a partner. Ask and answer questions with the prompts about what Claudia and Kenny have done in New York. Then write your questions and answers.**

1. Claudia and Kenny/arrive in New York

   *Have Claudia and Kenny arrived in New York?*

   *Yes, they have.*

2. they/enjoy/New York

   _____

   _____

3. they/go/to the Empire State Building

   _____

   _____

4. they/see/the Statue of Liberty

   _____

   _____

5. they/walk/in Central Park

   _____

   _____

6. they/eat/good food

   _____

   _____

7. they/buy/tickets for a Broadway show

   _____

   _____

8. they/visit/the Metropolitan Museum of Art

   _____

   _____

## 3 Practice

**Complete the conversation with wh- or yes/no questions in the present perfect.**

Sue: I haven't seen Claudia and Kenny all week. Where are they?

Pete: You didn't know? They've gone away on vacation.

Sue: Really! _Where have they gone?_ _____
<br>1

Pete: They've gone to New York.

Sue: How long _____
<br>2

Pete: They've been in New York for four days now.

Sue: _____
<br>3

Pete: They've seen the Empire State Building, St. Patrick's Cathedral, and Central Park.

Sue: _____ any interesting
<br>4

restaurants?

Pete: Oh, yes. They've eaten in Chinese, Korean, Greek, Brazilian, and Indian restaurants.

Sue: _____
<br>5

Pete: No, but they're going to visit the Metropolitan Museum of Art before they leave.

## 4 Practice

**Armando's roommate Daniel is a problem. Complete the dialogue with the present perfect of the verbs in parentheses.**

Armando: Daniel, I'm sorry, but it's time for you to find another place to live.

Daniel: Why? What's wrong?

Armando: What's wrong? You (be) _____ a terrible roommate.
<br>1

For example, today you (eat) _____ my food, you
<br>2

(drink) _____ my milk, and you
<br>3

(break) _____ my CD player.
<br>4

Daniel: Don't be so sensitive, Armando. I'll replace those things for you.

Armando: That's not all. You (not, pay) _____ the rent for
<br>5

two months. You (insult) _____ my sister, and you
<br>6

(try) _____ to steal my girlfriend. I
                7
(be) _____ very patient, but now it's time for you to
                8
leave.

Daniel:     Well, OK. I'll leave if you want. But...

Armando:  What?

Daniel:     I (spend) _____ all of my money. Could you lend me $500?
                            9

## 5 | Practice

**Complete the conversation with the present perfect of the verbs in parentheses.**

Marco:  What things (do) ___*have*___ you ___*done*___ up to now?
                              1                2
Tina:    Lots of things. I (wash) _____ the dishes, and I
                                          3
         (make) _____ the bed. I (go) _____
                     4                                              5
         to the store, and I (buy) _____ groceries. What have
                                              6
         you done?

Marco:  I (take) _____ a shower, I (do) _____
                        7                                              8
         my homework, and I (clean) _____ my room. And...oh, yes.
                                              9
         I (have) _____ lunch.
                        10

## 6 | Practice

**Work in pairs. Make a dialogue similar to the one in Practice 5 about yourselves.**

**Example:**
You:              What have you done today?
Your partner:  I've studied for the test tomorrow, and I've cleaned my room.
You:              I haven't studied for the test, but I've done all of my homework.

## 7 | Your Turn

**Think of things to do and places to see in the town where you are now. Make a list of five things to do or places to see. Ask other people what they have done in your town.**

**Example:**
You:              Have you been to the cathedral?
Your partner:  Yes, I have. Have you been to the zoo?
You:              No, I haven't. Have you visited the art museum?

## 6b  *For* and *Since*

This house has been here **since** 1925.
My grandmother has lived here **for** 50 years.

1. We use *for* with the present perfect when we are talking about a period or length of time that started in the past and continues to the present.

   I've lived here **for** three years.

2. We use *since* with the present perfect when we are talking about a point of time in the past such as a date, a month, or a day.

   I've worked here **since** August.
   She's been sick **since** Tuesday.

---

8  Practice

**Some of these time expressions are used with *for*. Others are used with *since*. Put them in the correct list.**

| | | |
|---|---|---|
| 2003 | I was a child | Monday |
| a long time | last month | my birthday |
| about a week | two months | six hours |
| New Year's Eve | last summer | ten minutes |
| eight o'clock | 30 seconds | three years |
| Friday evening | many years | yesterday |
| I moved here | May | |

| **I have been here...** | **I have been here...** |
|---|---|
| **for** | **since** |
| *a long time* | *2003* |
| _____ | _____ |
| _____ | _____ |
| _____ | _____ |
| _____ | _____ |
| _____ | _____ |
| _____ | _____ |
| | _____ |
| | _____ |
| | _____ |
| | _____ |

## 9  Practice

**Complete the sentences with *for* or *since*.**

**1.** Rob has had his car _____*for*_____ a year, but he wants to sell it.

**2.** He's had problems with it _____ the day he bought it.

**3.** The lights haven't worked _____ March.

**4.** It has made a funny noise _____ several weeks.

**5.** He has taken it to a mechanic every week _____ a month.

**6.** He has spent a lot of money on it every month _____ June.

**7.** He has run an advertisement in the newspaper every day _____ a week.

**8.** So far, he hasn't had a response _____ he ran the ad.

## 10  Your Turn

**Work with a partner. Ask questions with *how long* and the prompts. Your partner answers the questions using *for* or *since*.**

**Example:**
be in this country
You:              How long have you been in this country?
Your partner: I have been here for eight months.

be in this country     have your watch     live in your apartment     study in this class

## 6c  *Ever* and *Never*

A: Have you **ever** seen the Taj Mahal?
B: No, **never.**

1. We can use *ever* in questions, often with the present perfect. It means "at any time up to now."

2. When we use *ever* in present perfect tense questions, it comes between the subject and the past participle.

   Have you **ever** been to China?

3. We often use *never* (at no time) when we give a negative answer.

   No, I've **never** been to China.

---

**|1|  Practice**

**Interview the famous movie star La La Labore. Write questions with the prompts and give short answers.**

**1.** ever be/married

   *Have you ever been married?*

   Yes, _____*I have.*_____ I've been married eight times.

**2.** ever be/to Hollywood

   _____

   Yes, _____ I've been there many times.

**3.** ever drive/a Ferrari

_____

No, _____ I never drive. I have a chauffeur.

**4.** ever give/an interview on television

_____

Yes, _____ I've given interviews to famous journalists.

**5.** ever write/a book

_____

No, _____ Other people write about me.

**6.** ever sing/in a movie

_____

No, _____ I can't sing.

**7.** ever eat/caviar

_____

Yes, _____ I eat it for breakfast every day!

## 12 Practice

**Work with a partner. Ask questions with _have you ever_ and the prompts.**

**Example:**
fly in a helicopter
You:            Have you ever flown in a helicopter?
Your partner: Yes, I have. OR No, I never have. OR No, never.

1. fly in a helicopter
2. drive a truck
3. eat Thai food
4. go to Hawaii
5. have the flu
6. hold a snake
7. meet a millionaire

8. play baseball
9. sleep in a tent
10. speak to a famous person
11. swim in a river
12. take a photo of a lion
13. tell a lie
14. travel by boat

# 6d Already, Yet, and Just

They've **just** gotten married.
They've **already** had a ceremony.
They haven't gone on their honeymoon **yet.**

1. We use *yet* in negative sentences to say that something has not happened, but we think it will. *Yet* comes at the end of the sentence.

    The plane hasn't arrived **yet.**

2. We also use *yet* in questions to ask if something we expect to happen has happened.

    Has the plane arrived **yet?**

3. We use *just* if the action is very recent. *Just* comes before the past participle.

    I've **just** spoken to Tony.

4. We use *already* to say something happened before now or before it was expected to happen. *Already* comes before the past participle.

    I've **already** told you how to get there.

## 13 Practice

**A. Carlos and Rosa are in San Francisco on vacation. It's their last day. Read this list of things they want to do today. They have done some of these things, but they haven't done others yet. A check mark (√) shows what they have already done.**

1. √ get postcards
2. write postcards
3. have lunch
4. √ visit the Museum of Modern Art
5. √ see a show

6. buy souvenirs
7. ask the hotel for the bill
8. √ pack the suitcases
9. go to the post office
10. call the airline

**B. Write sentences with *already* and *yet*.**

1. *They've already gotten postcards.*
2. *They haven't written postcards yet.*
3. _____
4. _____
5. _____
6. _____
7. _____
8. _____
9. _____
10. _____

## 14 Your Turn

Write five sentences about things you've recently done and things you haven't done yet this week.

**Example:**
I've just paid the bills.
I've already done my homework.
I haven't called my mother yet.

1. _____
   _____
2. _____
   _____
3. _____
   _____
4. _____
   _____
5. _____
   _____

## 15 Your Turn

Work with a partner. Read each other's sentences from Practice 14. Ask and answer questions about what you've done and haven't done.

**Example:**
You:            Have you paid the bills yet?
Your partner: Yes, I have.

## 6e The Simple Past Tense OR The Present Perfect Tense

Antonia Beck **has been** to Turkey.
She **went** there in 2001.

1. We use the simple past tense when we are talking about the past. We use it for actions that happened in the past. We can state the specific time of the action.

    She **went** to Turkey in July, 2001. After a month, she **went** to Athens.

2. We use the present perfect for an action that happened in the past. The action has importance in the present. The specific time is unimportant, and we cannot state it.

    CORRECT:    Antonia **has been** to Turkey.
    INCORRECT: Antonia has been to Turkey ~~in 2001.~~

3. We use the simple past for an action that started and finished in the past.

    George **had** a headache for two hours this morning. (He doesn't have a headache now.)

4. We use the present perfect for an action that started in the past and is still continuing in the present.

    George **has had** a headache for two hours. (He still has a headache.)

---

### 16 Practice

**Complete the sentences with the simple past or present perfect of the verbs in parentheses.**

**1.** A: I (see) _____*saw*_____ Karen yesterday.

    B: Oh really? I (not/see) _____ her for weeks.

**2.** A: What (do) _____ you _____ last Saturday?

B: I (stay) _____ at home.

**3.** A: (write) _____ you _____ your essay yet?

B: Yes, I (finish) _____ it an hour ago.

**4.** A: (be) _____ you _____ to the United States?

B: Yes, I (go) _____ to Miami last summer.

**5.** A: I (know) _____ Tony for three years.

B: Really? When (meet) _____ you _____ him?

A: We (meet) _____ in college.

**6.** A: (eat) _____ you _____ at Mario's restaurant?

B: Yes, I _____. I (eat) _____ there last Saturday.

**7.** A: (ever, play) _____ you _____ _____ soccer?

B: Yes, I (play) _____ when I was a teenager.

**8.** A: (ask) _____ you _____ the teacher about your essay yet?

B: Yes, I (talk) _____ to her yesterday.

## |17| Practice

**Antonia Beck has made a lot of business trips in the last few years. Say which cities she has visited. Then say when she went there. Use the simple past and the present perfect.**

**Example:**
She has been to New York.
She went there in May, 2001.

| **2001** | | **2003** | |
|---|---|---|---|
| May | New York | February | Boston |
| September | Bangkok | April | Mexico City |
| December | Paris | October | Istanbul |

| **2002** | | **2004** | |
|---|---|---|---|
| March | Tokyo | January | Cairo |
| July | Chicago | July | Jakarta |
| September | Seoul | September | Rio de Janeiro |

## 6f  The Present Perfect Progressive Tense

Tony **has been waiting** for 45 minutes.

We form the present perfect progressive tense with *have/has* + the past participle of *be* (*been*) + verb + *-ing*.

| AFFIRMATIVE AND NEGATIVE STATEMENTS | | | |
|---|---|---|---|
| Subject | *Have/Has (Not)* | *Been* | Verb + *-ing* |
| I | **have**<br>**'ve** | | |
| You | **have not**<br>**'ve not**<br>**haven't** | | |
| He/She/It | **has**<br>**'s**<br><br>**has not**<br>**'s not**<br>**hasn't** | **been** | **waiting.** |
| We | **have**<br>**'ve** | | |
| They | **have not**<br>**'ve not**<br>**haven't** | | |

| YES/NO QUESTIONS | | | | SHORT ANSWERS | |
|---|---|---|---|---|---|
| *Have/Has* | Subject | *Been* | Verb + *–ing* | Yes, | No, |
| **Have** | I | | | you **have.** | you **haven't.** |
| | you | | | I/we **have.** | I/we **haven't.** |
| **Has** | he/she/it | **been** | **waiting?** | he/she/it **has.** | he/she/it **hasn't.** |
| **Have** | we | | | you **have.** | you **haven't.** |
| | they | | | they **have.** | they **haven't.** |

We use the present perfect progressive to talk about an action that began in the past and continues into the present. We can use this tense to show how long an activity has been in progress. We use the time words *for* and *since* for this.

> He **has been waiting for** 45 minutes.
> She **has been talking** on the phone **since** six o'clock.

## 18 Practice

**Complete the sentences with the present progressive or present perfect progressive of the verbs in parentheses.**

**A.**

A: Who (wait) _____*are*_____ you _____*waiting*_____ for?
                    1                          2

B: I (wait) _____ for the manager.
                        3

A: She (talk) _____ on the phone with a client for an hour. I'll tell
                          4

you when she's free.

**B.**

A: You look busy. What (do) _____ you _____?
                              1                        2

B: I (write) _____ my research paper.
                        3

A: How long (work) _____ you _____ on it?
                          4                      5

B: I (work) _____ on it since January.
                        6

**C.**

At the moment, I (sit) _____ in class. I (sit) _____
                              1                                          2

here for 20 minutes. We (learn) _____ about the present perfect
                                              3

progressive tense since the beginning of this class.

## 19 Practice

**Write answers using the present perfect progressive and a time expression with *for* or *since*.**

1. How long have you been going to this school?

   *I have been going to this school since September.*

2. How long have you been learning English?

   _____

**3.** How long have you been using this book?

_____

**4.** How long have you been sitting in this classroom today?

_____

**5.** How long have you been learning the present perfect tense?

_____

**6.** How long have you been doing this exercise?

_____

| 20 | **Your Turn** |

Work with a partner. Ask and answer questions about your lives with *how long* + the present perfect progressive. Use the list of verbs for ideas.

**Example:**
You:            How long have you been living in your house?
Your partner:  I've been living there for six months.

live                    stay                    study                    work

## 6g    The Present Perfect Tense OR The Present Perfect Progressive Tense

**Function**

Karen **has been talking** on the phone for two hours.
She **has made** four telephone calls.

1. We use the present perfect for an action that has just finished or that was finished at some unstated point in the past.

   He **has just missed** the bus.
   I **have missed** the bus, but I won't be late.

2. We use the present perfect progressive for an action that started in the past and continues into the present.

   Mr. Black **has been teaching** for nine years.

3. We use the present perfect to talk about a repeated action.

   She **has made** four telephone calls.

4. We use the present perfect progressive to emphasize the duration of the action.

   She **has been talking** on the phone for two hours.

5. With some verbs that take place over time, like *live, stay, study, teach,* and *work,* we can use either the present perfect or the present perfect progressive.

   He **has been teaching** for nine years.
   OR He **has taught** for nine years.

---

21 Practice

Complete the sentences with the present perfect or the present perfect progressive of the verbs in parentheses.

1. Carlos and Rosa are planning to buy a house. They

   (look) _have been looking_ for a house for a month. They

   (look) _____ at five houses, but they

   (not, find) _____ one that they like yet.

2. My grandfather (paint) _____ for ten years now. He

   (paint) _____ more than fifty paintings.

3. I (learn) _____ to drive for four months. I

   (take) _____ the driving test three times now and

   (not, pass) _____ yet.

4. John (write) _____ on his computer for an hour. He

   (already, send) _____ five e-mail messages to his friends.

5. Karen (drive) _____ for three hours now. She

   (drive) _____ almost 200 miles.

**6.** I (read) _____ this book for two weeks now, but I

(not, finish) _____ yet.

**7.** Jerry (work) _____ on a math problem for half an hour,

and he (not, find) _____ the answer yet.

**8.** I (cook) _____ for hours, and I

(just, burn) _____ the cake.

## 22 Practice

**Complete the sentences with the present perfect or the present perfect progressive of the verbs in parentheses.**

Dear Sarah,

I (mean) _____*have been meaning*_____ to write to you for weeks,
                      1

but you know how it is. Everything is fine here at home. I (just, finish)

_____ my second year at college, and I (get)
          2

_____ good grades. I (decide)
          3

_____ to get a job for the summer and save some
          4

money. So far, I (help) _____ Mom with the shopping
                  5

and the cooking.

Dad (sell) _____ the old car! He (buy)
             6

_____ a new one of the same make and color, of course! I
          7

(not/drive) _____ it yet. Mom is busy with redecorating the
          8

house. It (be) _____ a mess here. The painters (work)
          9

_____ as fast as they can, and I hope they will be done
          10

soon. The house will look great by the time you come.

I hope you (study) _____ hard!
                11

See you soon.

Your brother,

Tim

## 6h  The Past Perfect Tense

Candice was sad because her friends **hadn't asked** her to go biking with them.

We form the past perfect tense with *had* + the past participle of the verb.

| AFFIRMATIVE AND NEGATIVE STATEMENTS | | |
|---|---|---|
| Subject | *Had (Not)* | Past Participle |
| I | **had** | |
| You | **'d** | |
| He/She/It | | **left.** |
| We | **had not** | |
| They | **hadn't** | |

| YES/NO QUESTIONS | | | SHORT ANSWERS | |
|---|---|---|---|---|
| *Had* | Subject | Past Participle | Yes, | No, |
| **Had** | I | | you **had.** | you **hadn't.** |
| | you | | I/we **had.** | I/we **hadn't.** |
| | he/she/it | **left?** | he/she/it **had.** | he/she/it **hadn't.** |
| | we | | you **had.** | you **hadn't.** |
| | they | | they **had.** | they **hadn't.** |

1. We use the past perfect for a past action that happened before another past action.

2. We use the past perfect for the first action in time, and the simple past for the second action.

   **1st Action**          **2nd Action**
   When he **had saved** enough money, he **bought** a car.

3. The past perfect verb can come after the simple past verb. The verb tenses tell you which action happened first.

   **2nd Action**          **1st Action**
   He **bought** a car when he **had saved** enough money.

## 23 Practice

Complete the sentences with the simple past or past perfect of the verbs in parentheses.

**A.**

When I (get) _____*got*_____ home yesterday, the letter

(arrive) _____. I (open) _____ it
                 **2**                              **3**

and (read) _____ it. It said that they
                   **4**

(give) _____ the position to someone else because that person
              **5**

(have) _____ more experience.
              **6**

**B.**

When I (get) _____ home, my son
                    **1**

(eat, already) _____ dinner. He said he was hungry because he
                      **2**

(not, eat) _____ all day. Then, he (get) _____
                  **3**                                              **4**

sick because he (eat) _____ too much ice cream.
                              **5**

**Ken's mother and father-in-law are coming to stay for a few days. Look at the things Ken and his wife did and didn't do before their guests arrived. Write sentences using the past perfect tense.**

1. They changed the sheets.
2. They bought food.
3. They developed the photographs of their daughter.
4. They didn't prepare dinner.
5. They didn't rent any interesting movies.
6. They didn't do the laundry.
7. They washed the dishes.
8. They didn't clean the house.

Ken's mother and father-in-law arrived on Friday at 5:00 P.M. By that time,

1. _Ken and his wife had changed the sheets._

2. _By that time,_

3. _By that time,_

4. _By that time,_

5. _By that time,_

6. _By that time,_

7. _By that time,_

8. _By that time,_

## 25 Practice

**Work with a partner. Give two possible answers for each of these questions. Give one in the simple past and the other in the past perfect. Then write your answers. Use the ideas from the list or your own.**

| | | | |
|---|---|---|---|
| be unhappy | get a better offer | not bring/his wallet | study the night before |
| feel sick | her car/be stolen | not like/the menu | the neighbors/be loud |

**1.** Why did he fail the test?

*He failed the test because he felt sick during the test.*

*He failed the test because he had not studied the night before.*

**2.** Why did he leave his job?

_____

_____

**3.** Why did he leave the restaurant?

_____

_____

**4.** Why did she call the police?

_____

_____

## 26 Your Turn

**Think of a point in your life when your life changed, such as:**

**1.** you turned sixteen
**2.** you got your first car
**3.** you started/left school
**4.** you got married
**5.** the year 20XX

Write three things you had done before then.
Write three things that you hadn't done before then.

**Example:**
Before I turned sixteen, I hadn't driven a car.

## 6i    The Past Perfect Progressive Tense

Bob Blake was hot and nervous. He **had been sitting** in a meeting with his boss for two hours.

We form the past perfect progressive tense with *had been* + verb + *–ing*.

| AFFIRMATIVE AND NEGATIVE STATEMENTS | | |
|---|---|---|
| Subject | *Had (Not)* | *Been* + Verb + *-ing* |
| I | **had** | |
| You | **'d** | |
| He/She/It | | **been working.** |
| We | **had not** | |
| They | **hadn't** | |

| YES/NO QUESTIONS | | | SHORT ANSWERS | |
|---|---|---|---|---|
| *Had* | Subject | *Been* + Verb + *-ing* | Yes, | No, |
| **Had** | I | **been working?** | you **had.** | you **hadn't.** |
| | you | | I/we **had.** | I/we **hadn't.** |
| | he/she/it | | he/she/it **had.** | he/she/it **hadn't.** |
| | we | | you **had.** | you **hadn't.** |
| | they | | they **had.** | they **hadn't.** |

1. We use the past perfect progressive as the past of the present perfect progressive.

2. The past perfect progressive emphasizes the duration of an action that started and finished in the past.

| Past Perfect Progressive Tense | Present Perfect Progressive Tense |
|---|---|
| He **had been waiting** for me for an hour. (He isn't waiting now.) | He **has been waiting** for me for an hour. (He is still waiting now.) |

3. We also use the past perfect progressive to show the cause of an action that happened in the past.

**Result**          **Cause**
Her eyes were tired. She **had been working** on the computer for hours.

## 27 Practice

**What had they been doing? Complete the sentences using the verbs from the list and the past perfect progressive.**

dream          lie          run          try          walk          wait

1. Sophie's feet ached. She ___*had been walking*___ in her new shoes for hours.

2. Louis was angry. He _____ for Kim for 45 minutes.

3. Carmen woke up at 3:00 in the morning. She was frightened. She

   _____.

4. Ted was hot and out of breath when he came in. He _____ in the park.

5. Tony came in from the beach looking very red. He _____ in the sun too long.

6. The students were confused. They _____ to learn the past perfect progressive.

## 28 Your Turn

When was the last time:  • you were tired  • you were angry  • you were nervous

What had you been doing? How long had you been doing it? Tell your partner.

**Example:**
The last time I was tired was on Saturday. I had been cleaning the apartment all day.

# WRITING: Write a Friendly Letter

Write a letter to a friend about your recent experiences.

**Step 1. Think about things in your past and present life you can write about. Write the answers to these questions or others you can think of.**

**1.** What are you studying?

_____

**2.** How long have you been studying?

_____

**3.** What do you find easy/difficult/interesting?

_____

**4.** What have you been doing in your free time?

_____

**5.** Where is the last place you traveled to? What did you do there?

_____

**6.** What movies have you seen? What kind of sports have you been doing or have you watched on television?

_____

**7.** What special things have you bought?

_____

**8.** When will you talk to your friend again, or maybe see your friend?

_____

**Step 2. Rewrite the answers in the form of a letter. For more writing guidelines, see pages 407–411.**

**Step 3. Evaluate your letter.**

**Checklist**

_____ Did you include the date at the top of the letter?

_____ Did you start with a greeting such as "Dear Rosa"?

_____ Did you indent your paragraphs?

_____ Did you end with a closing such as "Sincerely," "Your friend," or "Love"?

_____ Did you sign your name at the bottom of your letter?

**Step 4. Edit your letter. Work with a partner or teacher to edit your sentences. Correct spelling, punctuation, vocabulary, and grammar.**

**Step 5. Write the final copy of your letter.**

# SELF-TEST

A Choose the best answer, A, B, C, or D, to complete the sentence. Mark your answer by darkening the oval with the same letter.

1. I _____ since 10:00 when the doorbell rang.

   A. was sleeping    Ⓐ Ⓑ Ⓒ Ⓓ
   B. have been sleeping
   C. slept
   D. had been sleeping

2. Sandy _____ a new computer last week. She likes it.

   A. bought    Ⓐ Ⓑ Ⓒ Ⓓ
   B. had bought
   C. was buying
   D. had been bought

3. Sam has lived in San Francisco _____ three years.

   A. since    Ⓐ Ⓑ Ⓒ Ⓓ
   B. for
   C. already
   D. yet

4. She _____.

   A. is just arrived    Ⓐ Ⓑ Ⓒ Ⓓ
   B. just arrive
   C. has just arrived
   D. arrived just

5. I _____ my homework.

   A. have done already    Ⓐ Ⓑ Ⓒ Ⓓ
   B. did already
   C. have already done
   D. arrived just

6. I _____.

   A. haven't finished yet    Ⓐ Ⓑ Ⓒ Ⓓ
   B. didn't finish yet
   C. haven't yet finished
   D. didn't yet finish

7. After he _____, he called a taxi.

   A. has packed    Ⓐ Ⓑ Ⓒ Ⓓ
   B. was packing
   C. pack
   D. had packed

8. I _____ such a strange story in my life.

   A. never heard    Ⓐ Ⓑ Ⓒ Ⓓ
   B. have never heard
   C. heard never
   D. have heard never

9. I _____ you since December.

   A. haven't saw    Ⓐ Ⓑ Ⓒ Ⓓ
   B. haven't seen
   C. didn't see
   D. not see

10. We _____ our trip to Thailand for a month. We have almost finished, and we are leaving next week.

   A. are planning    Ⓐ Ⓑ Ⓒ Ⓓ
   B. planned
   C. have been planning
   D. had planned

**B** **Find the underlined word or phrase, A, B, C, or D, that is incorrect. Mark your answer by darkening the oval with the same letter.**

1. <u>Have</u> you <u>yet</u> learned <u>all</u> <u>the</u> irregular past
      A       B        C  D
   participles?

   Ⓐ Ⓑ Ⓒ Ⓓ

2. <u>Have</u> you <u>study</u> English verb tenses <u>when</u>
      A       B                    C
   you <u>were</u> in high school?
       D

   Ⓐ Ⓑ Ⓒ Ⓓ

3. We <u>have been</u> <u>studying</u> the past tenses <u>for</u>
         A        B                   C
   the beginning of the <u>semester</u>.
                      D

   Ⓐ Ⓑ Ⓒ Ⓓ

4. Picasso <u>has painted</u> hundreds of paintings
             A
   <u>before</u> he <u>died</u> <u>in</u> 1973.
     B     C   D

   Ⓐ Ⓑ Ⓒ Ⓓ

5. My friend <u>had</u> not <u>been</u> <u>working</u> <u>since</u> the
            A        B     C    D
   company closed down two months ago.

   Ⓐ Ⓑ Ⓒ Ⓓ

6. <u>The</u> Science Museum <u>had</u> <u>been</u> closed <u>for</u>
    A                  B   C         D
   five days because of repairs, but it will
   open again next Monday.

   Ⓐ Ⓑ Ⓒ Ⓓ

7. <u>Have</u> you <u>seen</u> <u>ever</u> <u>the</u> Statue of Liberty
    A        B    C
   <u>in New York</u>?
      D

   Ⓐ Ⓑ Ⓒ Ⓓ

8. <u>How many</u> verb <u>tenses</u> <u>did</u> you <u>studied</u> up
      A           B    C      D
   to now?

   Ⓐ Ⓑ Ⓒ Ⓓ

9. <u>Have</u> you <u>see</u> <u>a kangaroo</u> when you <u>were</u>
    A      B    C               D
   in Australia last winter?

   Ⓐ Ⓑ Ⓒ Ⓓ

10. <u>Have</u> you <u>been</u> to London before you <u>were</u>
      A      B                        C
    there <u>last month</u>?
        D

    Ⓐ Ⓑ Ⓒ Ⓓ

# UNIT 7

# QUESTIONS AND PHRASAL VERBS

# 7a Yes/No Questions and Short Answers

A: Does he fight fires?
B: Yes, he does.

1. When forms of the verbs *be, have,* and *do* are used with other verb forms such as the base form, the *–ing* form, or the past participle, they are auxiliary verbs.

   He **is wearing** a firefighter's uniform. (*Is* is an auxiliary verb.)
   **Does** he **fight** fires? (*Does* is an auxiliary verb.)
   He **has fought** many fires. (*Has* is an auxiliary verb.)

2. Modal verbs such as *can, should,* and *will* are also auxiliary verbs.

   He **should** be careful on the job!

3. Auxiliary verbs are used to form tenses, questions, and negative statements.

4. There are 17 common auxiliary verbs in English that we use to make questions. Auxiliary verbs are also used to make short answers.

| YES/NO QUESTIONS | | | | SHORT ANSWERS | |
|---|---|---|---|---|---|
| Auxilary Verb | Subject | Base Verb or Base Verb + -ing or Past Participle | | Yes, | No, |
| **Am** | I | **disturbing** | you? | you **are.** | you **aren't.** |
| **Is** | it | **raining** | hard? | it **is.** | it **isn't.** |
| **Are** | they | **studying** | English? | they **are.** | they **aren't.** |
| **Was** | she | **studying** | English last year? | she **was.** | she **wasn't.** |
| **Were** | you | **trying** | to call me? | I **was.** | I **wasn't.** |
| **Do** | they | **like** | country music? | they **do.** | they **don't.** |
| **Does** | this school | **have** | a language lab? | it **does.** | it **doesn't.** |
| **Did** | it | **rain** | last night? | it **did.** | it **didn't.** |
| **Have** | they | **finished** | their work? | they **have.** | they **haven't.** |
| **Has** | Anne | **come** | home yet? | she **has.** | she **hasn't.** |
| **Had** | they | **eaten** | yet? | they **had.** | they **hadn't.** |
| **Can** | you | **swim** | well? | I **can.** | I **can't.** |
| **Could** | you | **ride** | a bike as a child? | I **could.** | I **couldn't.** |
| **Will** | they | **be** | here on time? | they **will.** | they **won't.** |
| **Would** | you | **go** | outside in a storm? | I **would.** | I **wouldn't.** |
| **Should** | you | **see** | a doctor? | I **should.** | I **shouldn't.** |
| **Must** | we | **stand** | in this line? | we **must.** | * |

*In this meaning, the negative short answer with *must* is "No, we don't have to."

## 1 Practice

**Match the questions with the short answers.**

_h_ **1.** Have you had lunch yet?

_____ **2.** Do you work in the city?

_____ **3.** Is it raining outside?

_____ **4.** Did you take the test yesterday?

_____ **5.** Can I borrow your car?

_____ **6.** Was the test difficult?

_____ **7.** Are your parents coming?

_____ **8.** Must I go with you?

**a.** Yes, it is.

**b.** No, you can't.

**c.** Yes, I do.

**d.** No, they aren't.

**e.** No, it wasn't.

**f.** No, I didn't.

**g.** Yes, you must.

**h.** Yes, I have.

## 2 Practice

**Write short answers to these questions.**

1. Is New York City the capital of the United States?

   _No, it isn't._

2. Was Elvis Presley a scientist?

   No, _____

3. Do they speak English in Australia?

   Yes, _____

4. Did Edison invent the computer?

   No, _____

5. Was Cleopatra Italian?

   No, _____

6. Does rice grow in China?

   Yes, _____

7. Can monkeys climb trees?

   Yes, _____

8. Are there pyramids in Turkey?

   Yes, _____

9. Were there cars 200 years ago?

   No, _____

10. Have humans been to the planet Jupiter?

    No, _____

## 3 Practice

**What kind of person are you? Complete the questions with the correct auxiliary verb. Then answer by checking Yes or No.**

1. _Are_ you shy?                           _____ Yes _____ No

2. _____ you like sports?                 _____ Yes _____ No

3. _____ you worry a lot?                 _____ Yes _____ No

4. _____ you get up early?                _____ Yes _____ No

5. _____ you lazy?                        _____ Yes _____ No

6. _____ you clean and tidy?              _____ Yes _____ No

7. _____ you cry when you watch a sad movie?  _____ Yes _____ No

8. _____ you get angry quickly?           _____ Yes _____ No

**9.** _____ friends very important to you?      _____ Yes _____ No

**10.** _____ you like to have fun a lot?      _____ Yes _____ No

**11.** _____ clothes important to you?      _____ Yes _____ No

---

**4** | **Your Turn**

**Ask your partner five yes/no questions. Use your own ideas or the ones in the list.**

**Example:**
friends
You:            Do you have a lot of friends?
Your partner:  Yes, I do.

friends          music          school          sports

---

## 7b  Questions with Wh- Words (*What, When, Where, Who(m), Why,* and *How*)

**Form**

A: **Where** do polar bears live?
B: They live in the Arctic.

A: **What** do they eat?
B: They eat seals and fish.

A: **When** do they have young?
B: In the spring.

1. We call words that start questions "wh- words" because most of them start with the letters *wh*.

2. When the verb in a question is the simple present or past tense of *be* (*am, is, are, was,* or *were*), we make questions by putting the verb before the subject.

| Wh- Word | Present or Past of *Be* | Subject |
|---|---|---|
| Who | **is** | **she?** |
| Where | **are** | **those students?** |
| Why | **were** | **you** late? |

3. For questions with all other verbs and tenses, we put an auxiliary verb before the subject.* The verb can be a base verb, an *–ing* verb, or a past participle.

| Wh– Word | Auxiliary Verb | Subject | Verb |
|---|---|---|---|
| Where | **have** | **you** | lived? |
| When | **does** | **she** | arrive? |
| What | **did** | **he** | do? |
| Why | **are** | **they** | leaving? |
| Who** | **can** | **you** | see? |
| How | **did** | **your team** | win? |

*When *who* or *what* is the subject of the question, we do not change the word order. See section 7c on page 166.

**In formal written English, the wh- word would be *whom*.

## Function

We use wh- words to ask for information about something.

1. We use *who(m)** to ask about a person.

    **Who(m)** were you calling?    I was calling Jill.
    **Who** took my dictionary?    Tom took your dictionary.

2. We use *what* to ask about a thing.

    **What** is she studying?    She's studying engineering.

3. We use *when* to ask about dates and times.

    **When** is the test?    It's on Monday at 9:00 A.M.

4. We use *where* to ask about places.

    **Where** do you live?    I live on Lemon Street.

5. We use *why* to ask for reasons.

    **Why** are you leaving?    I have to catch a train.

*In formal written English, *whom* is the object form of *who*. We usually use *who* for both subjects and objects in speech and informal writing.

## 5  Practice

**Who is the person? Read the answers and write questions with the words in parentheses. Then say who the person is.**

**A.**

**1.** Question: _When was she born?_

   Answer: She was born in 1929. (when)

**2.** Question: _____

   Answer: She was born in Philadelphia, Pennsylvania. (where)

**3.** Question: _____

   Answer: She married a prince. (who)

**4.** Question: _____

   Answer: She lived in Monaco. (where)

**5.** Question: _____

   Answer: She was famous for her fashionable clothes and her caring for people. (what)

**6.** Question: _____

   Answer: She died in a car accident in 1982. (when)

The person is _____

**B.**

**1.** Question: _____

   Answer: He was born in 1975. (when)

**2.** Question: _____

   Answer: He was born in Florida, in the United States. (where)

**3.** Question: _____

   Answer: He studied at Stanford University in California. (where)

**4.** Question: _____

   Answer: He started to play golf when he was three. (what)

**5.** Question: _____

   Answer: He became a professional in 1996. (when)

**6.** Question: _____

   Answer: He is famous because he is already one of the best players of all time, even though he is young. (why)

The person is _____

## 6 | Your Turn

Write a quiz about your country. Write five questions with *what, when, where, who,* and *why*. Ask the questions to the class.

**Example:**
What is the name of the lake in the north?
Where do most people live?

1. _____

2. _____

3. _____

4. _____

5. _____

# 7c  Questions with *Who* and *What* as the Subject

**Form**

**What** happened?
A man slipped on a banana peel.

**Who** was it?
It was my boss.

When *who* or *what* is the subject of a question, the word order is the same as in statements. If *who(m)* or *what* is the object of the question, the word order is in the question form.

| *Who/What* as Subject | *Who(m)/What* as Object |
|---|---|
| Who met you? | Who(m) did you meet? |
| What happened? | What did you see? |

166

Unit 7

## 7 | Practice

**Write questions with *who* or *what*. The underlined word is the answer.**

**1.** Pete saw <u>Karen</u> at the store yesterday.

_Who did Pete see at the store yesterday?_

**2.** <u>Pete</u> saw Karen at the store yesterday.

_____

**3.** Karen was buying <u>fresh strawberries</u>.

_____

**4.** <u>Karen</u> was buying fresh strawberries.

_____

**5.** <u>Karen</u> invited a friend for dinner yesterday.

_____

**6.** Karen invited <u>a friend</u> for dinner yesterday.

_____

## 8 | Practice

**A. Read this story about an accident.**

There was an accident this morning. It was 10:00, and it was raining. Bob saw a woman jogger crossing the street. Then he heard a loud bang. A white truck had suddenly stopped, and a red car had crashed into the back of the truck. Bob called 911 for the police and an ambulance. At about 10:15, the police and ambulance came. A police officer asked him questions.

**B. Complete the questions about the story with *who* or *what*.**

1. _Who_ saw the accident?
2. _____ caused the accident? The rain or the jogger?
3. _____ called 911?
4. _____ made the loud bang?
5. _____ happened to the driver of the white truck?
6. _____ happened to the jogger?
7. _____ happened to the driver of the red car?
8. _____ came at 10:15?
9. _____ asked questions?
10. _____ answered questions?

**C. With a partner, ask and answer the questions in part B. Use information from the story when possible. If not, use your imagination.**

**Example:**
You:          Who saw the accident?
Your partner:  Bob saw it.

# 7d  Questions with *Which* and *What*

**Which** woman has long curly hair?
**Which** woman has straight hair?

1. We use *what* or *which* to ask about people, places, and things.

2. We use *what* when the choices are not limited.

    **What** sports do you like?
    **What** authors do you like?

3. We use *which* when the choices are limited.

    **Which** is your favorite, swimming or tennis?
    **Which** author do you prefer, Agatha Christie or Steven King?

4. When using *which,* we can say *which, which* + a noun, or *which one.*

    **Which** do you prefer, Christie or King?
    **Which author** do you prefer, Christie or King?
    **Which one** do you prefer, Christie or King?

5. We can use *which* with singular or plural nouns.

    **Which places** did you visit?
    **Which place** was your favorite?

---

**9** Practice

**Complete the questions with *what* or *which*.**

Nina:     <u>Which</u> countries did you visit in Europe?
                 1

Claudia:   I went to France and Italy.

Nina:     _____ did you like better?
                 2

Claudia:   I loved France.

Nina:     _____ did you buy?
                 3

Claudia:   I bought some clothes and perfume.

Nina:     _____ country had the best clothes: France or Italy?
                 4

Claudia:   Italy had the best clothes.

Nina:     _____ one had the most perfumes?
                 5

Claudia:   France had the most perfumes. Tourists buy them tax free.

Claudia:   I have an Italian scarf for you, but you can choose the color.

              _____ one do you like—the red or the cream color?
                 6

Nina:       The red one. Thank you.

Nina:       _____ French cities did you visit?
                    7

Claudia:    I went to Paris, Lyon, Nice, and Cannes.

Nina:       _____ city was the most beautiful?
                    8

Claudia:    Paris, of course.

Nina:       _____ is a good time to visit Paris?
                    9

Claudia:    Anytime is good. I prefer spring.

Nina:       _____ month, April or May?
                    10

Claudia:    I prefer May; it's warmer.

Nina:       _____ country was cheaper, France or Italy?
                    11

Claudia:    They are about the same. My company paid for the trip—it was for business,

            you see.

## 10 Practice

**Work with a partner. Look at the photo of the two women on page 168.**

**Ask and answer questions with *which* or *what* about the women. Use the words in the list or your own ideas. You can answer like this:**
**The one on the right/left.**
**Neither one.**
**Both of them.**

**Example:**
You:            Which woman has curly hair?
Your partner:   The one on the left.

    curly hair
    dark hair
    glasses
    laughing
    a short-sleeved shirt
    smiling
    straight hair

# 7e  Questions with *How*

## Form / Function

**How long** is the blue whale?
It's about 100 feet long.

**How much** does it weigh?
It weighs more than 2,300 people.

**How big** is its mouth?
Its mouth can be 20 feet long.

1. We can use *how* alone, without a word such as *much* or *many*.

| Use | Example |
|---|---|
| We use *how* to ask about the way someone is or the way someone does something. | **How** did she sing? <br> She sang beautifully. <br> **How** do I look? <br> You look very handsome. <br> **How** do you change a flat tire? <br> It isn't difficult. I'll show you. |
| We use *how* to ask about a means of transportation. | **How** did you get here? <br> By plane./I flew. <br> By car./I drove. <br> By train./I took the train. <br> By bus./I took a bus. <br> On foot./I walked. |

2. We can use *how* with an adjective or an adverb.

| Use | Example |
|---|---|
| We use *how* + adjective/adverb to ask about qualities of things or how things are done. | **How old** are you? <br> I'm 22. <br> **How tall** is he? <br> He's five feet eight. <br> **How big** is it? <br> It's three feet across. <br> **How quickly** can you come? <br> In five minutes. <br> **How well** did he do on the test? <br> Pretty well. He got a B. <br> **How fast** was she driving? <br> Not very fast. Just 30 miles an hour. |

| Use | Example |
|---|---|
| We use *how often* to ask about the frequency that something happens. | **How often** do you have English class?<br>    I have class three times a week.<br>**How often** do you go to the gym?<br>    I usually go every day. |
| We can also say *how many times a day/week/month/year* to ask about frequency. | **How many times a week** do you have English class?<br>    I have class three times a week.<br>**How many times a month** do you go to the movies?<br>    I go once or twice a month. |
| We use *how much* and *how many* to ask about the amount of something. | |
| We use *how much* with noncount nouns. | **How much** money do you need?<br>    I need a lot of money.<br>**How much** time do we have?<br>    Not much. |
| We use *how many* with count nouns. | **How many** questions are there on the test?<br>    50.<br>**How many** sisters and brothers do you have?<br>    Just one sister. |
| We use *how far* to ask about the distance from one place to another. | **How far** is this school from your house?<br>    It's about ten blocks.<br>**How far** is New York from Los Angeles?<br>    About 3,000 miles. |
| We use *how long* to ask about a period of time. | **How long** have you been waiting?<br>    Not long. Just a few minutes.<br>**How long** did you stay in Houston?<br>    We stayed for one week. |
| We often ask and answer a question about length of time with *it takes* + time. | How long **does it take** to fly there?<br>    **It takes** about six hours.<br>How long **did it take** to write this essay?<br>    **It took** about three hours.<br>How long **will it take** for the rice to cook?<br>    **It will take** about 20 minutes. |
| We can also say *how many minutes/hours/days/weeks/months/years* to ask about length of time. | **How many years** is this passport good for?<br>    Ten years. |

3. We use *how about* to suggest something. We often use it in response to a statement or question.

| Statement or Question | How About | Noun/Pronoun/Gerund* |
|---|---|---|
| I don't know what to make for dinner. | | **spaghetti?** |
| What would you like to do tonight? | | **going** to a movie? |
| I need someone to go to the party with me. | **How about** | **me?** |
| We're cleaning the apartment. | | **giving** us some help? |

*A gerund is a verb + *-ing* that is used as a noun.

*What about* means the same thing as *how about*.

**What about** going to a movie?    OR    **How about** going to a movie?

## II  Practice

**Complete the questions about whales with *how, how big, how many/much, how fast, how long,* or *how often*.**

1. _How_____ does a whale breathe?

   It blows water high into the air and takes in fresh air.

2. _____ does it come to the surface to breathe?

   It comes to the surface every 15 minutes.

3. _____ is the blue whale's heart?

   Its heart is the size of a small car.

4. _____ kinds of whales are there?

   There are about 80 different kinds of whales.

5. _____ does it live?

   It lives for about 80 years.

6. _____ can it swim?

   It can swim 30 miles an hour.

7. _____ blue whales are there?

   There are about 5,000 blue whales.

8. _____ milk does a baby whale drink?

It drinks 100 gallons of its mother's milk each day.

9. _____ weight does the baby whale gain?

A baby whale gains eight pounds each hour!

## 12 Practice

**Complete the conversation with *how, how long, how many/much, how often,* and *how far.***

1. Man:     Passport, please. _____*How*_____ are you today, ma'am?

   Woman: I'm fine, thanks. And you?

2. Man:     Fine. _____ was your trip?

   Woman: Fine, thanks.

3. Man:     _____ did you stay out of the country?

   Woman: Not long. About three weeks.

4. Man:     _____ countries did you visit?

   Woman: Two countries: England and France.

5. Man:     _____ do you go to Europe?

   Woman: About once a year to visit friends.

6. Man:     _____ friends do you have in Europe?

   Woman: I have one friend in Oxford and one in Paris.

7. Man:     _____ is Oxford from London?

   Woman: It's about 50 miles, or 80 kilometers.

8. Man     _____ have you known this friend?

   Woman: I have known her for eight years.

9. Man:     _____ money do you have on you?

   Woman: I have about 200 dollars.

10. Man:     _____ gifts did you buy?

   Woman: I bought about seven gifts.

   Man:     Can I see them?

## 13 What Do You Think?

1. Where is this conversation taking place?
2. Who is the man?
3. Who is the woman?

## 14 Practice

**Write questions for which the underlined words are the answers. Use all wh- words:**
*who, what, where, when, why, which,* **and** *how.*

1. Lions live in <u>Africa and Asia</u>.

   *Where do lions live?*

2. Lions live in groups. There are <u>about six to 30 lions</u> in a group.

   _____

3. <u>The male lion</u> is the largest member of the cat family.

   _____

4. A male lion can weigh <u>up to 520 pounds (240 kilos)</u>.

   _____

5. Lions eat <u>other animals</u>.

   _____

6. The male lion sleeps for <u>about 20</u> hours a day.

   _____

7. Sometimes the male can go without food <u>for a week</u>.

   _____

8. The job of the male lion is to <u>make sure other lions do not come near the home of his family</u>.

   _____

9. Sometimes the male lion makes a loud roar or sound. You can hear the sound <u>five miles</u> away.

   _____

10. <u>The female</u> lion kills other animals for food.

    _____

11. She takes the food to <u>the home of the family</u>.

    _____

12. The female lions usually hunt <u>at night</u>.

    _____

13. <u>The female lion</u> takes care of the baby lions.

    _____

14. Lions are in danger <u>because people kill them for sport</u>.

    _____

**Practice**

**Write questions for which the underlined words are the answers. Use all wh- words.**

1. Bob is <u>an accountant</u>.

    *What is Bob?*

2. He lives <u>near Boston, in the United States</u>.

    _____

3. He travels to work <u>by subway</u>.

    _____

4. His wife's name is <u>Donna</u>.

    _____

5. They have <u>two</u> children.

    _____

6. The girl is <u>three</u>.

    _____

7. <u>The boy</u> is nine.

    _____

8. Bob plays with the children <u>after work</u>.

    _____

9. He likes football and baseball. He prefers <u>football</u>.

    _____

10. He watches football on television <u>because he doesn't have time to play</u>.

    _____

11. <u>His son</u> watches it with him.

    _____

12. His son plays football <u>at school</u>.

    _____

13. He usually watches <u>cartoons</u> with his daughter.

    _____

14. Donna and Bob take the children out <u>on Sundays</u>.

    _____

15. Donna and Bob love <u>their children</u>.

    _____

## 16 Practice

**Work with a partner. Make suggestions to visit three places in your city. Suggest the days and times you can both go. Use *how about* and *what about* to make suggestions.**

**Example:**

| | |
|---|---|
| You: | How about going to the park on Saturday? |
| Your partner: | OK. That's a good idea. What time? |
| You: | How about 10:30? |
| Your partner: | OK. |

# 7f  Tag Questions

**Form**

He's your brother, **isn't he?**

1. Tag questions are short questions at the end of a sentence. We form tag questions with the auxiliary verb from the first part of the sentence. The subject of the tag question at the end is always a pronoun—we do not repeat the noun. When we write, we always use a comma before the tag question.

   CORRECT:    John is your brother, **isn't he?**
   INCORRECT: John is your brother, isn't ~~John~~?

2. We make a tag question in the same way we make a regular question, but when the main sentence is positive, the tag question is usually negative.

   He is a farmer, **isn't he?**

3. When the first part of the sentence is negative, the tag question is usually positive.

   He isn't a businessman, **is he?**

4. When the verb in the first part of the sentence is in the simple present or the simple past of any verb except *be*, we use the auxiliaries *do, does,* or *did* in the tag question. When the first part of the sentence *be*, we use *be* again in the tag.

| AFFIRMATIVE VERB, NEGATIVE TAG | | NEGATIVE VERB, AFFIRMATIVE TAG | |
|---|---|---|---|
| Main Sentence | Tag | Main Sentence | Tag |
| She **likes** music, | **doesn't she?** | He **doesn't like** fish, | **does he?** |
| You **are** a student, | **aren't you?** | You **didn't** do it, | **did you?** |
| She**'s** learning English, | **isn't she?** | He **wasn't** nice to you, | **was he?** |
| We **had** fun, | **didn't we?** | We **didn't have** fun, | **did we?** |

**Note:** With the subject and verb *I am*, the tag question is *aren't I* or *am I not*.

| CORRECT: | I'm late, **aren't I?** |
|---|---|
| INCORRECT: | I'm late, ~~amn't I?~~ |
| CORRECT (very formal): | I'm late, **am I not?** |

## Function

1. We use tag questions when we want to check something we have said in the first part of the sentence.

   He lives in Utah, **doesn't he?** (The speaker is not sure and uses a tag question to check.)

2. We also use tag questions when we ask for agreement.

   The food is good, **isn't it?** (The speaker expects the answer "Yes.")
   You aren't angry, **are you?** (The speaker expects the answer "No.")

## 17 Practice

**Match the sentences with the tag questions.**

| ___d___ | **1.** It gets very cold in the winter, | **a.** didn't he? |
|---|---|---|
| _____ | **2.** You can't run that far, | **b.** does he? |
| _____ | **3.** He got the job, | **c.** couldn't she? |
| _____ | **4.** She could do it again, | **d.** doesn't it? |
| _____ | **5.** He doesn't like opera, | **e.** were you? |
| _____ | **6.** You weren't late, | **f.** can you? |

# 18 Practice

**Complete the conversation with the correct tag questions and short answers.**

Tina:   You went to Brazil, _____*didn't you*_____
                                    1

Jenny:  Yes, I _____
                        2

Tina:   They speak Portuguese there, _____
                                              3

Jenny:  Yes, they _____
                          4

Tina:   You speak Portuguese, _____
                                    5

Jenny:  No, I _____
                    6

Tina:   It was difficult to get around then, _____
                                                    7

Jenny:  No, it _____ I spoke English.
                      8

Tina:   A lot of people speak English there, _____
                                                    9

Jenny:  Many people in hotels and restaurants do.

Tina:   Rio is beautiful, _____
                                10

Jenny:  Yes, _____
                    11

Tina:   You had gone there before, _____
                                          12

Jenny:  Yes, a long time ago. You've been to Brazil, _____
                                                            13

Tina:   No, I _____
                    14

# 7g Phrasal Verbs

## Form / Function

Nick is **sitting down.**
He hasn't **picked up** the phone.

1. Many verbs in English consist of more than one word. These verbs have a verb plus a particle (an adverb such as *up or down*). These are phrasal verbs.

2. Sometimes we can guess the meaning of a phrasal verb.

   She walked into the room and **sat down.**
   When the president came into the room, everyone **stood up.**

   The phrasal verb *sit down* means "position yourself on a chair." The phrasal verb *stand up* means "get on your feet from a sitting position."

3. Many phrasal verbs have special meanings, for example:

   We **looked up** the words we didn't understand.

   The phrasal verb *look up* means "find information in a dictionary, encyclopedia, etc."

4. Some phrasal verbs do not take objects. In grammar, we call these intransitive phrasal verbs. Others do take objects. We call these transitive phrasal verbs.

   These two phrasal verbs do not take objects. They are intransitive.

| Subject | Phrasal Verb |
| --- | --- |
| We | **sat down** at the table. |
| They | **stood up** to sing the national anthem. |

These two phrasal verbs take objects. They are transitive.

| Subject | Phrasal Verb | Object |
| --- | --- | --- |
| I | **looked up** | **your number.** |
| The children | **put on** | **their coats.** |

## 19 Practice

**Underline the phrasal verbs in these sentences. If there is an object, circle it.**

1. Please <u>turn on</u> the (radio).
2. We told the dog to lie down.
3. I have a cold. I can't get over it.
4. She took off her coat and sat down.
5. What time do you get up in the morning?

## 7h Intransitive Phrasal Verbs

### Form / Function

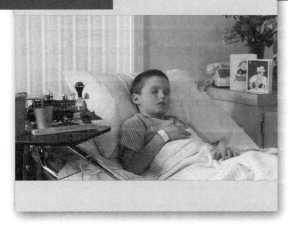

He's in the hospital.
He's **lying down.**

Here are some common phrasal verbs that are intransitive—they do not take objects.*

| Phrasal Verb | Meaning | Example |
|---|---|---|
| break down | to stop working (as a machine) | My car has **broken down** three times this month. |
| get back | to return | They **got back** from Seoul yesterday. |
| get up | to arise from bed; to arise from a sitting position | We **got up** late this morning. |
| lie down | to rest in a horizontal position | I have a headache. I'm going to **lie down.** |
| set out | to leave (on a trip) | The boys **set out** at 6:00 A.M. |
| sit down | to sit on a chair | You should **sit down** in a job interview. |
| stand up | to arise from a sitting position | You should **stand up** when you meet someone. |
| stay up | to keep awake | We **stayed up** late to watch a movie. |

*Some of these phrasal verbs can take objects, but the meaning is different. Like other verbs, phrasal verbs can have several meanings.

## 20 Practice

**Complete the paragraph with phrasal verbs from the list.**

| got back | lay down | set out | stood up |
|----------|----------|---------|----------|
| got up | sat down | stayed up | |

This morning, we _____*set out*_____ for Silver Mountain. The night before,
<sub>1</sub>

we _____ late to get everything ready. In the morning, we
<sub>2</sub>

_____ at 7:00. We walked for four hours before we _____
<sub>3</sub> <sub>4</sub>

to rest. We were tired. Julia was so tired that she _____ on the ground.
<sub>5</sub>

Finally, we _____ and continued our walk. When we got to the top of the
<sub>6</sub>

mountain, it was beautiful! Going back home was easier, and we _____ in
<sub>7</sub>

time for dinner.

## 21 Practice

**Complete the conversation with the correct phrasal verb in parentheses. Use the correct form of the phrasal verb.**

Karen: I feel so tired!

Jenny: _____*Sit down*_____ for a few minutes. Why are you so tired? (stay up/sit down)
<sub>1</sub>

Karen: I _____ until midnight last night. (stay up/break down)
<sub>2</sub>

Jenny: Why so late?

Karen: Because I didn't _____ from the library until then.
<sub>3</sub>

(set out/get back)

Jenny: Well, when did you _____ this morning? (lie down/get up)
<sub>4</sub>

Karen: At 7:00. Then I had to walk to school.

Jenny: Why?

Karen: Because my car _____ two blocks from my house.
<sub>5</sub>

(break down/set out)

Jenny: Oh no! Maybe you shouldn't sit down. Maybe you should _____!
<sub>6</sub>

(set out/lie down)

Your Turn

Tell your partner about a difficult day that you have had. Use some phrasal verbs without objects.

**Example:**
As soon as I got up, I knew that it would be a terrible day. I set out for work and discovered that my car had broken down.

## 7i   Transitive Phrasal Verbs: Separable

### Form / Function

Susan**'s looking up** a fact on the Internet.
She**'s looking** it **up.**

Many transitive phrasal verbs—phrasal verbs that have objects—can have their objects in two different positions. We call these *separable* phrasal verbs because the object can separate the verb from the particle. Separable phrasal verbs are very common in English.

1.  If a separable phrasal verb has a noun object, the object can come before or after the particle.

| Subject | Verb | Particle | Noun Object | Particle |
|---------|------|----------|-------------|----------|
| We | **turned** | **on** | the television. | |
| We | **turned** | | the television | **on.** |

2.  If the object is a pronoun (*me, you, him, her, us, it, them*), the object must come between the verb and the particle.

| Subject | Verb | Pronoun Object | Particle |
|---------|------|----------------|----------|
| We | **turned** | it | **on.** |

CORRECT:      We turned **it on.**
INCORRECT:   We turned ~~on it.~~

3. Here are some common separable phrasal verbs. See page 313 for more separable verbs.

| Phrasal Verb | Meaning | Example |
|---|---|---|
| call back | to call someone on the phone after he/she has called you | **Call** me **back** when you can. |
| fill out | to complete a form or questionnaire | You should **fill** this form **out** for the doctor. |
| find out | to find information about something | I **found** the answer **out** when I talked to my teacher. |
| look up | to find information in a dictionary, telephone book, encyclopedia, etc. | I need to **look up** the capital of Botswana. |
| pick up | to lift someone/something | Please **pick** the baby **up**. |
| put off | to delay something to a later date | We should **put** the party **off** for a week. |
| put on | to wear something | **Put** your sweater **on** before you go out. |
| put down | to put something on a surface like the floor or a table | I **put** your box **down** on the kitchen counter. |
| take off | to remove clothes from the body | It's hot in here. I'm going to **take off** my coat. |
| turn on | to start a machine | Please **turn** the oven **on**. |
| turn off | to stop a machine | I can't hear you. **Turn** the radio **off**. |
| throw out/away | put something into the garbage or trash | I accidentally **threw** my homework **out**. |
| wake up | stop somebody from sleeping | I **woke up** the baby. |
| write down | write something on a piece of paper | I **wrote** the directions **down**, but now I can't find them. |

## 23 | Practice

**Complete the sentences with the correct phrasal verb from the list.**

| | | |
|---|---|---|
| call back | put down | turn off |
| fill out | put off | turn on |
| find out | put on | wake up |
| look up | take off | write down |
| pick up | throw out | |

1. My eyes are open at six every morning, but I __*wake up*__ my husband at 6:30.

2. Then I take a shower and _____ my clothes _____.

3. I _____ the television to listen to the news.

4. Before I leave, I _____ the television _____.

5. When I get to the office, I _____ my coat.

6. I _____ my bag on the floor, next to my desk.

7. Then, I _____ the phone.

8. I listen to my calls and _____ important messages _____ on a note pad.

9. When a person says it's urgent and gives me a number, I _____ the person _____.

10. I read all the mail. I _____ letters that I don't want.

11. I don't pay the bills immediately. I _____ some of them _____.

12. Sometimes I _____ a questionnaire. I think it's fun.

13. I can't remember numbers, so I _____ phone numbers _____ all the time.

14. On my lunch break, I call home and _____ what my teenagers are doing.

## 24 Practice

**Write answers using separable phrasal verbs and pronouns.**

1. What do you do with a form or questionnaire?

   _I fill it out._____

2. What do you do with old papers or things you do not want anymore?

   _____

3. What do you do with your shoes, shirt, or pants before you go to bed?

   _____

4. What do you do when a baby is crying in her bed?

   _____

5. What do you do with the television, faucet, or light?

   _____

# 7j   Transitive Phrasal Verbs: Inseparable

Amanda **ran into** Jane yesterday.

1. Some transitive phrasal verbs with objects cannot have an object between the verb and the particle. We call these *inseparable* phrasal verbs. The object can only go after the verb and the particle.

   CORRECT:    Amanda **ran into** Jane yesterday.
   INCORRECT:  Amanda ran ~~Jane into~~ yesterday.

2. There are fewer inseparable phrasal verbs than separable phrasal verbs. Here are some common ones.

| Phrasal Verb | Meaning | Example |
|---|---|---|
| come across | to find by chance | How did you **come across** that book? |
| get into | to enter a car/taxi | We're late! **Get into** the car and let's go! |
| get off | to leave a bus/train/plane | Where do we **get off** the bus? |
| get on | to enter a bus/train/plane | Here's the bus. Let's **get on** it. |
| get out | leave a car/taxi | We're there. Let's **get out** of the car. |
| get over | to recover | She has **gotten over** the flu. |
| go over | to review | Be sure to **go over** phrasal verbs before the test! |
| look after | to take care of | I have to **look after** the children today. |
| look into | to investigate | The police are **looking into** the accident. |
| run into | to meet by chance | I **ran into** an old high school friend yesterday. |

## 25 Practice

**Complete the sentences with the correct phrasal verb from the list. Use the correct tense of the phrasal verb.**

get into       get on       get over       look into
get off         get out      look after

Last night, Jackie had a problem with her bank account, and she needed to

_____*look into*_____ it. She stayed up until 11:30 P.M. This morning she got up
       1

very late! She quickly _____ a taxi and went to work. When she
                        2

_____ of the taxi she felt dizzy. She was trying to _____
      3                                       4

a bad cold that she had had for a week. She told the people at the office she was going

home. She did not want to go out for a few days until she was better. She said her

husband could _____ her when she was at home. To _____ and
                  5                                  6

_____ a bus in this cold weather was not going to help her get better.
    7

## 26 Practice

**Write complete answers to these questions.**

1. What are some kinds of transportation you get on and off?

   *You get on and off buses and trains.*

2. What are some forms of transportation you get into and out of?

   _____

3. What are some things or people you look after?

   _____

4. What are some illnesses that you have gotten over?

   _____

5. Tell about someone you have run into on the street.

   _____

6. What topics have you looked into for your classes?

   _____

**Some of these sentences have errors in the use of phrasal verbs. If a sentence has an error, rewrite it correctly. If it does not have an error, write "Correct." Some of the phrasal verbs are separable and some are inseparable.**

1. Let's put the meeting off until 2:00 this afternoon.

   _Correct_

2. This glass is broken. I'm going to throw out it.

   _This glass is broken. I'm going to throw it out._

3. Sarah had a bad cold, but she got over it quickly.

   _____

4. You should put on your gloves before you go outside.

   _____

5. The baby was sleeping, but the phone woke up her.

   _____

6. I want to go the directions over before we start the trip.

   _____

7. What a beautiful painting! Where did you come across it?

   _____

8. Can you look some sales numbers up for Mr. Clark?

   _____

9. My brother called me this morning. I need to call back him.

   _____

10. Charles ran an old friend into this morning.

    _____

11. Here's the questionnaire. Fill out it in ink, please.

    _____

# WRITING: Write a Questionnaire

Write questions about games or customs.

**Step 1. Work with a partner. You want to find out what other people know about a topic such as the Olympic games or a custom in your country. Use the question words and forms you have learned in this unit to write a questionnaire with 20 questions.**

**Examples:**
What are the Olympic games?
Which country will host the Olympic games next time?
When will the Olympic games be held?
Which Olympic sport is your country good at?

**Step 2. Evaluate your questionnaire. For more writing guidelines, see pages 407–411.**

**Checklist**

_____ Did you write 20 questions?

_____ Are all of your questions about the same general topic?

_____ Do you know the answer to each question?

_____ Are your questions clear?

**Step 3. Edit your questions. Work with a partner or your teacher to edit the questions. Correct spelling, punctuation, vocabulary, and grammar.**

**Step 4. Make copies of your questionnaire. Ask people to write their answers. Report the results to the class.**

# SELF-TEST

A  **Choose the best answer, A, B, C, or D, to complete the sentence. Mark your answer by darkening the oval with the same letter.**

1.  I can't study with the television on. Could you _____?

    **A.** turn off it    Ⓐ Ⓑ Ⓒ Ⓓ
    **B.** turn on it
    **C.** turn it off
    **D.** turn off television

2.  If you don't know the meaning of the word, _____ in the dictionary.

    **A.** look up it    Ⓐ Ⓑ Ⓒ Ⓓ
    **B.** look it up
    **C.** look out it
    **D.** look the word

3.  Sue: _____ did you live in Texas?
    Tom: Three years.

    **A.** When    Ⓐ Ⓑ Ⓒ Ⓓ
    **B.** How many
    **C.** What time
    **D.** How long

4.  Sue: _____ didn't you write?
    Tom: Because I didn't have your address.

    **A.** Why    Ⓐ Ⓑ Ⓒ Ⓓ
    **B.** What
    **C.** How
    **D.** Which

5.  He never eats broccoli, _____?

    **A.** doesn't he    Ⓐ Ⓑ Ⓒ Ⓓ
    **B.** eats he
    **C.** isn't he
    **D.** does he

6.  Tom: _____ is that bird?
    Sue: It's an eagle.

    **A.** Which    Ⓐ Ⓑ Ⓒ Ⓓ
    **B.** What
    **C.** How
    **D.** Who

7.  You haven't seen my keys, _____?

    **A.** did you    Ⓐ Ⓑ Ⓒ Ⓓ
    **B.** you have
    **C.** don't you
    **D.** have you

8.  Joe: _____ wake me up at 7:00?
    Anne: Yes, I will.

    **A.** Will you    Ⓐ Ⓑ Ⓒ Ⓓ
    **B.** Would you
    **C.** Can you
    **D.** Could will

9.  _____ going?

    **A.** What are you    Ⓐ Ⓑ Ⓒ Ⓓ
    **B.** Where you are
    **C.** Where are you
    **D.** Where you

10. Billy: _____ crying?
    Susie: No, I'm not.

    **A.** You are    Ⓐ Ⓑ Ⓒ Ⓓ
    **B.** Why are you
    **C.** You
    **D.** Are you

**B** **Find the underlined word or phrase, A, B, C, or D, that is incorrect. Mark your answer by darkening the oval with the same letter.**

1. How <u>many</u> does <u>it</u> <u>take</u> <u>to drive</u> to New
        A      B   C   D
   York from here?

2. <u>Did</u> they <u>came</u> <u>back</u> from <u>their</u> vacation?
   A       B     C       D

3. We <u>don't</u> <u>always</u> <u>have to</u> communicate
       A     B     C
   with words, <u>have</u> we?
               D

4. We <u>have</u> apple pie <u>and</u> cherry pie. <u>What</u>
       A          B          C
   kind <u>would you</u> like?
        D

   Ⓐ Ⓑ Ⓒ Ⓓ

5. Here is <u>a form</u>. You <u>have to</u> fill in <u>it</u> and
          A          B       C
   give <u>it</u> to the passport control officer.
      D

   Ⓐ Ⓑ Ⓒ Ⓓ

6. I can't remember <u>the things</u> I <u>have to</u> do
                    A       B
   every day, so I write down <u>them</u> <u>on</u> a
                       C   D
   piece of paper.

   Ⓐ Ⓑ Ⓒ Ⓓ

7. They <u>don't</u> have <u>any</u> children, <u>do</u> they
        A       B         C
   <u>have</u>?
   D

   Ⓐ Ⓑ Ⓒ Ⓓ

8. The weather report <u>didn't</u> say <u>anything</u>
                  A      B
   about rain today, <u>did</u> <u>he</u>?
               C   D

   Ⓐ Ⓑ Ⓒ Ⓓ

9. You will <u>be</u> <u>back</u> <u>on</u> Monday as usual, <u>will</u>
          A   B   C                D
   you?

   Ⓐ Ⓑ Ⓒ Ⓓ

10. Brenda <u>was</u> very sick <u>with</u> a bad cold, but
           A          B
    now <u>she's</u> getting it <u>over</u>.
         C         D

    Ⓐ Ⓑ Ⓒ Ⓓ

# UNIT 8

## MODAL AUXILIARIES AND RELATED FORMS

# 8a  *Can, Could,* and *Be Able To* to Express Ability

<table>
<tr><td>Form</td></tr>
</table>

Fred **could play** football last year, but he **can't play** football now.

1. We use the modal auxiliary *can* + a base verb to express ability in the present or future, and *could* + a base verb to express ability in the past.

2. Like all modals, *can* and *could* take the same form for all persons. There is no *–s* ending in the third person singular.

3. We put *not* after *can, could,* and other modals to form the negative. Many modals can be contracted in their negative form.

| Affirmative | Negative Full Form | Negative Contraction |
|---|---|---|
| can | cannot | can't |
| could | could not | couldn't |

Note that the full negative form of *can* is written as one word: *cannot.* The full negative form of other modal auxiliaries is written as two words: *could not; should not.*

| CAN: ABILITY IN THE PRESENT OR FUTURE | | | | COULD: ABILITY IN THE PAST | | | |
|---|---|---|---|---|---|---|---|
| Subject | Can Cannot Can't | Base Verb | | Subject | Could Could Not Couldn't | Base Verb | |
| I | | | | I | | | |
| You | **can** | | | You | **could** | | |
| He/She/It | **cannot** | **play** | now. later. | He/She/It | **could not** | **play** | then. |
| We | **can't** | | | We | **couldn't** | | |
| They | | | | They | | | |

4. We put *can, could,* and other modals before the subject to form questions.

| QUESTIONS | | | | SHORT ANSWERS | |
|---|---|---|---|---|---|
| *Can* | Subject | Base Verb | | Yes, | No, |
| **Can** | I | | now? later? | you can. | you can't. |
| | you | **play** | | I/we can. | I/we can't. |
| | he/she/it | | | he/she/it can. | he/she/it can't. |
| | we | | | you can. | you can't. |
| | they | | | they can. | they can't. |

5. We can use *be able to* to express ability in the present, past, and future.

| *ABLE TO:* ABILITY IN THE PRESENT | | | | |
|---|---|---|---|---|
| Subject | Form of *Be* | *Able To* | Base Verb | |
| I | **am** | | | |
| You | **are** | | | |
| He/She/It | **is** | **able to** | **play** | now. |
| We | **are** | | | |
| They | | | | |

| *ABLE TO:* ABILITY IN THE PAST | | | | |
|---|---|---|---|---|
| Subject | Form of *Be* | *Able To* | Base Verb | |
| I | **was** | | | |
| You | **were** | | | |
| He/She/It | **was** | **able to** | **play** | yesterday. |
| We | **were** | | | |
| They | | | | |

| *ABLE TO:* ABILITY IN THE FUTURE | | | | |
|---|---|---|---|---|
| Subject | Form of *Be* | *Able To* | Base Verb | |
| I | | | | |
| You | | | | |
| He/She/It | **will be** | **able to** | **play** | tomorrow. |
| We | | | | |
| They | | | | |

1. We use *can* + a base verb to express ability in the present or future.

   She **can speak** Japanese.
   He **can play** tennis very well.
   I **can help** you in 15 minutes.

2. We use *could* + a base verb to express ability in the past.

   When I was young, I **could run** five miles.
   I **couldn't drive** five years ago.

3. *Am/is/are able to* and *was/were able to* have the same general meaning as *can* and *could*. *Can* and *could* are more common in speech.

   I wanted to call you, but I **couldn't remember** your phone number.
   I wanted to call you, but I **wasn't able to remember** your phone number.

4. When we want to suggest that something is frustrating or difficult, we usually use *be able to*.

   I tried very hard, but I **wasn't able to do** all of my math problems.
   After I spoke to my teacher, I **was able to do** them.

5. When we talk about a future ability that we do not have in the present, we use *will be able to*.

   Next year, I**'ll be able to drive.**

6. We must use *be able to,* not *can,* with some grammatical structures, such as with another modal and in the present perfect tense.

   CORRECT:     You should be able to do this problem.
   INCORRECT:   You ~~should can~~ do this problem.

   CORRECT:     I have been able to swim since I was six.
   INCORRECT:   I ~~can have swum~~ since I was six.

---

## 1 │ Practice

**Fred has a broken leg and broken arms. What can he do? What can't he do? Complete the sentences with *can* or *can't* and one of the verbs from the list.**

| | | | |
|---|---|---|---|
| eat | listen | shake | watch |
| hold | put on | talk | wear |

1. He _____can't wear_____ his shoes.

2. He _____ his meals by himself.

3. He _____ a glass of water in his hands.

4. He _____ hands with visitors.

5. He _____ television.

6. He _____ to the doctors and nurses and visitors.

7. He _____ his clothes by himself.

8. He _____ to the radio.

## 2 Practice

**Complete the sentences with *could* or *couldn't*.**

Tarzan was a human who was born in a jungle. He _____could_____ survive there
_____1_____

because apes took care of him as their own baby. As Tarzan grew, he _____
                                                                              2

do many things that the apes _____ do. He _____ climb
                                      3                          4

trees. He _____ swing from tree to tree. He _____ find nuts
                5                                              6

and fruit to eat.

One day, some European men in the jungle saw the strange man. They _____
                                                                              7

understand how he lived there. They tried to speak with him, but he _____
                                                                              8

speak. He _____ make only animal noises. The men took Tarzan
                9

back to Europe with them. They taught him many things. After some time, he

_____ speak French. He _____ also walk and eat like other
        10                              11

people in Europe.

## 3 What Do You Think?

1. What other things could Tarzan do in the jungle?
2. What things could he do after he lived in Europe for a while?

## 4 Your Turn

**You are going on a trip to the jungle for two weeks. Choose six things you need to take with you to survive. What do you need them for? Use *can*.**

**Example:**
I need a blanket so I can cover myself at night.

## 5 Practice

**Joe likes outdoor activities. Rewrite the sentences using the correct form of *be able to* in place of *can/could* + a verb.**

1. It's summer now. Joe and his friends can play baseball outdoors.

   *It's summer now. Joe and his friends are able to play baseball outdoors.*

2. He can go hiking in the mountains.

   _____

3. He can play tennis now, and he can also play it in the fall.

   _____

4. He can't go ice skating now, but he could go ice skating last winter.

   _____

5. Last winter, he couldn't go skiing because he didn't have the money.

   _____

6. He and I can go mountain climbing now.

   _____

7. We can't go mountain climbing in the winter because it's too dangerous then.

   _____

## 6 Practice

**Check the correct completion for the sentences. Sometimes both choices are possible.**

1. √ can't                    I ... cook very well, so I'm taking a course.
   √ am not able to

2. ___ can                    When I finish this course, I ... make Chinese food.
   ___ will be able to

3. ___ can                    I ... make stir-fried dishes now.
   ___ am able to

4. ___ couldn't               Before taking this course, I ... make spaghetti sauce.
   ___ wasn't able to

5. ___ could                  I ... learn how to make cakes, but it took me a long time.
   ___ was able to

**6.** ___ can            If I work hard, I might ... make some French dishes soon.

   ___ be able to

**7.** ___ will be able to    When this course is over, I ... give my family better meals.

   ___ am able to

**8.** ___ can            Also, I should ... save money.

   ___ be able to

**9.** ___ can            My instructor says that you spend less money if you ...

   ___ are able to       cook well.

## 8b *May I, Could I,* and *Can I* to Ask for Permission

**Form**

**Can I have** another napkin?

| QUESTIONS | | | | ANSWERS | |
| --- | --- | --- | --- | --- | --- |
| Modal | Subject | Base Verb | | Affirmative | Negative |
| **May** | | | the phone? | Yes, of course. | I'm sorry. It's for office use only. |
| **Could** | I | **use** | | Certainly. | |
| | | | | Sure.* | |
| **Can** | | | | No problem.* | |
| **May** | I | **help** | you? | Yes, please. | No, thanks. |
| **Can** | | | | | |
| *These expressions are informal English. | | | | | |

1. We use *may I, can I,* and *could I* + a base verb to ask for permission to do something. *May I* is the most polite, or formal, of the three. We often use *may I* when speaking to someone who is older, who is in authority over us, or whom we do not know.

2. *Could I* is more polite or formal than *can I. Could I* is a good choice for most situations.

3. *Can I* is often used between people who know each other well.

In these sentences, a customer asks for a form from a bank teller.

| | | |
|---|---|---|
| FORMAL | **May I take** one of these? | (They do not know each other.) |
| | **Could I take** one of these? | (They might or might not know each other.) |
| INFORMAL | **Can I take** one of these? | (They have been speaking together or they know each other.) |

---

**7** Practice

**Complete the conversations with *may I, can I,* or *could I*. In some sentences, there is more than one correct answer.**

**1.** Student:     _May I_____ hand in my homework tomorrow, please?

  Teacher:   No, you may not.

**2.** Student:   _____ have some more time to finish the essay?

  Teacher:   No, absolutely not.

**3.** Student:   _____ borrow your grammar book?

  Classmate:   Sure.

**4.** You:   _____ use your computer?

  Classmate:   No problem.

**5.** You:   _____ have a scholarship application?

  School Clerk:   Sure.

**6.** You:   _____ speak with Professor Jones?

  Secretary:   She's not here right now. _____ take a message?

## 8 | Practice

**Work with a partner. Ask and answer questions with *may I, can I,* and *could I.***

**Example:**
You are at a friend's house. You want to use the phone.
You:           Can I use the phone?
Your partner:  Yes, sure.

1. You are at a friend's house. You want to use the telephone.
2. You want to sit next to a person you don't know in a fast food restaurant.
3. You are in a restaurant. You ask for the check.
4. You are in a shoe store. You want to try on the black shoes in the window in size 10.
5. You are talking to the teacher. You want to come to class late tomorrow because you have a doctor's appointment.
6. You are at a friend's house. You want a glass of water.
7. The teacher is carrying a lot of books. You want to help her carry the books.
8. You are on the phone with a friend. The doorbell rings. You want to call your friend back later.

## 8c  *Can, Could,* and *Would* to Make Requests

### Form

**Could you meet** me
later for a movie?

| QUESTIONS | | | | ANSWERS | |
| --- | --- | --- | --- | --- | --- |
| Modal | Subject | Base Verb | | Affirmative | Negative |
| *Can* | | | | Yes, of course. | Sorry, I can't. |
| *Could* | you | wait | a minute, please? | Certainly. | I'd like to, but I don't have time. |
| | | | | Sure.* | |
| *Would* | | | | Okay.* | |

*These expressions are informal English.

1. We use *would you, could you,* and *can you* + a base verb to ask someone to do something. The meaning of these three modals is the same when we use them to make a request.

2. Although they have the same meaning, *would* and *could* are more formal than *can*. We generally use *could* and *would* when we make requests of strangers, older people, or people in authority. We use *would, could,* and *can* with friends and family members.

   To a stranger: **Could/Would** you **send** the report, please?
   To a friend: **Could/Would/Can** you **come** here for a second?

3. We use *please* to make requests more polite. We use *please* especially with *would* or *could*. *Please* usually comes after the subject or at the end of the sentence. When *please* comes at the end of the sentence, we put a comma before it.

   Would you **please** sign this?
   Could you sign this, **please**?

## 9 Practice

**Work with a partner. Make requests with *can you, could you,* and *would you*. More than one answer is possible.**

1. You are speaking to your brother.

   You: _____Can you_____ hold this for me?

   Brother: Sure.

2. You are speaking to a bank teller.

   You: _____ give me the balance of my checking account,

   please?

   Bank Teller: Certainly. It's $506.25. Is there anything else I can do for you?

3. You are speaking to your boss.

   You: _____ look over this report, please?

   Boss: I can't do it now, but I'll do it as soon as I can.

4. You are speaking to a flight attendant.

   You: _____ bring me some water, please?

   Flight Attendant: Certainly.

**5.** You are speaking to a doctor.

You: _____ give me the same prescription as last time,

please?

Doctor: Of course.

## 10 Practice

**Work with a partner. Make requests and answer them with *can, could,* and *would*. More than one answer is possible.**

**1.** Ask a stranger to ...

**a.** tell you the way to the exit.

_Could you tell me the way to the exit, please?_

**b.** hold the elevator.

_____

**2.** Ask your roommate to ...

**a.** answer the door.

_____

**b.** help you with your homework.

_____

**3.** Ask your brother to ...

**a.** turn off the television.

_____

**b.** carry the groceries for you.

_____

**4.** Ask a server at a restaurant to ...

**a.** bring you the menu.

_____

**b.** tell you about today's special.

_____

**5.** Ask a travel agent to ...

**a.** check for the cheapest fare.

_____

**b.** send you the ticket.

_____

# 8d  *May, Might,* and *Could* to Express Possibility

That's dangerous! He **may fall!**

| Subject | Modal (+ *Not*) | Base Verb |
|---|---|---|
| I<br>You<br>He/She/It<br>We<br>They | **may**<br>**may not***<br>**might**<br>**might not***<br>**could**** | **go.** |

\*In this meaning, we do not contract *may* and *might* with *not*.
\*\*In this meaning, we do not use *could* in the negative.

## Function

1. We use *may, might,* or *could* + a base verb to express something that is possible now or in the future. *May, might,* and *could* mean "perhaps."

   She **may fall** and **break** something.
   OR She **might fall** and **break** something.
   OR She **could fall** and **break** something.
   OR **Perhaps** she will fall and break something.

2. Remember, we also use *could* + a base verb to mean past ability, to ask permission, and to make requests. We also use *may* + a base verb to ask for permission.

   I **could run** very fast when I was young.
   **Could** I **take** one of these?
   **Could** you **help** me, please?
   **May** I **take** one of these, please?

3. When expressing possibility, we do not use *may* in Yes/No questions. *Might* can be used in Yes/No questions, but it is very formal.

| | |
|---|---|
| CORRECT: | Could that answer be correct? |
| CORRECT (very formal): | Might that answer be correct? |
| INCORRECT: | ~~May~~ that answer be correct? |

4. In this meaning, we do not use *could* in the negative.

| | |
|---|---|
| CORRECT: | Our flight may not be late. |
| CORRECT: | Our flight might not be late. |
| INCORRECT: | Our flight ~~could not~~ be late. (This sentence means "It is impossible for our flight to be late.") |

## 11 Practice

**Donald worries about everything. Complete the sentences with *may, might,* or *could* and one of the words or phrases from the list. More than one answer is possible.**

| | | |
|---|---|---|
| bite him | divorce him | have an accident |
| catch a cold | get sunburned | have bacteria in it |
| crash | | |

1. He doesn't fly because he thinks the plane _____ *might crash.* _____
2. He doesn't like to go to the beach because he _____
3. He doesn't go to the zoo because he thinks an animal _____
4. He doesn't go out when it's raining because he _____
5. He doesn't drive because he _____
6. He doesn't eat in a restaurant because the food _____
7. He doesn't want to get married because his wife _____

## 12 Practice

**Underline the correct verb in parentheses.**

Ann:     What's for dinner?

Betty:   We (are having / may have) chicken. It's in the oven.
                    1

Ann:     When will it be ready?

Betty:   I'm not sure. It (will / may) be ready in half an hour.
                    2

Ann:      What time is John coming?

Betty:    I don't know. It depends on the traffic. He (may / will) be late.
                                                              3

Ann:      Is Ted coming at 7:00?

Betty:    Yes. He called. He's on his way. He (will / may) be here at seven for sure.
                                                            4

Ann:      Are we having dessert?

Betty:    Yes, we (are / might). It's in the refrigerator.
                         5

Ann:      It's the doorbell. Who can it be?

Betty:    I don't know. It (is / may be) Ted.
                              6

## 13 Practice

**Carla and George are waiting for their friend to arrive from the airport. He is late, and they are getting worried. Read their conversation. Underline the correct form in parentheses. If both forms are possible, underline both of them.**

George:   (Could / May) his flight be late?
               1

Carla:    Maybe, or he (could / may) be caught in traffic.
                              2

George:   I don't think so. There isn't much traffic at this time.

Carla:    There (might not / mightn't) be a lot of traffic, but perhaps he got lost on the way.
                       3

George:   (May / Could) we call him?
            4

Carla:    I tried, but he didn't answer. His cell phone (might not / couldn't) be turned on.
                                                              5

George:   Let's call the airline. They (may / might) have some information about the flight.
                                             6

Carla:    Good idea. Oh! I see lights in the driveway. (Might / Could) that be his car?
                                                             7

## 14 Your Turn

**Write two things you may/might (not) do for each of these times.**

**Example:**
Tonight, I may do my homework, or I might call my parents.

**1.** Tonight, _____

**2.** This weekend, _____

**3.** Next year, _____

## 8e  *Maybe* OR *May Be*

Antonio is thinking about a young woman he saw.
"**Maybe** she's not married," he thinks.

1. *Maybe* (one word) and *may be* (two words) both express possibility.

2. *Maybe* (one word) is an adverb. It comes in front of a subject and a verb. It means "perhaps" or "possibly."

    **Maybe** she's not married.

3. *May be* (two words) is used as the verb of a sentence.

    She **may be** married.

---

**15** | Practice

**Antonio saw an attractive woman on the street yesterday. Her name is Angelica. Complete the sentences with *may be* or *maybe*.**

1. Her name is Angelica. _____*Maybe*_____ she's French.

2. Or, she _____ Italian. He doesn't know.

3. He doesn't know what she does. _____ she's a dancer.

4. Yes, she _____ a ballet dancer.

5. He saw Angelica for the first time yesterday. Why didn't he see her before?

    _____ she doesn't live in this town.

6. Yes, she _____ from out of town.

7. He said, "Hello," and asked, "What's your name?" She didn't say anything. _____ she doesn't understand English.

8. At first Antonio thought, "She _____ from another country." So he said slowly, "My name is Antonio. What is your name?"

9. She looked at him. There was something in her eyes. _____ she thought he was impolite.

10. Then she said, "Angelica." _____ it wasn't her real name. Then she ran away.

## 16  What Do You Think?

**Finish the story about Antonio and Angelica. Use *maybe* and *may be*.**

## 17  What Do You Think?

**Work in pairs or groups. Look at the two photos. Use *may, might,* or *maybe* to make guesses about what you think these objects are.**

A.

1. _____
2. _____
3. _____
4. _____

B.

1. _____
2. _____
3. _____
4. _____

**Your Turn**

Say three good things and three bad things that may happen to you this year. Use *maybe* or *may be*.

**Example:**
Maybe I'll pass my English exam.
If I don't pass, I may be in the same class again!

## 8f  *Let's* and *Why Don't We* to Make Suggestions; *Why Don't You* to Give Advice

### Form / Function

**SUGGESTIONS**

1. We can make suggestions with *let's* and *why don't we* + a base verb. They have the same meaning.

2. *Let's* is a contraction of *let* + *us*. We usually say and write *let's*. *Let us* is very formal. We rarely use it.

3. *Let's* includes you and one or more other people.

| AFFIRMATIVE | | | | |
|---|---|---|---|---|
| *Let's* | Base Verb | | Ways to Agree | Ways to Disagree |
| **Let's** | **watch** | TV. | Good idea. Sure. OK. Fine with me. | I'd rather not. Let's ... instead. Let's not. |
| | **go** | dancing. | | |
| | **eat** | now. | | |

| NEGATIVE | | | | |
|---|---|---|---|---|
| *Let's Not* | Base Verb | | Ways to Agree | Ways to Disagree |
| **Let's not** | **watch** | TV. | I agree. Good idea. Sure. OK. | Oh, I'd really like to. Why not? |
| | **go** | dancing. | | |
| | **eat** | now. | | |

| *Why Don't We* | Base Verb | | Ways to Agree | Ways to Disagree |
|---|---|---|---|---|
| **Why don't we** | **watch** | TV? | Good idea. | I'd rather not. |
| | **go** | dancing? | Sure. | Let's not. |
| | **eat** | now? | OK. | Let's ... instead. |

**ADVICE**

4. We use *why don't you* + a base verb to give friendly advice to someone.

| Why Don't You | Base Verb | | Ways to Agree | Ways to Disagree |
|---|---|---|---|---|
| **Why don't you** | **rest** | a little? | Good idea. OK. I will. | I have no time. I'm OK. |
| | **go** | to the doctor? | | |
| | **take** | an aspirin? | | |

| 19 | Practice

**Make suggestions with *let's* or *why don't we* and one of the ideas in the list or with your own ideas.**

| | |
|---|---|
| buy her a gift | hurry |
| go get a pizza | stay home and watch TV |
| go for a walk | study together in the library |
| go see it | watch it |

1. It's a beautiful day.

    *Why don't we go for a walk?*

2. There's a good movie at the movie theater here.

    _____

3. It's raining again tonight. I don't want to go out. What should we do?

    _____

4. I'm hungry, but there's nothing to eat here.

    _____

5. There's a good football game on TV now.

    _____

6. It's Carol's birthday next Monday.

    _____

7. We have a test tomorrow.

    _____

8. Class starts in a few minutes.

    _____

## 20 Practice

Look at these problems. Give advice to your friend with *why don't you* and one of the ideas from the list, or use your own ideas.

ask her what she wants          call the store
go to the dentist               put on a sweater
have a cup of coffee            take an aspirin
have a piece of fruit           tell him/her what happened

**1.** Your friend: I can't find my credit card. I think I left it in the department store today.

You: _Why don't you call the store?_

**2.** Your friend: I left my essay for my English class at home. My teacher wants it today.

You: _____

**3.** Your friend: I have a terrible headache.

You: _____

**4.** Your friend: I don't know what to get my mother for her birthday.

You: _____

**5.** Your friend: I have a toothache.

You: _____

**6.** Your friend: I'm cold.

You: _____

**7.** Your friend: Reviewing for the test is making me sleepy.

You: _____

**8.** Your friend: I'm hungry, but I don't have time to eat lunch right now.

You: _____

## 21 Your Turn

Work with a partner or the class. Name three problems that you have.

**Example:**
You:            I'm gaining weight.
Your partner:  Why don't you eat less?

## 22 Your Turn

Make three suggestions for a place and time for a class party. Use *let's* or *why don't we*. Give answers.

**Example:**
You:            Why don't we have the party in a hotel?
Your partner:  No, that's too expensive.

# 8g  *Should, Ought To,* and *Had Better* to Give Advice

I broke my friend's CD player.
**Should** I **buy** a new one for him?

### ADVICE

| AFFIRMATIVE STATEMENT | | | NEGATIVE STATEMENT | | |
|---|---|---|---|---|---|
| Subject | Modal | Base Verb | Subject | Modal + *Not* | Base Verb |
| You | **should** **ought to** | **buy** a new one. | You | **should not** **shouldn't** | **lie** about it. |

1. We use *should* and *ought to* + base verb to say what is the best or right thing to do. *Should* and *ought to* have the same meaning.

2. We usually do not use *ought to* in questions, negative sentences, and short answers. We use *should* instead.

    You **shouldn't stay** up late. You have an exam tomorrow.

    **Should** I **send** a card?
    Yes, you **should.**

### STRONG ADVICE OR WARNING

| AFFIRMATIVE STATEMENTS | | | NEGATIVE STATEMENTS | | |
|---|---|---|---|---|---|
| Subject | Modal | Base Verb | | Subject | Modal + *Not* | Base Verb |
| You | **had better** | **hurry.** | | We | **had better not** | **wait.** |
| We | **'d better** | **eat** | now. | She | **'d better not** | **leave.** |

3. We use *had better* to give a strong recommendation. *Had better* often suggests a warning and is stronger than *should* or *ought to*. The speaker expects the action to happen. The contraction of *had better* is *'d better*.

    It's raining. You **had better take** an umbrella.
    We**'d better not be** late or we'll miss the plane.

4. We rarely use *had better* in questions.

## 23 Practice

**Say what Sandra should or should not do.**

1. She doesn't do her homework.

   _She should do her homework._

2. She goes out with her friends every night.

   _____

3. She never goes to the gym.

   _____

4. She always eats out.

   _____

5. She drinks a lot of coffee.

   _____

6. She stays out at dance parties all night.

   _____

7. She wears dirty shoes inside the house.

   _____

8. She stays in bed until noon on weekends.

   _____

9. She lends her car to her friends.

   _____

10. She spends all her money on clothes and make-up.

    _____

## 24 Practice

**Benny is overweight and is not feeling well. He eats, smokes, and works too much. Use**
*had better* **or** *had better not* **with the words in parentheses to give him strong advice.**

1. (eat less) _You had better eat less._
2. (drink a lot of soft drinks) _____
3. (drink too much coffee) _____
4. (get more exercise) _____
5. (use less salt) _____
6. (eat lots of snacks) _____
7. (work overtime often) _____
8. (see a doctor) _____

Modal Auxiliaries and Related Forms

## 25 What Do You Think?

**What is your advice for Benny?**

**Example:**
He'd better lose some weight.

## 26 Practice

**Give strong advice in these situations. Write a sentence with *had better* and a sentence with *had better not*.**

1. I'm going out, and it's starting to rain.

   _You had better take an umbrella._

   _You'd better not go out._

2. I think I have a temperature.

   _____

   _____

3. I might miss an important interview. I have to be there in ten minutes.

   _____

   _____

4. I have to go by car, but there isn't much gas in it.

   _____

   _____

5. I am driving too fast. The speed limit is 40 miles an hour.

   _____

   _____

## 27 Your Turn

**Say what you had better do to keep healthy. Say what you had better not do.**

**Example:**
I'd better exercise more, and I'd better not smoke.

## 8h Prefer ... to, Like ... Better Than, and Would Rather to Express Preference

### Form / Function

I **prefer** playing football **to** basketball.

1. We can use *prefer ... to* to express preferences. We can use a noun or a gerund as an object after *prefer*. (A gerund is a verb + –*ing* used as a noun.)

| Subject | *Prefer* | Object | *To* | Object |
|---------|----------|--------|------|--------|
| I | **prefer** | football | **to** | basketball. |
| | | playing football | | playing basketball. |

2. We can also use *like* with *better than* or other comparative forms to express preferences. We can use a noun or a gerund as an object after *like*.

| Subject | *Like* | Object | Comparative Form | Object |
|---------|--------|--------|------------------|--------|
| I | **like** | football | **better than** | basketball. |
| | | playing football | | playing basketball. |

3. We can also use *would rather (not)* to express preferences. We use *than* when we talk about two things.

| Subject | *Would Rather (Not)* | Base Verb | Object | *Than* | Object |
|---------|---------------------|-----------|--------|--------|--------|
| I | **would rather**<br>**'d rather** | **play** | football | **than** | (play) basketball. |
| | **would rather not***<br>**'d rather not*** | **play** | football. | | |

*We do not use the negative form *wouldn't* in sentences with *would rather + than*.

4. *Prefer ... to, like ... better,* and *would rather* have the same meaning. We use them to say what we prefer to do, or that we like one thing more than another.

> I **prefer** salad **to** soup.
> OR I **like** salad **better** than soup.
> OR I'**d rather** have salad than soup.

5. In questions with *would rather,* we often use *or.*

> Would you rather have salad **or** soup?

|28| Practice

**Complete the sentences with *than, to,* and *or.***

1. I'd rather sit by the window _____*than*_____ sit at the back of the restaurant.

2. I like the table by the window better _____ the table at the back.

3. I prefer the table by the window _____ the table at the back.

4. I like rice better _____ potatoes.

5. I prefer rice _____ potatoes.

6. I'd rather have rice _____ potatoes.

7. Would you rather have fish _____ meat?

8. I prefer having fish _____ having meat.

9. Do you like eating fish better _____ eating meat?

10. Would you rather pay cash _____ pay with a credit card?

11. I prefer paying with a credit card _____ paying cash.

12. I like paying by credit card better _____ paying cash.

|29| Practice

**Write sentences with *I'd rather* or *I prefer* and one of the items from the list.**

| | | |
|---|---|---|
| eat later | go now | phone them |
| go by plane | go to a restaurant | stand |
| take a taxi | watch a video | |

1. Let's take the bus.

   (prefer) _I prefer taking a taxi._

2. Would you like to sit down?

   (rather) _____

**3.** Shall we eat at home?

(prefer) _____

**4.** Do you want to watch TV?

(rather) _____

**5.** Shall we drive there?

(prefer) _____

**6.** Would you like to write a thank you card?

(rather) _____

**7.** Do you want to stay a few more minutes?

(prefer) _____

**8.** Would you like to eat now?

(prefer) _____

## 30 Your Turn

**What would you rather do? Use *I'd rather* to write what you prefer.**

**Example:**
play football or soccer
I'd rather play soccer than football.

**1.** play football or soccer

_____

**2.** live in the country or the city

_____

**3.** be married or be single

_____

**4.** drink tea or coffee

_____

**5.** do homework or watch TV

_____

# 8i *Have To*, *Have Got To*, and *Must* to Express Necessity

She **doesn't have to work** today.

## *HAVE TO:* PRESENT AND FUTURE

| AFFIRMATIVE STATEMENTS | | | NEGATIVE STATEMENTS | | |
|---|---|---|---|---|---|
| Subject | *Have/Has To* | Base Verb | Subject | *Not Have To* | Base Verb |
| I | **have to*** | | I | **do not have to** | |
| You | | | You | **don't have to** | |
| He/She/It | **has to*** | **work.** | He/She/It | **does not have to** **doesn't have to** | **work.** |
| We | **have to*** | | We | **do not have to** | |
| They | | | They | **don't have to** | |

*We do not contract *have to* and *has to* with the subject.

CORRECT:　　I have to work.
INCORRECT:　I've to work.

| YES/NO QUESTIONS | | | | SHORT ANSWERS | |
|---|---|---|---|---|---|
| *Do/Does* | Subject | *Have To* | Base Verb | Yes, | No, |
| **Do** | I | | | you **do.** | you **don't.** |
| | you | | | I/we **do.** | I/we **don't.** |
| **Does** | he/she/it | **have to** | **work?** | he/she/it **does.** | he/she/it **doesn't.** |
| **Do** | we | | | you **do.** | you **don't.** |
| | they | | | they **do.** | they **don't.** |

## HAVE TO: PAST

| AFFIRMATIVE STATEMENTS | | | NEGATIVE STATEMENTS | | |
|---|---|---|---|---|---|
| Subject | *Had To* | Base Verb | Subject | *Not Have To* | Base Verb |
| I<br>You<br>He/She/It<br>We<br>They | **had to*** | **work.** | I<br>You<br>He/She/It<br>We<br>They | **did not have to**<br>**didn't have to** | **work.** |

\*We do not contract *had to* with the subject.

CORRECT:     I had to work.
INCORRECT: ~~I'd~~ to work.

| YES/NO QUESTIONS | | | | SHORT ANSWERS | |
|---|---|---|---|---|---|
| *Did* | Subject | *Have To* | Base Verb | Yes, | No, |
| **Did** | I<br>you<br>he/she/it<br>we<br>they | **have to** | **work?** | you **did.**<br>I/we **did.**<br>he/she/it **did.**<br>you **did.**<br>they **did.** | you **didn't.**<br>I/we **didn't.**<br>he/she/it **didn't.**<br>you **didn't.**<br>they **didn't.** |

## HAVE GOT TO: PRESENT AND FUTURE

| Subject | *Have/Has Got To* | Base Verb | |
|---|---|---|---|
| I<br>You | **have got to**<br>**'ve got to** | **work** | now.<br>later.<br>tomorrow. |
| He/She/It | **has got to**<br>**'s got to** | | |
| We<br>They | **have got to**<br>**'ve got to** | | |

## MUST: PRESENT AND FUTURE

| Subject | Modal | Base Verb | |
|---|---|---|---|
| I<br>You<br>He/She/It<br>We<br>They | **must** | **work** | now.<br>tonight.<br>next week. |

1. *Must, have to,* and *have got to* have almost the same meaning. They all mean that it is necessary to do something.

2. *Must* is the strongest form. We use *must* in requirements, rules, and laws. We often use *must* in written instructions.

   > You **must take** an entrance exam. (School requirements)
   > Drivers **must signal** before they turn right or left. (Driver's manual)

3. When *must* expresses necessity, we use it only to refer to the present or the future. To refer to the past, we use *had to.*

   > CORRECT:    I had to work last Saturday.
   > INCORRECT:  I ~~must work~~ last Saturday.

4. We usually use *have to* and *have got to* in everyday conversation. *Have to* and *have got to* have the same meaning.

   > It's Saturday, but I **have to work.**
   > It's Saturday, but I**'ve got to work.**
   > I **had to work** last Saturday, too.

5. We do not usually use *have got to* in questions and negative statements.

6. We use *have got to* only to refer to present and future necessity. To refer to the past, we use *had to.*

   > CORRECT:    We had to finish this homework.
   > INCORRECT:  We ~~had got to~~ finish this homework.

---

[31] Practice

**Change the written information with *must* to a spoken form with *have to* or *have got to.***

**1.** All students must register and pay fees.

   *All students have to register and pay fees.*

**2.** All students must register before taking courses.

   _____

**3.** Every student must take an English placement exam.

   _____

**4.** Every new student must attend orientation during registration week.

   _____

**5.** Students must apply for parking permits during registration.

_____

**6.** Students must present registration forms on the first day of classes.

_____

[32] **Practice**

**This is Mr. Krone and his two children, Bill and Jane. What do they have to do every day?**

|  | **Mr. Krone** | **Bill and Jane** |
|---|---|---|
| Get up | 7:00 | 7:30 |
| Leave home | 7:30 | 8:00 |
| Be at the office | 8:30 | — |
| Be at school | — | 8:30 |
| Go to bed | 11:30 | 10:00 |

**1.** Mr. Krone _____*has to*_____ get up at 7:00 in the morning to go to work.

**2.** Bill and Jane _____ get up at 7:30 to go to school.

**3.** Mr. Krone _____ leave home at 7:30 in the morning to go to work.

**4.** Bill and Jane _____ leave home at 8:00 to go to school.

**5.** Bill and Jane _____ be at school at 8:30.

**6.** Mr. Krone _____ be at the office at 8:30.

**7.** Mr. Krone _____ go to bed at 11:30 in the evening because he is always very tired.

**8.** Bill and Jane _____ go to bed at 10:00.

**33** Practice

A. Mr. Krone had a busy week. Match each situation with what he had to do.

**Situations**                                      **He had to ...**

_____  **1.** He got sick.                        **a.** work overtime

_____  **2.** He had a lot of work.               **b.** take it to the mechanic

_____  **3.** His car broke down.                 **c.** write a big check

_____  **4.** His taxes were due.                 **d.** go to the doctor

_____  **5.** Mrs. Krone was traveling.           **e.** rest

_____  **6.** He got very tired.                  **f.** do all the cooking

B. Now write a sentence with *had to* for each solution.

**1.** _He had to go to the doctor because he got sick._

**2.** _____

**3.** _____

**4.** _____

**5.** _____

**6.** _____

**34** Practice

Work with a partner. Write questions about what Mr. Krone had to do last week.

**1.** A: _Did Mr. Krone have to go to the dentist?_

   B: No, he didn't.

**2.** A: _____

   B: No, he didn't.

**3.** A: _____

   B: Yes, he did.

**4.** A: _____

   B: No, he didn't.

**5.** A: _____

   B: Yes, he did.

**6.** A: _____

   B: No, he didn't.

Practice

**Underline the correct form in parentheses. If both forms are correct, underline both of them.**

1. Bonnie (<u>has to</u> / <u>has got to</u>) travel to Seoul, Korea next month.
   <sub>1</sub>

2. She doesn't have a passport, so she (had to / had got to) apply for one last week.
   <sub>2</sub>

3. Before she applied for her new passport, she (must / had to) have her picture taken.
   <sub>3</sub>

4. When she gets to Seoul, she (must / has got to) visit many customers.
   <sub>4</sub>

5. The director of her company in Korea (has to / must) introduce her to them.
   <sub>5</sub>

6. When she returns home, she (must / had to) write letters to everyone she met in Seoul.
   <sub>6</sub>

Your Turn

**Write three things you had to do last week and three things you have to/have got to do this week.**

**Example:**
Last week, I had to do my laundry. This week, I've got to write an important essay.

## 8j Must Not to Forbid and Not Have To to Express Lack of Necessity

**Form / Function**

Look at the sign!
We **mustn't swim** here.

1. We use *must not* + a base verb to say that something is not allowed or is forbidden. *Must not* is stronger than *should not*.

223
Modal Auxiliaries and Related Forms

| Subject | Modal + *Not* | Base Verb |
|---|---|---|
| I | | |
| You | | |
| He/She/It | **must not** **mustn't** | **park** here. |
| We | | |
| They | | |

2. We use *not have to* to show that something is not necessary. (See page 218 for the forms of *not have to*.)

Tomorrow is Sunday. You **don't have to** get up early.
I **had to** get up early yesterday.

## 37 Practice

**Look at the following instructions about flights and planes. Then write sentences with *mustn't* or *don't have to*.**

1. It isn't necessary for you to fasten your seat belt all through a flight, but it's a good idea.

   *You don't have to fasten your seat belt all through a flight.*

2. It is forbidden to smoke on the aircraft.

   *You must not smoke on the aircraft.*

3. It isn't necessary for you to carry your medications with you, but it's a good idea.

   _____

4. It isn't necessary for you to put labels on your luggage, but it's a good idea in case it gets lost.

   _____

5. It is forbidden to carry knives or sharp objects in your carry-on luggage.

   _____

6. It is forbidden to carry more than two pieces of carry-on luggage.

   _____

7. It isn't necessary to carry breakable objects in your carry-on luggage, but if you don't, they might get broken.

   _____

8. It isn't necessary for you to stay in your seat all through the flight.

   _____

9. It is forbidden to leave your luggage unattended.

   _____

**10.** It is forbidden to take items from strangers on the aircraft.

_____

**11.** It isn't necessary to eat light meals, but you might feel better if you do.

_____

**12.** It is forbidden to take fruits and other foods from one country to another.

_____

## 38 Practice

Look at these washing labels on clothes. Say what they mean. Use *must, must not,* or *don't have to.*

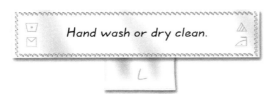

**1.** <u>You don't have to dry clean this clothing.</u>

**5.** _____

_____

**2.** _____

_____

**6.** _____

_____

**3.** _____

_____

**7.** _____

_____

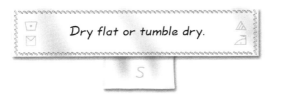

**4.** _____

_____

**8.** _____

_____

Modal Auxiliaries and Related Forms

## 39 Practice

**You are going for a vacation in the sun in the Caribbean. You will be staying at a nice hotel. What mustn't you forget? What do you not have to take?**

1. blankets
2. a coat
3. gloves
4. a grammar book

5. knives and forks
6. my passport
7. my plane tickets
8. a suit

9. my sunglasses
10. a swimsuit

1. *I don't have to take blankets.*

2. _____

3. _____

4. _____

5. _____

6. *I mustn't forget my passport.*

7. _____

8. _____

9. _____

10. _____

## 40 Your Turn

**You are going for a weekend at a friend's house. Write three things you mustn't forget to take with you and three things you don't have to take.**

**Example:**
I mustn't forget my toothbrush.

**Things I mustn't forget**

1. _____

2. _____

3. _____

**Things I don't have to take**

1. _____

2. _____

3. _____

# 8k  *Must* to Make Deductions

A: Who is that woman? Is she a student?
B: I don't know, but I've seen her go into the teachers' room.
A: Oh. She **must be** a teacher. She **must not be** a student.

1. We use *must* for deductions, or guesses, from facts that we know. *Must* expresses what is logical in the situation.

   | Fact: | Tony has three houses and four cars. |
   | Deduction: | He **must** be rich. |

2. We use *must not* for a negative deduction.

   | Fact: | Tony has three companies. He works very hard. |
   | Deduction: | He **must not** have a lot of free time. |

3. Remember, we also use *must* to express strong necessity, and we use *must not* when we forbid something.

   You **must** do your homework.
   You **must not** drive when the traffic light is red.

Three people are having breakfast in a hotel. Some of their belongings are on their tables. What can you tell about their owners? Complete the sentences with *must*.

**A.**

**1.** The owner _____ *must be a woman.*

**2.** The owner _____

**3.** The owner _____

**B.**

**1.** The owner _____

**2.** The owner _____

**3.** The owner _____

**C.**

**1.** The owner _____

**2.** The owner _____

**3.** The owner _____

## 42 Your Turn

Work with a partner. Look at the photos of the two people. Make deductions based on what you see in the photos. Make three sentences for each photo using *must* or *must not*.

**Example:**
He must be a doctor.
She must be a photographer.

# 81 Imperatives

**Form**

1. We use the base form of the verb in imperative sentences. The verb is always the same form.

2. We use the imperative to address one or more people. The subject of the sentence, *you*, is understood. It is not stated.

   **Open** the window.

3. We can use **please** at the beginning or at the end of the sentence. At the end of the sentence, it must follow a comma.

   **Please** open your books.
   Open your books, **please.**

4. For the negative, we use *do not* or *don't* before the base form of the verb.

   **Do not** enter.
   **Don't** be late!

We use the imperative to tell someone to do something. Imperatives are used for these purposes.

| Function | Example |
|---|---|
| 1. Commands | **Wash** your hands. |
| 2. Requests | Please **turn off** the lights. |
| 3. Directions | **Turn** right at the traffic light. |
| 4. Instructions | **Cook** for 15 minutes. |
| 5. Warnings | **Be** careful. |
| 6. Advice | **Get** some sleep. |

## 43 Practice

**Complete the teacher's instructions with verbs in the list. Use *don't* where necessary.**

| | | | | |
|---|---|---|---|---|
| be | close | make | sit | talk |
| chew | do | open | stop | work |

1. _Close_____ your books.

2. _____ to your neighbor in class.

3. _____ gum in class.

4. _____ sentences with these words.

5. _____ your books to page 210.

6. _____ with your partner.

7. _____ homework in class.

8. _____ quiet!

9. _____ down.

10. _____ that noise!

**Add two more of your own.**

11. _____

12. _____

## 44 Practice

**Work with a partner. Give advice to a friend in these situations. Use affirmative and negative imperatives.**

1. I have a cold.

   _Don't go to school. Stay home and rest. Drink lots of tea with lemon._

   _____

2. I can't fall asleep at night.

   _____

   _____

3. My computer won't start.

   _____

   _____

4. My grades are bad.

   _____

   _____

5. I can't save money.

   _____

   _____

## 45 Your Turn

**Give instructions. You are going on a long vacation. Your friend is coming to your home every day to take care of things. Make a list of six things for your friend to do.**

### THINGS TO DO

1. _Take the mail in._
2. _____
3. _____
4. _____
5. _____
6. _____

# WRITING: Write a Friendly Letter

**Write a letter to a friend about changes in your life.**

**Step 1. Read the situation.**

You have been accepted at a famous university to study for your Bachelor of Arts degree. The university is famous, but it is not in your city. You have to leave home and move far away. You are writing a letter to a friend explaining the changes in your life.

**Step 2. Think about these facts and write sentences using modals.**

**1.** move to a new city or country
**2.** make new friends
**3.** live in the school dorm or find a cheap apartment
**4.** leave things behind
**5.** not come home for long periods

**Step 3. Rewrite the sentences as a paragraph as in the model letter below. For more writing guidelines, see pages 407–411.**

> May 1, 20XX
>
> Dear Paul,
>     I'm writing to tell you that I got accepted at the University of
> _____ . It's a famous university, but it is not in my city, so I have
> to go live there. I'm going next month. I have to do many things.
>
>
>
>     Your friend,

**Step 4. Evaluate your paragraph.**

**Checklist**

_____ Did you write the letter in correct letter form?
_____ Did you indent your paragraph?
_____ Did you use some modal auxiliaries in your sentences?

**Step 5. Work with a partner to edit your paragraph. Check spelling, punctuation, and grammar.**

**Step 6. Write a final copy of your paragraph.**

# SELF-TEST

**A**  **Choose the best answer, A, B, C, or D, to complete the sentence. Mark your answer by darkening the oval with the same letter.**

1. You _____ put that blouse in the washing machine. It says dry clean only.

    A. must          Ⓐ Ⓑ Ⓒ Ⓓ
    B. mustn't
    C. don't have to
    D. have to

2. I _____ read until I was six.

    A. can't          Ⓐ Ⓑ Ⓒ Ⓓ
    B. shouldn't
    C. couldn't
    D. mustn't

3. _____ I borrow your pen, please?

    A. May          Ⓐ Ⓑ Ⓒ Ⓓ
    B. Would
    C. Should
    D. Will

4. I _____ go to the market. I need some eggs for this cake.

    A. might          Ⓐ Ⓑ Ⓒ Ⓓ
    B. could
    C. must
    D. mustn't

5. We _____ leave now. It's getting late.

    A. could          Ⓐ Ⓑ Ⓒ Ⓓ
    B. should
    C. might
    D. are able to

6. Sam:  What should we have for lunch?
   Kate: _____ pizza?

    A. Why don't we have      Ⓐ Ⓑ Ⓒ Ⓓ
    B. I'd rather have
    C. We'd better have
    D. We have to have

7. _____ you open the door for me, please?

    A. May          Ⓐ Ⓑ Ⓒ Ⓓ
    B. Could
    C. Should
    D. Might

8. I'm sorry, I _____ to play football with you next week. I'm going out of town.

    A. can't          Ⓐ Ⓑ Ⓒ Ⓓ
    B. don't have
    C. won't be able
    D. must not

9. I don't know her. She _____ a student.

    A. maybe          Ⓐ Ⓑ Ⓒ Ⓓ
    B. may be
    C. 'd rather be
    D. should

10. _____ You are going to fall.

    A. You may be careful.      Ⓐ Ⓑ Ⓒ Ⓓ
    B. You could be careful.
    C. You are careful!
    D. Be careful!

Modal Auxiliaries and Related Forms

**B** Find the underlined word or phrase, A, B, C, or D, that is incorrect. Mark your answer by darkening the oval with the same letter.

1. You <u>don't</u> <u>have be</u> <u>a</u> citizen <u>to get</u> a
        A    B   C        D
   driver's license.

   Ⓐ Ⓑ Ⓒ Ⓓ

2. <u>You</u> must <u>to drive</u> with a seatbelt <u>in</u> this
    A      B  C            D
   country.

   Ⓐ Ⓑ Ⓒ Ⓓ

3. In most <u>movie theaters</u>, senior citizens
            A
   <u>can't</u> <u>have to</u> pay full price for <u>a movie</u>.
     B    C              D

   Ⓐ Ⓑ Ⓒ Ⓓ

4. The store <u>maybe</u> very <u>crowded</u> tomorrow
            A       B
   because <u>there is</u> <u>a</u> big sale.
          C   D

   Ⓐ Ⓑ Ⓒ Ⓓ

5. You <u>could</u> not <u>sign</u> <u>anything</u> before
       A     B   C
   reading <u>it</u> carefully.
           D

   Ⓐ Ⓑ Ⓒ Ⓓ

6. <u>Would</u> you <u>rather see</u> a movie <u>to</u> stay at
    A       B          C
   home and <u>watch</u> a video?
           D

   Ⓐ Ⓑ Ⓒ Ⓓ

7. <u>You better</u> <u>study</u> more, or you <u>might</u> not
    A      B           C
   <u>pass</u> the class.
    D

   Ⓐ Ⓑ Ⓒ Ⓓ

8. Karen <u>was</u> able <u>change</u> <u>the</u> flat tire
         A       B   C
   <u>by herself</u> yesterday.
     D

   Ⓐ Ⓑ Ⓒ Ⓓ

9. You <u>mightn't</u> try <u>to take</u> the entrance
       A       B
   exam without <u>preparing</u> for <u>it</u> first.
             C     D

   Ⓐ Ⓑ Ⓒ Ⓓ

10. We <u>must</u> to work overtime last week
       A
    <u>in order to</u> <u>finish</u> <u>the project</u> by the
         B     C     D
    deadline.

    Ⓐ Ⓑ Ⓒ Ⓓ

# UNIT 9

## GERUNDS AND INFINITIVES

## 9a Gerund as Subject and Object

Form

**Climbing** rocks is dangerous.
Melanie loves **climbing** rocks.

1. To form a gerund, we add *–ing* to the base form of the verb. See page 406 for spelling rules for adding *–ing* to the base form of verbs.

| Base Verb | Gerund |
|-----------|-----------|
| climb | **climbing** |
| go | **going** |
| run | **running** |
| watch | **watching** |

2. We can use a gerund like a noun. It can be the subject or the object of a sentence.

| Subject | Verb | Object |
|---------|------|--------|
| **Climbing** rocks | takes | a lot of energy. |

| Subject | Verb | Object |
|---------|------|--------|
| Melanie | loves | **climbing** rocks. |

3. We can use a gerund as the subject of a question.

   Is **climbing** rocks dangerous?

## 1 Practice

**Complete the sentences with the gerund form of the verbs in the list. You may use a verb more than one time.**

| drive | fly | sleep | watch |
|-------|-----|-------|-------|
| fish | play | wash | |

1. _Flying_____ in an airplane is not really dangerous.
2. John is afraid of _____ in an airplane. He travels by car.
3. He loves his car and enjoys _____ it.
4. On Sundays, his favorite pastime is _____ his car.
5. _____ football is too tiring for John.
6. He prefers _____ football on television.
7. His favorite sport is _____ in a river.
8. _____ in a river is relaxing for John.
9. He likes _____ his dirty clothes in the washing machine.
10. John also likes _____ late on Sundays.

## 2 Practice

**Say which activities in the list are easy and which are difficult for you. Use gerunds in your answers.**

**Example:**
I think cooking is difficult.

| cook | ride a horse | ski | write letters |
|------|--------------|-----|---------------|
| dance | run | swim | |
| learn English | sing | water ski | |
| read | skate | windsurf | |

## 3 Your Turn

**Say five things that you like or that you think are fun.**

**Example:**
Dancing is fun.
I love listening to music.

Gerunds and Infinitives

# 9b Verb + Gerund

We **enjoy skiing** in the mountains. Little Jamie came with us this year.

1. We can use a gerund as the object of certain verbs. Here are some of the verbs.

| | | | |
|---|---|---|---|
| consider | finish | keep on | quit |
| discuss | give up | not mind | start |
| dislike | imagine | postpone | stop |
| enjoy | keep | put off | think about |

2. We use a gerund after the verb *go* for some activities.

| | | | |
|---|---|---|---|
| go **bowling** | go **dancing** | go **jogging** | go **shopping** |
| go **camping** | go **fishing** | go **running** | go **sightseeing** |
| go **climbing** | go **hiking** | go **sailing** | go **swimming** |

## 4 Practice

**Complete the sentences with the gerund form of the verb in parentheses.**

1. After Mike stopped (work) _____working_____, he went
   (bowl) _____ with his friends.

2. Ted was considering (visit) _____ his sister next week, but he
   postponed (go) _____ for another two weeks.

3. It didn't stop (rain) _____, so we put off (go) _____
   until later.

4. Timmy quit (watch) _____ cartoons when he started
   (go) _____ to school.

5. My parents keep (tell) _____ me rock climbing is dangerous, but it's
   hard to give up (do) _____ something I enjoy.

6. I enjoy (receive) _____ letters, but I always put off
   (reply) _____ to them.

7. We postponed (go) _____ on the trip until next weekend.

8. I don't mind (go) _____ sightseeing, but we must go
   (shop) _____ later.

9. He finished (do) _____ his homework, and then he went
   (jog) _____.

10. I gave up (fix) _____ my car, and I am considering
    (buy) _____ a new one.

## 5 Your Turn

**Complete the chart with two things you enjoy doing, dislike doing, and don't mind doing. Then ask two classmates about themselves and complete the chart.**

**Example:**
I enjoy going to the movies. I dislike cleaning the house, but I don't mind cooking.

| Student | Enjoy Doing | Dislike Doing | Don't Mind Doing |
|---------|-------------|---------------|------------------|
| 1. Me   |             |               |                  |
| 2.      |             |               |                  |
| 3.      |             |               |                  |

**Your Turn**

**What do you like to do for fun? Write three things with *go* + a gerund.**

**Example:**
I like going shopping. I also like going fishing and bowling.

1. _____

2. _____

3. _____

# 9c  Verb + Infinitive

## Form / Function

She **tried to give** him his medicine, but he **refused to open** his mouth.

We use an infinitive (*to* + the base form of a verb) after certain verbs. Here are some of the verbs.

| agree | expect | manage | pretend | would like |
|-------|--------|--------|---------|------------|
| appear | forget | mean | promise | would love |
| can't afford | hope | need | refuse | would prefer |
| can't wait | intend | offer | try | |
| decide | learn | plan | want | |

## 7 Practice

**Complete the sentences with the infinitive form of the verbs in the list.**

**A.**

be          break in          catch          get into          steal

Someone tried ___*to break in*___ to my office last week. He planned
1
_____ some of my files. He managed _____
2                                              3
the building. He passed by the security officer. He pretended _____ an
4
electrician. When the security officer tried _____ him, he ran away.
5

**B.**

ask          go          take          visit

I have an old friend in Montreal, Canada. I promised _____ her. I'm
1
planning _____ in November. I wanted _____ you about
2                                              3
the weather. Do I need _____ a heavy coat with me?
4

**C.**

find          give          quit          take care of

My company refused _____ me a week off. I need
1
_____ my sick mother. So I decided _____ my job. I'll try
2                                              3
_____ another job later.
4

**D.**

build          buy          do          finish          fix

We can't afford _____ a new house, so we decided
1
_____ this one up. For example, we need _____ another
2                                              3
bathroom. I have learned _____ the plumbing, and I plan
4
_____ the new bathroom next month.
5

**E.**

| drive | fix | pay |
|---|---|---|

I can't wait _____ my new car on the highway. I can't afford
                  1

_____ a mechanic to repair it if it breaks down, so I will learn how
     2

_____ it myself.
     3

# 9d  Verb + Gerund or Infinitive

**Function**

Oli **loves waterskiing.**
He **loves to waterski** in Hawaii.

We can use a gerund or an infinitive after certain verbs. The meaning is the same.
Here are some examples.

| like | hate | can't stand | continue |
|---|---|---|---|
| love | begin | start | try |

## 8 | Practice

Complete the sentences with a gerund and an infinitive of each of the verbs given.

**1.** do

Ted hates _____*doing*_____ his homework.

Ted hates _____*to do*_____ his homework.

**2.** sit

He likes _____ in front of the television.

He likes _____ in front of the television.

**3.** argue

He doesn't like _____

He doesn't like _____

**4.** wait

He can't stand _____ in long lines.

He can't stand _____ in long lines.

**5.** go out

He loves _____ with his friends on weekends.

He loves _____ with his friends on weekends.

## 9 | Your Turn

**Use the sentences in Practice 8 to make statements about yourself. They don't have to be true.**

**Example:**
I like doing my homework.

## 10 | Practice

**Complete the sentences with the gerund or the infinitive of the verbs in parentheses. Sometimes two answers are possible.**

**A.**

Gary is learning (play) _____*to play*_____ the guitar. He wants
1

(write) _____ his own music, and he hopes (become) _____
2                                                                3

a famous guitarist one day. He would like (make) _____ a lot of money
4

and travel around the world.

243

**B.**

Janet would like (be) _____ an artist because she loves

(draw) _____. She has decided (go) _____ to art school

next year. A famous art school in New York agreed (give) _____ her a

scholarship. Without it, she could not afford (go) _____.

**C.**

Amy wants (become) _____ an actress. Her parents would like her

(go) _____ to college and become a dentist. She refuses

(listen) _____ to their advice and plans (go) _____

to Los Angeles next year.

**D.**

Tony doesn't like (study) _____. He loves (repair) _____

all kinds of things, but he prefers (repair) _____ cars. He wants

(be) _____ a mechanic. He hopes (have) _____ his own

garage one day.

## II Practice

**Complete the sentences with the infinitive or gerund form of the verb in parentheses.**

**A.**

Kate and Ben can't afford (go) _____*to go*_____ on vacation this year, but they

intend (save) _____ enough money to travel to Europe next year. They

would like (visit) _____ three or four countries. They are really looking

forward to (go) _____.

**B.**

Michael hates (clean) _____ his apartment. He would like
<sub>1</sub>

(have) _____ someone clean it for him, but he can't afford
<sub>2</sub>

(pay) _____ them. He manages (do) _____
<sub>3</sub> <sub>4</sub>

some cleaning before people come to visit. Usually he puts off (clean) _____
<sub>5</sub>

until the last day or hour.

## 12  Your Turn

**Write 10 sentences about your friends or family members. Use the verbs from List 1 followed by a gerund or an infinitive. You can use the ideas in List 2, or you can use your own ideas.**

**Example:**
My sister likes sewing.
My friend Charles loves playing chess.

**List 1**

| dislike | enjoy | like | love | not mind |
|---------|-------|------|------|----------|

**List 2**

| cook | listen to rock music | ride motorcycles |
|------|---------------------|------------------|
| dance | play chess | sew |
| eat healthy food | play sports | stay out late with friends |
| exercise | read about philosophy | watch soap operas |

1. _____
2. _____
3. _____
4. _____
5. _____
6. _____
7. _____
8. _____
9. _____
10. _____

# 9e  Preposition + Gerund

Ken is good **at** skateboarding.

1. We can use a gerund after a preposition. The gerund is the object of the preposition.

    I apologize **for being** late.

2. Prepositions can follow certain verbs and adjectives.

| Prepositions Following Verbs | | Prepositions Following Adjectives | |
|---|---|---|---|
| apologize **for** | insist **on** | capable **of** | interested **in** |
| approve **of** | succeed **in** | excited **about** | pleased **about** |
| believe **in** | think **about** | fond **of** | tired **of** |
| care **about** | worry **about** | good **at** | sad **about** |

I am **thinking about** leaving early today. (verb + preposition)
He is **good at** skateboarding. (adjective + preposition)

## 13 Practice

**Complete the conversation with the gerund form of the verb in parentheses.**

Tony: I'm tired of (do) _____*doing*_____ the same thing every day.
                     **1**

Ken: Well, what are you good at?

Tony: I'm good at (skateboard) _____ and (surf) _____.
                             **2**                         **3**

      I dream about (go) _____ to Hawaii one day.
                         **4**

Ken: Can't you think of (do) _____ anything else?
                         **5**

Tony: I have always been interested in (write) _____ for a newspaper.
                                        **6**

      I have often thought of (be) _____ a journalist. I'm not afraid
                                 **7**

      of (go) _____ to dangerous places.
              **8**

Ken: But it's hard work!

Tony: I don't care about (work) _____ hard as long as I enjoy it. I don't
                            **9**

      even care if I don't get paid for (do) _____ it.
                                              **10**

## 14 Your Turn

**Complete the sentences about yourself. Then tell a partner about yourself.**

**Example:**
I'm good at swimming.

I'm good at _____

I'm not very good at _____, but I'm excellent at

_____

I'm interested in _____

I believe in _____

I look forward to _____

# 9f  Infinitive of Purpose

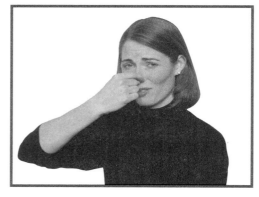

We hold our nose **to show** that something smells bad.

We put a finger to our mouth **to ask** for quiet.

We cross our middle and index fingers **to wish** good luck.

1. We use an infinitive to talk about the reason or purpose for doing something (why someone does something).

   I went to the cafeteria **to have** some lunch.
   He's going to the supermarket **to buy** groceries.

2. In more formal English, we use *in order to*.

> She left early **in order to avoid** the heavy traffic.
> We're saving money **in order to buy** a new car.

3. We can also use *for* to show purpose. We use a noun after *for*.
> I went to the cafeteria **for** lunch.
> He's going to the supermarket **for** milk and bread.

## 15 Practice

**Where did you go yesterday? Why did you go to these places?**

**A. Match the words in column A with those in column B.**

| A | | B | |
|---|---|---|---|
| _f_ | **1.** buy | **a.** | a car |
| _____ | **2.** cash | **b.** | a check |
| _____ | **3.** eat | **c.** | a flight |
| _____ | **4.** learn | **d.** | lunch |
| _____ | **5.** mail | **e.** | some letters |
| _____ | **6.** rent | **f.** | some clothes |
| _____ | **7.** reserve | **g.** | Spanish |

**B. Use the phrases in part A to write sentences about the following places.**

**1.** the post office

  *I went to the post office to mail some letters.*

**2.** the department store

  _____

**3.** the bank

  _____

**4.** the travel agency

  _____

**5.** a fast food restaurant

_____

**6.** a car rental agency

_____

**7.** night school

_____

## 16 Practice

**Complete the sentences with *to* or *for*.**

1. I go to school _____ *to* _____ learn English.
2. We go to school _____ get an education.
3. Some people need English _____ get a better job.
4. We need a grammar book _____ learn the rules.
5. We need a dictionary _____ vocabulary.
6. We use the Internet _____ do research.
7. I sometimes use my computer _____ do homework.
8. Our teacher sometimes uses videos _____ discussion.
9. Our teacher always gives us lots of exercises _____ homework.
10. We always have a lot of homework _____ do.
11. The library is a good place _____ do research.
12. It has computers _____ Internet searches.

## 17 Your Turn

**Say why you do these things. Use *for* or *to* in your answers.**

**Example:**
go on vacation
I go on vacation to relax and for fun.

| go on vacation | play sports | work |
| go to school | save money | |

## 18 Practice

**A. Match the ideas in column A with those in column B.**

|  | A | | B |
|---|---|---|---|
| _b_ | **1.** He's studying hard | **a.** | keep in shape |
| _____ | **2.** She's exercising | **b.** | pass the test |
| _____ | **3.** I turned up the volume | **c.** | get there by tomorrow |
| _____ | **4.** We must drive all night | **d.** | hear the news better |
| _____ | **5.** He must save money | **e.** | study for the test |
| _____ | **6.** We're going to the library | **f.** | buy a motorbike |

**B. Use *in order to* to write sentences with the phrases in Part A.**

**1.** _He's studying hard in order to pass the test._ _____

**2.** _____

**3.** _____

**4.** _____

**5.** _____

**6.** _____

## 19 Your Turn

**Complete the sentences to explain the meaning of some gestures in your country or culture.**

**1.** _We kiss both cheeks_ _____ to say hello to a friend.

**2.** _____ to say goodbye to a friend.

**3.** _____ to say something is good.

**4.** _____ to say something is bad.

**5.** _____ to say someone is crazy.

# 9g  Adjective + Infinitive

We were **amazed to see** a man walking in space.

1. We can use an infinitive after certain adjectives. Here are some of the adjectives.

| | | |
|---|---|---|
| afraid | frightened | sad |
| difficult | glad | safe |
| disappointed | happy | sorry |
| easy | pleased | surprised |
| foolish | right | wrong |

I am **pleased to see** you.
She was **surprised to get** a letter.

2. We can also use adjectives with infinitives after **it.**

**It** is **difficult to speak** English.
**It** is **important to finish** on time.

## 20 Practice

**Complete the sentences with the infinitive of the verbs in the list.**

| | | |
|---|---|---|
| eat | get off | travel |
| fasten | get on | watch |
| find | have | |
| fly | learn | |

1. People say it's dangerous _____*to fly*_____ on a plane.

2. I wasn't afraid _____ by plane.

3. Then I was disappointed _____ that the flight was delayed.

4. I was the first _____ the plane.

5. I was the last _____ the plane when it landed.

6. I was surprised _____ such tasty food.

7. It was necessary _____ the seat belt for take off and landing.

8. I was glad _____ a movie on the flight.

9. I was happy _____ my feet on the ground again.

10. I was pleased _____ my friends waiting for me.

## 21 Practice

**Rewrite the sentences using *it* and an infinitive.**

1. Learning to use a computer is easy.

   *It is easy to learn to use a computer.* _____

2. Being polite to customers is important.

   _____

3. Making mistakes when you speak English is normal.

   _____

4. Traveling to new countries is interesting.

   _____

5. Meeting people is fun.

   _____

6. Living in Tokyo is expensive.

   _____

7. Being on time is essential.

   _____

**8.** Waiting for more than 10 minutes is unusual here.

_____

**9.** Picking up a poisonous snake is dangerous.

_____

**10.** Taking tests is necessary.

_____

# 9h *Enough* and *Too* with Adjectives and Adverbs; *Enough* and *Too* with Infinitives; *Enough* with Nouns

## Form / Function

He is not **big enough** to wear the suit.
The suit is **too big** for him to wear.

1. We use *enough* after adjectives and adverbs but before nouns. *Enough* means that there is the right amount of something—not too much and not too little.

| ADJECTIVE/ADVERB + *ENOUGH* | | | |
|---|---|---|---|
| Subject | Verb | Adjective/Adverb + *Enough* | Infinitive |
| She | isn't | old **enough** | to drive. |
| It | is | warm **enough** | to swim. |
| He | swims | fast **enough** | to win the race. |

| ENOUGH + NOUN | | | |
|---|---|---|---|
| Subject | Verb | *Enough* + Noun | Infinitive |
| I | have | **enough** eggs | to make an omelet. |
| He | has | **enough** money | to buy a CD. |

| 2. | We use *too* before adjectives and adverbs. *Too* means "more than enough." | | |
|---|---|---|---|
| Subject | Verb | *Too* + Adjective/Adverb | Infinitive |
| I | am | **too** tired | to go out. |
| He | writes | **too** well | to fail the test. |

[22] Practice

**Can you do these things? Answer each question with *too* or *enough*. You may use the adjectives in the list in your answers.**

| | | | | |
|---|---|---|---|---|
| big | fast | rich | slow | tall |
| brave | funny | serious | small | weak |
| dangerous | poor | short | strong | |

1. Can you touch the ceiling?

   *No, I can't. I'm not tall enough to reach the ceiling. OR I'm*
   *too short to reach the ceiling.*

2. Can you carry a 60-pound suitcase?

   _____

   _____

3. Can you make people laugh?

   _____

   _____

4. Can you jump from an airplane?

   _____

   _____

5. Can you run a mile in one minute?

   _____

   _____

6. Can you put a whole apple in your mouth at one time?

   _____

   _____

7. Can you buy a palace?

   _____

   _____

**Practice**

**Complete the sentences with *too* or *enough*.**

1. I got up _____*too*_____ late this morning.

2. I ran to the bus stop, but I wasn't fast _____ to catch the bus.

3. At work, I had a client who talked _____ much.

4. I wanted to see my boss, but he didn't have _____ time to talk to me.

5. The day was _____ long.


# 9i  *Be Used To* + Gerund and *Be Accustomed To* + Gerund

## Form / Function

I'm **not used to eating** this kind of food. I'm also **not accustomed to eating** with chopsticks. I'm **used to eating** with a knife and fork.

1. We use *be used to* + gerund or *be accustomed to* + gerund to talk about something that we are familiar with because we have done it often. *Be used to* and *be accustomed to* have the same meaning.

   I **am used to eating** with chopsticks.
   I **am accustomed to eating** with chopsticks.

2. Do not confuse *be used to* + gerund with *used to* + base verb. We use *used to* + base verb to talk about something that happened or was true in the past, but it is different or not true now.

   I **used to eat** with chopsticks when I lived in Japan. (Now I don't.)

## 24 Practice

**Complete the sentences with *be used to* or *used to* plus the verbs in parentheses.**

1. I (write) _____*used to write*_____ on a typewriter many
   years ago. Now I write on a computer. At first it was hard, but now I
   (write) _____*am used to writing*_____ on my computer and can't live
   without it.

2. My brother (live) _____ in London, but
   now he lives in New York. It was strange for him at first, but now he
   (live) _____ in New York, and he loves the
   lifestyle.

3. I have to be at work at 7:00 every morning, so I
   (go) _____ to bed early. I'm
   (not/go) _____ to bed late.

4. Before I got this job, I used to get up late. Now I have to be at work at 8:00 in the
   morning. It was difficult, but now I (get) _____
   up early.

5. Yukio didn't like American food when he first arrived, but now he
   (eat) _____ it.

6. I am getting up at 6:00 tomorrow morning to go to the airport. I
   (not/get up) _____ early. I
   (get up) _____ at around 8:00.

7. Suzy found Japan strange at first. For example, she
   (not/take off) _____ her shoes before going into
   a house.

8. For six months after I bought the car, I
   (not/drive) _____ it much, but now I
   (drive) _____ it, and I love it.

**Your Turn**

Work with a partner. Ask and answer questions with *be used to* or *be accustomed to*.

**Example:**
What time are you accustomed to getting up?
I'm accustomed to getting up at 6:30 in the morning.

1. What time are you accustomed to/used to ...
   a. getting up?
   b. going to bed?
   c. eating lunch?
   d. eating dinner?
2. What language are you accustomed to speaking at home?
3. What are you accustomed to drinking in the morning with breakfast?
4. What are you used to eating for breakfast?

# 9j  *Be Supposed* + Infinitive

## Form / Function

Son, you**'re supposed to tell** us where you are going!

| Subject | Be (Not) Supposed | Infinitive | |
|---------|-------------------|------------|---|
| He | **was supposed** | **to write** | to me. |
| You | **are supposed** | **to help** | your mother at home. |
| We | **aren't supposed** | **to go** | into that room. |

We use *be supposed* + infinitive to talk about something that is expected of someone or something.

> It **is supposed to rain** tomorrow. (That is what the weather bureau predicted.)
> Kevin **is supposed to be** home by ten. (His parents have told him to do this.)

## 26 Practice

Kevin is supposed to be home by 10:00 every evening. Which of the following things is he supposed to do or not supposed to do?

1. be on time for meals _He is supposed to be on time for meals._

2. wear dirty shoes inside the house _He is not supposed to wear dirty shoes inside the house._

3. play loud music until three in the morning _____

4. stay out all night on weekends _____

5. tell his parents where he is going _____

6. tell his parents if he is going to get home later than usual _____

7. talk back to his parents _____

8. leave plates of food and glasses of soda in his room _____

9. use his father's computer without permission _____

10. help his mother lift things when he is at home _____

## 27 Your Turn

Imagine you have a daughter who is fifteen years old. She doesn't like school, doesn't do her homework, and barely passes her exams. She is only interested in clothes, make up, and going out with her friends. She always asks you for more and more spending money every week. She doesn't work. Make sentences about what you think she is supposed to do and you, her parents, are supposed to do.

**Example:**
She is supposed to do her homework.

# WRITING: Describe Personal Qualities

Write a paragraph about your personal qualities.

**Step 1. Choose one of these topics:**
1. You want a pen pal in another country.
2. You want to find a future husband/wife.
3. You want to find a roommate to share your apartment.

**Step 2. Answer these questions about yourself. Write down your answers. You can add other questions if you wish. Use gerunds and infinitives in some of your answers.**
1. What do you like/don't like doing?
2. What do you hate/love?
3. What are you interested in?
4. What do you enjoy doing?
5. What are you good at doing?
6. What are you used to doing?
7. What do you need to do for the future?

**Step 3. Write your information in the form of a paragraph. For more writing guidelines, see pages 407–411.**

**Step 4. Evaluate your paragraph.**

**Checklist**

_____ Did you indent your paragraph?

_____ Did you give information about yourself?

_____ Did you give information that would help you reach your goal (finding a pen pal, a husband or wife, or a roommate)?

**Step 5. Edit your paragraph. Work with a partner or your teacher to check your spelling, punctuation, vocabulary, and grammar.**

**Step 6. Write your final copy.**

# SELF-TEST

A   Choose the best answer, A, B, C, or D, to complete the sentence. Mark your answer by darkening the oval with the same letter.

1. It is important _____ on time.

   A. to be        Ⓐ Ⓑ Ⓒ Ⓓ
   B. being
   C. to being
   D. be

2. I went to the bank _____ some traveler's checks.

   A. for to get   Ⓐ Ⓑ Ⓒ Ⓓ
   B. for getting
   C. getting
   D. to get

3. She was happy _____.

   A. see me       Ⓐ Ⓑ Ⓒ Ⓓ
   B. me seeing
   C. to see me
   D. to seeing me

4. This coffee is _____ for me.

   A. to sweet     Ⓐ Ⓑ Ⓒ Ⓓ
   B. too sweet
   C. enough sweet
   D. two sweet

5. It wasn't _____ to the beach.

   A. too warm go      Ⓐ Ⓑ Ⓒ Ⓓ
   B. enough warm to go
   C. warm enough to go
   D. too warm to going

6. He loves _____ on the pond in the winter.

   A. skate        Ⓐ Ⓑ Ⓒ Ⓓ
   B. go skating
   C. to go skating
   D. going skate

7. _____ an easy form of exercise for most people.

   A. Run is       Ⓐ Ⓑ Ⓒ Ⓓ
   B. To run
   C. Running is
   D. Running

8. He left without _____ goodbye.

   A. to say       Ⓐ Ⓑ Ⓒ Ⓓ
   B. saying
   C. say
   D. to saying

9. Thank you _____ me with my homework.

   A. to help      Ⓐ Ⓑ Ⓒ Ⓓ
   B. helping
   C. for helping
   D. for to help

10. We aren't _____ this cold weather.

    A. accustomed to    Ⓐ Ⓑ Ⓒ Ⓓ
    B. accustom
    C. accustom to
    D. accustomed

261

Gerunds and Infinitives

**B** Find the underlined word or phrase, A, B, C, or D, that is incorrect. Mark your answer by darkening the oval with the same letter.

1. <u>Watch</u> sports on television <u>is</u> <u>a lot of</u> <u>fun</u>.
   A                  B   C    D

   Ⓐ Ⓑ Ⓒ Ⓓ

2. <u>It is</u> dangerous for anybody <u>to going</u>
   A                          B
   <u>jogging</u> in this park <u>at night</u>.
   C              D

   Ⓐ Ⓑ Ⓒ Ⓓ

3. Some people <u>are</u> <u>good at</u> and <u>have</u> a
   A     B         C
   talent for <u>learn</u> languages.
   D

   Ⓐ Ⓑ Ⓒ Ⓓ

4. We <u>were</u> considering <u>to go</u> on vacation in
   A               B
   June, but we <u>postponed</u> <u>it</u> for another
   C    D
   month.

   Ⓐ Ⓑ Ⓒ Ⓓ

5. Some students <u>go</u> to the library
   A
   <u>to studying</u> because <u>it</u> is <u>quiet</u>.
   B             C   D

   Ⓐ Ⓑ Ⓒ Ⓓ

6. The summers <u>are</u> usually <u>warm</u> in this part
   A       B
   of the country, but this year <u>it is</u> supposed
   C
   to <u>being</u> cool.
   D

   Ⓐ Ⓑ Ⓒ Ⓓ

7. I <u>wasn't</u> <u>accustomed</u> to <u>eat</u> with
   A     B         C
   chopsticks until I <u>went</u> to Japan.
   D

   Ⓐ Ⓑ Ⓒ Ⓓ

8. Many students <u>use</u> the Internet <u>for</u>
   A                B
   do <u>their</u> <u>research</u>.
   C   D

   Ⓐ Ⓑ Ⓒ Ⓓ

9. In some countries, <u>it is necessary</u> <u>to pass</u>
   A          B
   an entrance exam before <u>enter</u> <u>a</u> university.
   C   D

   Ⓐ Ⓑ Ⓒ Ⓓ

10. <u>Traveling</u> to new <u>countries</u> <u>are</u> interesting
    A               B   C
    <u>for</u> most people.
    D

    Ⓐ Ⓑ Ⓒ Ⓓ

# UNIT 10

# COMPARATIVE AND SUPERLATIVE FORMS

# 10a Adjectives and Adverbs

Basketball players are **tall.**
They throw the ball **quickly**
and **accurately** into the net.

1. We can make adverbs by adding –*ly* to many adjectives. Sometimes the spelling of the adjective changes before –*ly* is added.

| Spelling Rule | Adjective | Adverb |
|---|---|---|
| To form most adverbs, add –*ly* to the adjective. | quick | quick**ly** |
| | accurate | accurate**ly** |
| | dangerous | dangerous**ly** |
| | safe | safe**ly** |
| If the adjective ends in *l*, add –*ly*. | wonderful | wonderful**ly** |
| | careful | careful**ly** |
| If the adjective ends in *le*, drop the *e* and add –*y*. | gentle | gent**ly** |
| | subtle | subt**ly** |
| If the adjective ends in a consonant + *y*, drop the *y* and add –*ily*. | easy | eas**ily** |
| | noisy | nois**ily** |

2. Some adverbs are irregular. Some have the same form as the adjective or a completely different form.

| Adjective | Adverb |
|---|---|
| good | well |
| fast | fast |
| hard | hard |
| early | early |
| late | late |

3. Adjectives can go before nouns.

He is a **tall** man.

Adjectives can also go after verbs such as *appear, be, become, feel, get, look,* and *seem.*

He is **tall.**
He looks **good.**

4. Most adverbs go after verbs and objects, but adverbs of frequency usually go before all verbs except *be.* An adverb of frequency tells how often something happens. (See page 6 for more information on adverbs of frequency.)

| Subject | Adverb of Frequency | Verb | Object |
|---------|---------------------|------|--------|
| He | **always** | eats | breakfast. |

| Subject | Verb | Object | Other Adverb |
|---------|------|--------|--------------|
| She | drives | the car | **dangerously.** |
| He | speaks | | **softly.** |

5. Adverbs can also go before adjectives, other adverbs, and past participles.

He was **surprisingly** polite.

## Function

1. Adjectives describe nouns. They have the same form in the singular and plural.

He is a **tall** player. They are **tall** men. (The adjective *tall* describes the nouns *player* and *men.*)

2. Adverbs describe verbs, adjectives, or other adverbs.

He plays **well.** (*Well* describes the verb *plays.*)
He is **incredibly** fast. (*Incredibly* describes the adjective *fast.*)
He plays **amazingly** well. (*Amazingly* describes the adverb *well.*)

## 1   Practice

**Underline the correct word.**

1. It was Mary's birthday, but she was (<u>miserable</u> / miserably).

2. She was waiting (impatient / impatiently) to get a phone call.

3. No one called to wish her a (happy / happily) birthday.

4. (Sudden / Suddenly), she heard the mailman.

5. She ran to the door (quick / quickly).

6. There was an envelope. She opened it (anxious / anxiously).

7. She was (disappointed / disappointedly). It was an advertisement.

8. Mary felt (sad / sadly).

9. Then her friend called (unexpected / unexpectedly).

10. Mary's friend told her to come to her house (immediate / immediately).

11. Mary put on her (new / newly) dress and left.

12. She arrived at her friend's house and knocked on the door (soft / softly).

13. Her friend opened the door (slow / slowly).

14. All her family and friends were there. They all sang "Happy Birthday" (loud / loudly).

---

2 **Your Turn**

**Write how you think you do the actions in the list.**

**Example:**
speak
I think that I speak quickly, but I walk slowly.

1. speak
2. dress
3. walk
4. study
5. sing

---

# 10b Participles as Adjectives

She's **irritated.**

1. We can often use present participles and past participles of verbs as adjectives.

2. We form present participles with the base verb + *–ing*. We form regular past participles with the base verb + *–ed*. See the spelling rules for *–ing* and *–ed* forms on page 406.

| Base Form | Present Participle | Past Participle |
|---|---|---|
| amuse | amus**ing** | amus**ed** |
| annoy | annoy**ing** | annoy**ed** |
| bore | bor**ing** | bor**ed** |
| excite | excit**ing** | excit**ed** |
| frighten | frighten**ing** | frighten**ed** |
| interest | interest**ing** | interest**ed** |
| irritate | irritat**ing** | irritat**ed** |
| relax | relax**ing** | relax**ed** |
| surprise | surpris**ing** | surpris**ed** |

## Function

1. Past participles used as adjectives describe someone's feelings.

   She felt **relaxed.**
   The boys were **excited** during the game.

   To show what caused the feeling, we can use a prepositional phrase. Most past participles take the preposition *by*. Others take other prepositions. For example, *interested* takes *in*.

   We were amused **by the children's behavior.**
   He was frightened **by the loud noise.**
   They are interested **in astronomy.**

2. Present participles used as adjectives describe the person or thing that produces the feeling.

   She was having a **relaxing** vacation.
   The boys were watching an **exciting** football game.

## 3 Practice

**Underline the correct word.**

1. This was a very (<u>fascinating</u> / fascinated) book.
2. At first I thought it was (boring / bored), but it wasn't.
3. The story was very (exciting / excited).
4. I was very (interested / interesting) in the people in this book.
5. I was (surprised / surprising) by the ending of the story.
6. I was (shocked / shocking) to know it was based on a true story.
7. It is (frightening / frightened) to know that these things can really happen.
8. I read the book quickly because it was so (interested / interesting).
9. I am (interesting / interested) in reading another book by the same author.
10. I don't think I will be (disappointed / disappointing).

## 4 Practice

**Alan and Brenda have been on vacation. Read the dialogue and underline the correct participle in parentheses.**

Alan:   I was (<u>surprised</u> / surprising) at how good the weather was.
         1

Brenda: Yes, it was really sunny. It was (surprising / surprised).
                                                2

Alan:   It was good to lie in the sun. It was so (relaxed / relaxing).
                                                      3

Brenda: There was a lot to see, too. The museum was (interested / interesting).
                                                         4

Alan:   Yes, I was (interesting / interested) in many things there.
                      5

Brenda: I was (fascinating / fascinated) by the king's furniture.
                  6

Alan:   Yes, the furniture was (fascinating / fascinated).
                                    7

Brenda: But I was (tiring / tired) after the museum.
                      8

Alan:   Yes, it was (tired / tiring).
                       9

Brenda: Now I am (exhausted / exhausting).
                     10

Alan:   Vacations are always (exhausted / exhausting).
                                  11

**Your Turn**

Write one sentence with each of the words in the list.

| bored | interested | surprised |
|-------|-----------|-----------|
| boring | interesting | surprising |

1. *I think that history is interesting.*
2. _____
3. _____
4. _____
5. _____
6. _____

## 10c Adjectives After Verbs

**Form / Function**

The coffee **smells good.**

1. We can use adjectives after verbs of existence, such as *be, get\*, become,* and *seem.*

   He **seems nice.**
   **Be quiet!**
   I'm **getting hungry.**

2. We can also use adjectives after verbs of the senses like *look, feel, sound, taste,* and *smell.*

   You **look tired.**
   The coffee **smells good.**
   This soup **tastes strange.**

\* In this meaning, *get* usually means *become.*

## 6 Practice

**Guests are coming to Ann's house this evening, but things have gone wrong. Complete the sentences with one of the words from the list.**

| burned | happy | short | tired |
|--------|-------|-------|-------|
| dirty | miserable | sweet | wet |

1. Ann isn't happy today. She feels ___*miserable.*___

2. She was cooking and cleaning for hours and hours. She got _____

3. She forgot about the cake in the oven. The cake got _____

4. She went out and it started to rain. She had no umbrella. She got

   _____

5. The dog came in with muddy feet. The floor got _____

6. She put sugar instead of salt in the soup. The soup tasted _____

7. She tried on her new dress but it seemed _____

8. Luckily, when her guests came, they had a good time. She felt _____

## 7 Practice

**Underline the correct word.**

1. Tony was getting (<u>hungry</u> / hungrily).

2. The dinner was (ready / readily).

3. The soup smelled (good / well).

4. It tasted (good / well).

5. Tony finished the soup (quick / quickly).

6. His grandmother had cooked (good / well).

7. She cooked some (specially / special) pasta for him.

8. It looked (delicious / deliciously).

9. He looked at the dish (hungry / hungrily).

10. He ate it (quickly / quick) because it was so good.

11. Tony was (happy / happily).

Your Turn

**Make four sentences about you or your partner. Use some of the verbs from the list.**

| | | |
|---|---|---|
| be | get | smell |
| become | look | sound |
| feel | seem | taste |

**Example:**
I am happy today. I feel good.
My partner looks tired today. I think she is getting nervous about the test.

# 10d *As + Adjective + As; As + Adverb + As*

## Form

May and June are twins.
May is **as tall as** June.

1. We can use *as...as* with adjectives and adverbs.

| ADJECTIVES | | | | | |
|---|---|---|---|---|---|
| Subject | Verb *(+ Not)* | *As* | Adjective | *As* | |
| May | is<br>isn't | **as** | tall<br>old<br>good<br>funny | **as** | June. |

| ADVERBS | | | | | |
|---|---|---|---|---|---|
| Subject | Verb (+ *Not*) | *As* | Adverb | *As* | |
| May | learns<br>doesn't learn | as | quickly | as | June. |
| | runs<br>doesn't run | | fast | | |
| | studies<br>doesn't study | | hard | | |
| | laughs<br>doesn't laugh | | loudly | | |

2. We can add an auxiliary verb or repeat the first verb at the end of the sentence.

> May is as funny as June.
> May is as funny as June **is.**
> May plays as beautifully as June.
> May plays as beautifully as June **does.**
> May plays as beautifully as June **plays.**

## Function

1. We use *as ... as* to show that two people or two things are the same or equal.

> May is **as old as** June. (May and June are the same age.)

2. We use *not as ... as* for the negative form.

> May is **not as funny as** June.

3. When we use *not as ... as* instead of the comparative, it sometimes sounds more polite.

> Ben is **shorter than** Jim.
> Ben is **not as tall as** Jim.

---

9 Practice

**Use the prompts to write sentences with *as ... as* or *not as ... as*.**

1. autumn/cold/winter

   *Autumn is not as cold as winter.*

2. the month of September/long/the month of June

   _____

**3.** in the United States, September/hot/July

_____

**4.** in the winter months, California/cold/New York

_____

**5.** days in winter/long/days in summer

_____

**6.** September/popular/July for vacations in North America

_____

**7.** in autumn, plants/grow/fast/in spring

_____

**8.** in summer, people/dress/heavily/in winter

_____

**9.** in autumn, flowers/are/colorful/in spring

_____

**10.** in summer, it/rain/frequently/in spring

_____

## 10 Practice

**Many languages have sayings that include a phrase similar to _as ... as_. Complete the following sayings with words from the list. Then explain how they are different in another language that you know.**

| | | | | |
|---|---|---|---|---|
| a bird | a feather | clockwork | ink | sugar |
| a dog | a mouse | gold | snow | the sky |

**1.** Mary made a cake. The cake was as light as ___*a feather.*___

**2.** This melon is sweet. It is as sweet as _____

**3.** Nobody noticed that Tina had come home. She was as quiet as _____

**4.** We left the children with my sister for the weekend. The children were happy and were as good as _____

**5.** The coffee she made was very strong, and it was as black as _____

**6.** She had beautiful blue eyes. They were as blue as _____

**7.** He left home and moved to the city. Then he felt as free as _____

**8.** The fish I ate for dinner was bad, and I was as sick as _____

**9.** George comes to the office at exactly the same time every day. He is as regular as

_____

**10.** Harry was not old, but his hair was as white as _____

## 11 Your Turn

**Compare yourself today with the way you were five years ago.**
**Use *as ... as* or *not as ... as*.**

**Example:**
study hard
Today, I study as hard as I did five years ago.
OR Today, I don't study as hard as I did five years ago.

1. study hard
2. be happy
3. be healthy
4. be poor
5. sleep late

# 10e Comparative Forms of Adjectives and Adverbs

**Form**

Fifty years ago, office machines were **slower than** today.

1. Adjectives and adverbs form their comparatives in the same ways.

| SHORT ADJECTIVES AND ADVERBS | | | | | |
|---|---|---|---|---|---|
| Adjective + *-er* + *Than* | | | Adverb + *-er* + *Than* | | |
| A typewriter is | slow**er than** | a computer. | She can type | fast**er than** | I can. |

| LONG ADJECTIVES AND ADVERBS | | | | | |
|---|---|---|---|---|---|
| *More/Less* + Adjective + *Than* | | | *More/Less* + Adverb + *Than* | | |
| A computer is | **more** useful **than** | a typewriter. | She types | **less** accurately **than** | I do. |

2. We use these rules for spelling the comparative forms of short (one syllable) adjectives and adverbs and for two-syllable adjectives ending in –y.

| Spelling Rule | Adjective | Comparative Adjective | Adverb | Comparative Adverb |
|---|---|---|---|---|
| Add –er to most one-syllable adjectives and adverbs. | cheap | cheap**er than** | fast | fast**er than** |
| If a one-syllable adjective or adverb ends in e, or a two-syllable adjective ends in le, add –r. | wide | wide**r than** | late | late**r than** |
| | simple | simple**r than** | | |
| If a one-syllable adjective ends in a single vowel plus a consonant, double the consonant and add –er. | hot | hot**ter than** | | |
| If a two-syllable adjective ends in a consonant plus y, change the y to i and add –er. | noisy | nois**ier than** | | |

3. Some adjectives and adverbs have irregular comparative forms.

| Adjective | Adverb | Comparative Form for Both |
|---|---|---|
| good | well | **better than** |
| bad | badly | **worse than** |
| far | far | **farther/further than** |

4. We use these rules for using the –er form or the more form of the comparative.

| Rules for Using -er or More | Adjectives | Adverbs |
|---|---|---|
| Use –er with one-syllable adjectives and adverbs. | small**er than** | fast**er than** |
| Use –er with two-syllable adjectives that end in a consonant + y. | pretti**er than** | |
| Use more + adjective/adverb + than with most adjectives and adverbs of two syllables or more. | **more** popular **than** | **more** seriously **than** |
| Some two-syllable adjectives use –er or more. | angri**er/more** angry **than** | |
| | simpl**er/more** simple **than** | |
| | clever**er/more** clever **than** | |
| | friendli**er/more** friendly **than** | |
| | gentl**er/more** gentle **than** | |
| | narrow**er/more** narrow **than** | |
| | quiet**er/more** quiet **than** | |
| | polit**er/more** polite **than** | |
| | common**er/more** common **than** | |
| | pleasant**er/more** pleasant **than** | |

5. We can use a noun after *than*. We can also use a subject pronoun or a possessive noun or pronoun + a verb after *than*. We can omit the verb.

   I am taller than **my mother (is).**          I am taller than **she (is).**
   My hair is darker than **my mother's (is).**  My hair is darker than **hers (is).**
   I study harder than she **(does).**           I study harder than she **(studies).**

6. We can use *less* before an adjective or adverb with two or more syllables.

   He is **less serious** than she is.
   She speaks **less fluently** than he does.

   We do not usually use *less* with one syllable adjectives or adverbs. Instead, we use *not as* (adjective/adverb) *as*.

   CORRECT:      This CD is**n't as good as** the other one.
   INCORRECT:    This CD is ~~less good than~~ the other one.

   CORRECT:      She is**n't** singing **as well as** she usually does.
   INCORRECT:    She is singing ~~less well than~~ she usually does.

## Function

1. We use comparative forms of adjectives and adverbs to show the difference between two things.

   Watching television is **more relaxing than** ironing.

2. We use **less** to show a lower degree.

   This test was **less difficult than** the last test.

3. If we use a pronoun after *than*, and if we omit the verb, we can use either a subject pronoun or an object pronoun. In formal English, we use a subject pronoun, but in informal English, we use an object pronoun.

   FORMAL:    She is taller than **I.**
   INFORMAL:  She is taller than **me.**

   If we include the verb, we must use a subject pronoun.

   She is taller than **I am.**

4. We use *very* to describe adjectives and adverbs; however, we use *much* with comparative forms of adjectives and adverbs.

   It's **very** cold today.
   It's **much** colder today than yesterday.

## 12 Practice

**Complete the sentences with the comparative form of the words in parentheses.**

1. A bicycle is (quiet) _____ *quieter than* _____ a car.

2. A bicycle is (cheap) _____ a car.

3. A bicycle is (easy to park) _____ a car.

4. A car goes (fast) _____ a bicycle.

5. A car is (expensive) _____ a bicycle.

6. A car is (comfortable) _____ a bicycle.

7. In China, a bicycle is (popular) _____ a car.

8. A bicycle runs (economically) _____ a car.

9. A bicycle is (light) _____ a car.

10. A car is (difficult to use) _____ a bicycle.

## 13 Practice

**Complete the sentences with the comparative form of the words in parentheses.**

**A.**

Ted:     You look like your mother.

Nancy: People say that. But, she's really (tall) _____ *taller* _____
         _____ *than* _____ _____ *I* _____. My hair
              **2**                        **3**

         is (light) _____ *lighter* _____ _____ *than* _____
                              **4**                        **5**

         _____ *hers* _____ .
                   **6**

Ted:     Are her eyes (dark) _____
                                        **7**

         _____ _____?
                **8**            **9**

Nancy: No. Her eyes are a little (light) _____
                                                    **10**

         _____ _____.
                **11**            **12**

**B.**

Jane:    I want to fly to Los Angeles tomorrow morning. Are there any flights

         that are (early) _____ *earlier* _____ _____ *than* _____
                              **1**                        **2**

         the one at 10:00 in the morning?

Travel Agent: Yes, there is. Flight 1620 is at 5:30. And flight 1535 is

(late) _____ _____ flight 1620.
                    3                 4
It leaves at 7:00.

Jane:          Are there a lot of people on the 5:30 flight?

Travel Agent: No. The 7:00 flight is usually much (crowded) _____
                                                                              5
_____ _____ the 5:30 flight.
           6                 7

Jane:          I think the 5:30 flight will work (well) _____
                                                              8
_____ the 7:00 flight. Will it be (cheap)
           9
_____ _____ the later flight?
          10                11

Travel Agent: No, in fact it's $10 (expensive) _____
                                                          12
_____ _____ the other flights.
          13                14


**C.**

Ann:      Do we have to walk (far) _____
                                          1
_____ this?
          2

Ken:      Just a little (long) _____. Let's take a rest. Are you
                                      3
feeling (good) _____ _____
                        4                   5
before?

Ann:      I feel (exhausted) _____ _____
                                      6                   7
_____ before.
          8


**D.**

Jim:        The computers in the library are (old) _____
                                                          1
_____ the one I have at home!
           2

Linda:      They need to get (modern) _____
                                              3
_____ computers, but they are very expensive, aren't they?
           4

Jim:        Not really. Today, many electronic things are (cheap) _____
                                                                              5
_____ they were a few years ago.
           6

## 14 Practice

**Compare each pair of nouns. Use the adjectives. Write your opinion.**

1. cats/dogs—friendly

   _Dogs are friendlier than cats. OR Cats are friendlier than dogs._

2. fish/lizards—beautiful

   _____

3. spiders/snakes—dangerous

   _____

4. little boys/little girls—noisy

   _____

5. Los Angeles/Chicago—interesting

   _____

6. summers in New York/summers in London—hot

   _____

## 15 Practice

**Complete the sentences using a comparative form of an adverb and your own additional information. You can use the adverbs from the list or your own.**

| cautiously | dangerously | high |
| comfortably | fast | slowly |

1. The bullet trains in Japan go _faster than the trains in the United States._
2. The space shuttle flies _____
3. City buses go _____
4. Passengers in a large car usually travel _____
5. In fast traffic, you should drive _____
6. 100 years ago, people traveled _____ _____

## 16 Practice

**Complete the sentences with *much* or *very*.**

1. Learning another language is _____ very _____ difficult.
2. Learning another language is _____ more difficult than learning geography.

3. English books are _____ expensive these days.

4. Dictionaries are _____ more expensive than books.

5. Chinese is _____ hard.

6. Chinese is _____ harder than English as a language.

7. English spelling rules are _____ unreliable.

8. English grammar rules are _____ more reliable than spelling rules.

---

### 17 | Your Turn

**Write five sentences comparing people in your family. Use adjectives or adverbs.**

**Example:**
My father is older than my mother.

1. _____

2. _____

3. _____

4. _____

5. _____

# 10f  Superlative Forms of Adjectives and Adverbs

## Form

My wedding day was **the happiest** day of my life.

1. Adjectives and adverbs form their superlative forms in the same ways.

| SHORT ADJECTIVES AND ADVERBS | | | | | |
|---|---|---|---|---|---|
| *The* + Adjective + *-est* | | | *The* + Adverb + *-est* | | |
| Mt. Everest is | **the** high**est** | mountain. | She runs | **the** fast**est** | of us all. |

| LONG ADJECTIVES AND ADVERBS | | | | | |
|---|---|---|---|---|---|
| *The Most/Least* + Adjective | | | *The Most/Least* + Adverb | | |
| Which is | **the most** dangerous | city? | He works | **the most** happily | of us all. |

2. We use the definite article **the** before superlative adjectives and adverbs.

> The Crown is **the** best hotel in town.
> It has **the** most expensive restaurant.

3. The spelling rules for short comparative adjectives and adverbs on page 275 also apply to short superlative forms.

| Adjective or Adverb | Comparative | Superlative |
|---|---|---|
| late | late**r than** | **the** late**st** |
| hot | hot**ter than** | **the** hot**test** |
| noisy | nois**ier than** | **the** nois**iest** |

4. Some adjectives and adverbs are irregular.

| Adjective | Adverb | Comparative Form (Both) | Superlative Form (Both) |
|---|---|---|---|
| good | well | **better** | **best** |
| bad | badly | **worse** | **worst** |
| far | far | **farther/further** | **farthest/furthest** |

## Function

1. We use superlative forms of adjectives and adverbs to compare three or more things.

2. We use *–est* and *most* in superlatives to show the highest degree.

> Antarctica is **the** cold**est** place in the world.
> Tokyo is **the most** crowded city in the world.

3. We use *the least* to show the lowest degree.

> Antarctica is **the least** populated place in the world.

4. We often use the preposition *in* after superlatives. We use *in* with nouns of locations such as *the world,* countries, and cities; and with group nouns such as *the class, my family,* and *the group.*

> Ted is the best student **in the class.**
> The elephant is the biggest land animal **in the world.**
> Sarte is the most expensive restaurant **in New York City.**

Comparative and Superlative Forms

5. We often use the preposition *of* with expressions of time and quantity, and with plural nouns.

> I know three very good restaurants, but this one is the best **of all.**
> Yesterday was the longest day **of the year.**
> He is the youngest **of the students.**

6. We do not use **least** with one-syllable adjectives.

> CORRECT:    John is the shortest of my three brothers.
> INCORRECT: John is ~~the least tall of~~ my three brothers.

## 18 Practice

**Complete the sentences with the superlative form of the words in parentheses.**

1. Our teacher is Ms. Flint. She gives (clear) _____ *the clearest* _____ explanations of all the teachers.

2. Ms. Flint thinks Linda's handwriting is (neat) _____ handwriting of all the students in the class.

3. We think Peter speaks English (fluently) _____ in our class.

4. All the teachers give us homework, but Ms. Flint gives (difficult) _____ homework.

5. Terry is always the first person to arrive in class. He comes to class (early) _____.

6. Fred is a funny student. He's (humorous) _____ student in the class.

7. Kate takes the class seriously. She's (responsible) _____ student in the class.

8. Tony works (hard) _____ of all the students.

9. He is also (good) _____ student in the class.

10. He gets (high) _____ grades on the tests.

11. He answers the teacher's questions (easy) _____ of us all.

12. Then there is George. He is (bad) _____ student in the class.

## 19 Practice

**Complete the sentences with the correct words.**

1. The blue whale is _____the_____ biggest _____of_____ all the animals.

2. The giraffe is _____ tallest animal _____ the world.

3. The elephant is _____ biggest _____ all the animals on land.

4. People think the lion is the king and _____ strongest _____ the animals.

5. The ostrich is _____ biggest bird _____ the world.

6. The snail is _____ slowest animal _____ all.

7. Lions sleep for _____ greatest part _____ the day.

8. Antarctica has _____ least number of land animals _____ the world.

## 20 Your Turn

**Imagine there is a fire in your house. You can only take five things away. Which of the five things from the list will you take with you? Think about which is the least expensive, the most expensive, etc. Then discuss your decisions with your partner and the rest of the class. Use comparative forms with the words and phrases in the list or use your own ideas.**

**Example:**
My old photographs are the most important of all, so I will take them.
My radio is the easiest to replace, so I won't take it.

| | | |
|---|---|---|
| beautiful | cheap | valuable |
| hard/easy to replace | important | useful |

1. your passport
2. your favorite book
3. old photographs
4. your computer
5. an antique vase

6. your sunglasses
7. your jewelry
8. your cell phone
9. your music CDs
10. your radio

# 10g Comparative and Superlative Forms of Nouns

Of all my favorite foods, ice cream
has **the most calories.**

**COMPARATIVE NOUNS**

1. We use *more* to compare both count and noncount nouns.

> This class has **more students** than that one does.
> Our teacher gives us **more homework** than your teacher does.

2. We use *fewer* with count nouns. We use *less* with noncount nouns.

> This class has **fewer students** than that one does.
> Our teacher gives us **less homework** than your teacher does.

**SUPERLATIVE NOUNS**

3. We use *the most* with superlative count and noncount nouns.

> This class has **the most students.**
> Our teacher gives us **the most homework.**

4. We use *the fewest* with count nouns. We use *the least* with noncount nouns.

> This class has **the fewest students.**
> That teacher gives **the least homework.**

## AS ... AS WITH NOUNS

We can use *as ... as* with count and noncount nouns. We use *many* with count nouns and *much* with noncount nouns.

| Count Noun | She has | as | many | CDs | as | I do. |
|---|---|---|---|---|---|---|
| Noncount Noun | | | much | money | | |

## Function

1. We use the comparative forms of nouns with *more, fewer,* and *less* to compare the different quantities of two nouns.

   I have **more** homework than my friend.
   My friend has **less** homework than I do.
   Your class has **fewer** tests than our class does.

2. We use the superlative forms of nouns with *the most, the fewest,* and *the least* to show the largest and smallest quantity in a group of two or more.

   Tony's class gets **the most** homework.
   Your class has **the fewest** tests.

3. We use *as ... as* to show that things or people are the same in two situations.

   I have 100 CDs. Amy has 100 CDs.
   I have **as many CDs** as Amy (has).

## 21 Practice

**Look at the chart and then complete the sentences.**

| Food (per 100 gm) | Protein | Carbohydrate | Fat | Calories (kcal) |
|---|---|---|---|---|
| Bread | 7.3 | 40 | 2.4 | 200 |
| Pasta | 2.0 | 14 | 0.4 | 60 |
| Pizza | 15.0 | 37 | 10.0 | 280 |
| Rice | 6.0 | 52 | 0.4 | 225 |
| Ice cream | 4.0 | 21 | 10.0 | 190 |

1. Bread has _____*more*_____ protein than pasta.
2. Pizza has _____ protein.

**3.** Ice cream has _____ protein than rice.

**4.** Pizza has _____ fat as ice cream.

**5.** Rice has _____ carbohydrate than bread.

**6.** Pasta has _____ fat as rice.

**7.** Bread has _____ calories than pizza.

**8.** Pizza has _____ calories.

**9.** Pasta has _____ calories.

**10.** Pasta has _____ calories than rice.

## 22 Practice

**Look at the following chart and complete the sentences.**

|  | City A | City B | City C |
|---|---|---|---|
| People |  |  |  |
| Crime |  |  |  |
| Pollution |  |  |  |
| Doctors |  |  |  |
| Universities |  |  |  |
| Rainfall (a year) |  |  |  |

**1.** City C has ___*the most*___ people.

**2.** City A has _____ people.

**3.** City A has _____ pollution than City C.

**4.** City A has _____ doctors than City C.

**5.** City C has _____ doctors than City A.

**6.** City B has _____ doctors as City C.

**7.** City A has _____ universities.

**8.** City C has _____ universities.

**9.** City A has _____ universities than City B.

**10.** City C has _____ rainfall.

**11.** City A has _____ rainfall.

**12.** City C has _____ rainfall than City B.

## 23 Your Turn

**Write five sentences comparing your class with another class, or yourself with someone else that you know. You may use the items from the list to compare.**

**Example:**
grammar
We study more grammar than the other class.

| conversation | grammar | homework | students | tests |

# 10h The Double Comparative

## Form / Function

Buildings are getting **taller and taller.**

1. We use "comparative and comparative" to show that something increases or decreases all the time.

   The weather is getting **colder and colder.**
   Things are getting **more and more expensive.**

2. We can use these sentence structures to show that two things change together or that one thing depends on another thing. The second part of the comparative is often the result of the first part.

| *The* + Comparative Clause | *The* + Comparative Clause |
| --- | --- |
| The more you study, | the more you learn. |
| The sooner we leave, | the sooner we'll get there. |

| *The* + Comparative | *The* + Comparative Clause |
| --- | --- |
| The harder the test, | the more you learn. |
| The more people in the room, | the hotter it will get. |

## 24 Practice

**Rewrite the sentences about the world today using "comparative *and* comparative" with the underlined adjectives.**

1. The world's population is getting <u>big</u>.

   *The world's population is getting bigger and bigger.*

2. The air is becoming <u>polluted</u>.

   _____

3. Technology is getting <u>sophisticated</u>.

   _____

4. People's lives are getting <u>long</u>.

   _____

5. Computers are getting <u>advanced</u>.

   _____

6. Life is getting <u>complicated</u>.

   _____

7. Buildings are getting <u>tall</u>.

   _____

8. Medicine is getting <u>good</u>.

   _____

9. Forests are becoming <u>small</u>.

   _____

10. The problem of feeding the world's people is getting <u>bad</u>.

    _____

## 25 Practice

**Complete the sentences with "*the* + comparative clause, *the* + comparative clause" or with "*the* + comparative + comparative clause."**

1. If the hotel is famous, it is expensive.

   *The more famous* _____ the hotel, _____ *the more expensive* _____
   it is.

2. The hotel is near the beach. It is crowded.

   _____ the hotel is to the beach,
   _____ it is.

3. The room is big. The price is high.

_____ the room, _____ the

price is.

4. If you reserve early, the room is good.

_____ you reserve, _____

room you get.

5. The hotel is far from downtown. It is cheaper.

_____ the hotel is from downtown,

_____ it is.

6. You pay more. The service is good.

_____ you pay, _____

service you get.

7. The hotel is near the highway. It is noisy.

_____ the hotel is to the highway,

_____ it is.

## 26  Your Turn

**A.**
**Write two sentences about your class or school. Use "comparative and comparative."**

**Example:**
We have more and more tests every year.

1. _____

2. _____

**B.**
**Write two sentences about how you learn. Use "*the* + comparative, *the* + comparative clause."**

**Example:**
The better the textbook, the more I learn.

1. _____

2. _____

## 10i  *The Same As, Similar To, Different From, Like,* and *Alike*

### Form / Function

1. We use *the same* and *the same ... as* to say that things are the same.

   John has a black 2002 Toyota. Jane has a black 2002 Toyota.
   John's car is **the same** color **as** Jane's.
   John's car is **the same** year **as** Jane's car.
   Their cars are **the same.**

2. We use *like* and *alike* to say that things are the same or almost the same. *Like* and *alike* are used in different structures.

   | Noun | Be + Like | Noun |
   |---|---|---|
   | John's car | **is like** | Jane's car. |

   | Noun | Noun | Verb + Alike |
   |---|---|---|
   | John's car | and Jane's car | **are alike.** |
   | Betty | and Cathy | **look alike.** |

   We can also use *alike* with a plural noun or pronoun.

   The twins dress **alike.**
   They talk **alike.**
   They think **alike.**

3. We use *similar* and *similar to* to say that things are different in small ways.

   John has a black Toyota. Paul has a black Mazda. Both cars are small.
   John's car is **similar to** Paul's car.
   John and Paul's cars are **similar.**

4. We use *different* and *different from* to say that things are quite different. We usually use *from* after the adjective *different*. The grammatically correct word is *different from* although some people use *different than* in everyday conversation.

   John has a black Toyota. Mike has a red Volkswagen.
   John's car is **different from** Mike's car.
   John and Mike's cars are **different.**

---

## 27  Practice

**Underline the correct form.**

1. Mike and Jane live in the town of Homa. Mike lives in

   (the same town / <u>the same town as</u>) Jane.

2. They both live in (the same / the same as) town.

3. Mike and Jane were born in Homa and have lived there all their lives. Mike talks (like / alike) Jane.

4. Mike and Jane talk (like / alike).

5. Ted is Mike's brother. He lives in the town of Chester. Ted lives in a (different / different from) town.

6. Mike and Ted live in (different / different from) towns.

7. Ted looks (like / alike) Mike.

8. Ted and Mike look (like / alike).

9. Mike's truck is (similar / similar to) Ted's truck.

10. Mike's and Ted's trucks are (similar / similar to).

11. Ted is a mechanic. Mike is an engineer. Mike's job is (different / different from) Ted's job.

12. Mike's and Ted's jobs are (different / different from).

## 28 Your Turn

**Work with a partner or a group. Compare the four houses.**

**Example:**
The first house and the third house are alike.

**House 1**

**House 2**

**House 3**

**House 4**

# WRITING: Write a Comparative Paragraph

Write a paragraph that compares your life today with your life five years ago.

**Step 1. Think about the following parts of your life today and five years ago. Make notes in the chart.**

|  | Then | Now |
|---|---|---|
| 1. Schools/classes attended |  |  |
| 2. Homework |  |  |
| 3. Friends |  |  |
| 4. Free time |  |  |
| 5. Interests |  |  |
| 6. Money |  |  |
| 7. Responsibilities |  |  |

**Step 2. Write sentences about your life then and now. In general, is your life better now than it was? Why or why not?**

**Step 3. Choose some of your sentences and write them in a paragraph. Give reasons why your life is better or worse now. Write a title to your paragraph, for example, "My Life Then and Now." For more writing guidelines, see pages 407–411.**

> *My Life Then and Now*
>
> *Five years ago I attended high school. Now I attend college. The college is farther from my home, and I don't have as many friends there. In college, I have to work harder, and ...*

**Step 4. Evaluate your paragraph.**

**Checklist**

_____ Did you write a title and put it in the right place?

_____ Did you indent the first paragraph?

_____ Did you say why your life is better or worse now?

**Step 5. Edit your work. Work with a partner to edit your paragraph. Correct spelling, punctuation, vocabulary, and grammar.**

**Step 6. Write your final copy.**

# SELF-TEST

**A  Choose the best answer, A, B, C, or D, to complete the sentence. Mark your answer by darkening the oval with the same letter.**

**1.** Mary is _____ Tina.

**A.** as much tall as    Ⓐ Ⓑ Ⓒ Ⓓ
**B.** as tall than
**C.** as tall as
**D.** as taller as

**2.** As we walked, it got darker and _____.

**A.** darker    Ⓐ Ⓑ Ⓒ Ⓓ
**B.** more dark
**C.** the darker
**D.** the darkest

**3.** This question is _____ than the others.

**A.** the less difficult    Ⓐ Ⓑ Ⓒ Ⓓ
**B.** less difficult
**C.** least difficult
**D.** less difficulter

**4.** This is _____ building in the city.

**A.** the most oldest    Ⓐ Ⓑ Ⓒ Ⓓ
**B.** the oldest
**C.** oldest
**D.** most oldest

**5.** The more you study, _____.

**A.** the more you learn    Ⓐ Ⓑ Ⓒ Ⓓ
**B.** the more than you learn
**C.** you learn more
**D.** more you learn

**6.** It's _____ here in the country than in the city.

**A.** more peacefully    Ⓐ Ⓑ Ⓒ Ⓓ
**B.** more peaceful
**C.** peacefuller
**D.** the more peaceful

**7.** The Bellevue is _____ of the five hotels in this area.

**A.** the least expensive    Ⓐ Ⓑ Ⓒ Ⓓ
**B.** least expensive
**C.** the less expensive.
**D.** the least expensivest

**8.** Ted is a _____ his brother.

**A.** better student from    Ⓐ Ⓑ Ⓒ Ⓓ
**B.** better student than
**C.** gooder student than
**D.** best student

**9.** Carol drives _____ than her sister.

**A.** more careful    Ⓐ Ⓑ Ⓒ Ⓓ
**B.** more carefully
**C.** carefulier
**D.** the more carefully

**10.** The older she gets, the _____ she becomes.

**A.** quieter    Ⓐ Ⓑ Ⓒ Ⓓ
**B.** more quieter
**C.** quiet
**D.** quietlier

Comparative and Superlative Forms

**B** **Find the underlined word or phrase, A, B, C, or D, that is incorrect. Mark your answer by darkening the oval with the same letter.**

1. This year, computers <u>are</u> <u>more cheap</u> <u>than</u>
   A         B              C
   <u>last year</u>.
   D

   Ⓐ Ⓑ Ⓒ Ⓓ

2. Our neighbors bought a television set
   that <u>is</u> twice <u>so</u> <u>expensive</u> as <u>ours</u>.
        A        B      C            D

   Ⓐ Ⓑ Ⓒ Ⓓ

3. This is the <u>most funniest</u> movie I <u>have</u>
              A                        B
   <u>ever</u> <u>seen</u>.
   C      D

   Ⓐ Ⓑ Ⓒ Ⓓ

4. <u>The more</u> time I spend with my
   A
   grandmother, <u>the</u> more <u>than</u> she
                 B           C
   appreciates <u>it</u>.
               D

   Ⓐ Ⓑ Ⓒ Ⓓ

5. It is <u>getting</u> <u>the</u> warmer and <u>warmer</u> as
          A         B                  C
   spring <u>approaches</u>.
          D

   Ⓐ Ⓑ Ⓒ Ⓓ

6. My mother and <u>I</u> <u>are</u> <u>like</u> in <u>character</u> and
                  A    B    C           D
   physical appearance.

   Ⓐ Ⓑ Ⓒ Ⓓ

7. My English teacher <u>is</u> <u>different</u> <u>to</u> my
                       A       B         C
   History teacher <u>in many ways</u>.
                   D

   Ⓐ Ⓑ Ⓒ Ⓓ

8. I am <u>very</u> <u>interesting</u> <u>to see</u> the new
         A        B            C
   exhibit at <u>the Science Museum</u>.
              D

   Ⓐ Ⓑ Ⓒ Ⓓ

9. There are many <u>interested</u> <u>sights</u> <u>to see</u>
                   A          B       C
   <u>in New York City</u>.
   D

   Ⓐ Ⓑ Ⓒ Ⓓ

10. My job and Tony's job <u>are</u> <u>similar</u> each
                          A       B
    <u>other</u> <u>in many ways</u>.
    C       D

    Ⓐ Ⓑ Ⓒ Ⓓ

# UNIT 11

# THE PASSIVE VOICE

# 11a Active and Passive Voice Verbs: Simple Present, Simple Past, Present Perfect, Past Perfect, and Future Tenses

## Form

The Eiffel Tower **was built** in 1889.
It **was designed** by Gustave Eiffel.
It **is made** of iron, and it **has been repaired** many times.
It **is visited** by millions of tourists every year.

1. A sentence with an active voice verb has a subject, a verb, and an object.

| Subject | Active Verb | Object |
|---|---|---|
| Gustave Eiffel | **designed** | the Eiffel Tower. |

2. A sentence with a passive voice verb has a subject, a verb, and sometimes an agent.

| Subject | Passive Verb | Agent |
|---|---|---|
| The Eiffel Tower | **was designed** | (by Gustave Eiffel). |

3. We form the passive voice with *be* + a past participle. The verb *be* can be in any form: *am/is/are, was/were, has been/have been/had been, be,* and so on. We put the past participle after the form of *be*.

4. For regular verbs, the past participle ends in *–ed*. The past participle of irregular verbs is usually different.

| Type of Verb | Base Form | Past Participle |
|---|---|---|
| **Regular** | visit | visited |
| **Irregular** | write | written |

See page 404 for a list of irregular verbs.

| Tense | Active Voice | Passive Voice |
|---|---|---|
| **Simple Present** | Mr. Stone teaches me. | I **am taught** by Mr. Stone. |
| | Mr. Stone teaches Joe. | Joe **is taught** by Mr. Stone. |
| | Mr. Stone teaches us. | We **are taught** by Mr. Stone. |
| **Simple Past** | Mr. Stone taught me. | I **was taught** by Mr. Stone. |
| | Mr. Stone taught us. | We **were taught** by Mr. Stone. |
| **Present Perfect** | Mr. Stone has taught me. | I **have been taught** by Mr. Stone. |
| | Mr. Stone has taught him. | He **has been taught** by Mr. Stone. |
| **Past Perfect** | Mr. Stone had taught me. | I **had been taught** by Mr. Stone. |
| | Mr. Stone had taught us. | We **had been taught** by Mr. Stone. |
| **Future** | Mr. Stone is going to teach us. | We **are going to be taught** by Mr. Stone. |
| | Mr. Stone will teach me. | I **will be taught** by Mr. Stone. |
| | Mr. Stone will teach us. | We **will be taught** by Mr. Stone. |
| **Modals** | Mr. Stone can teach us. | We **can be taught** by Mr. Stone. |
| | Mr. Stone should teach us. | We **should be taught** by Mr. Stone. |

5. If we change an active voice sentence to a passive voice sentence, the object of the active voice sentence becomes the subject of the passive voice sentence.

   In a passive sentence, we can express the subject of the active voice sentence as an agent. The agent is stated in a prepositional phrase with *by*.

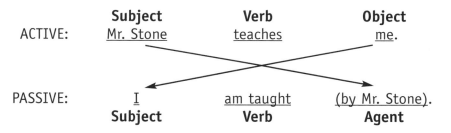

6. We can form the passive voice only with transitive verbs—verbs that have an object.

| Subject | Verb | Object |
|---|---|---|
| Paolo | wrote | the essay. |

The verb *wrote* has an object, so it is transitive, and we can make the sentence passive.

The essay **was written** (by Paolo).

We cannot use the passive form if the verb is intransitive. An intransitive verb does not have an object.

| Subject | Intransitive Verb |
|---------|-------------------|
| The book | fell. |
| The plane | will arrive. |

INCORRECT:  The book ~~was fallen~~.
INCORRECT:  The plane ~~will be arrived~~.

## Function

Millions of hamburgers **are eaten** every day in the United States.

We use the passive when we do not know who does an action or if it is not important or necessary to say who does something.

A Van Gogh painting **was stolen** from the National Gallery. (We do not know who stole it.)

## 1 Practice

**Change these sentences from the active voice to the passive voice.**

**1.** Helen invites me.

    _I am invited by Helen._

**2.** Helen invites Ted.

    _____

**3.** Helen invites us.

    _____

**4.** Helen invited me.

_____

**5.** Helen invited us.

_____

**6.** Helen has invited Jessica.

_____

**7.** Helen has invited them.

_____

**8.** Helen had invited me.

_____

**9.** Helen had invited them.

_____

**10.** Helen will invite Tony.

_____

**11.** Helen is going to invite us.

_____

## 2 | Practice

**Change the sentences into passive where possible. When a sentence cannot be changed into passive (because the verb is intransitive), write "No change."**

**1.** I went for an interview last week.

_No change._

**2.** The president of the company conducted the interview.

_The interview was conducted by the president of the company._

**3.** He asked questions in English.

_____

**4.** I replied in English.

_____

**5.** I left with a smile on my face.

_____

**6.** A letter from the company arrived yesterday.

_____

**7.** My father opened the letter.

_____

**8.** The president of the company wrote the letter.

_____

**9.** The job was mine!

_____

---

**3** Practice

**What happens when you go to the doctor? Rewrite the sentences in the simple present passive.**

**1.** The nurse weighs you.

  _You are weighed (by the nurse)._

**2.** The nurse takes your temperature.

  _____

**3.** The doctor takes your blood pressure.

  _____

**4.** The doctor listens to your heart.

  _____

**5.** The doctor examines your chest.

  _____

**6.** The doctor looks at your throat.

  _____

**7.** The doctor checks your lungs.

  _____

**8.** The doctor sends you to the technician.

  _____

**9.** The technician takes blood samples.

  _____

**10.** The doctor then writes a prescription.

  _____

**4** Practice

**Complete the sentences with the simple past passive form of the verbs in parentheses.**

**1.** The world's biggest explosion (cause) _____was caused_____ by a volcano on the island of Krakatoa in Indonesia in 1883.

2. The explosion (hear) _____ in India and Australia.

3. Half the island (destroy) _____.

4. Only a few people (kill) _____ by the explosion.

5. A very big wave, about 35 meters high, (create) _____ by the explosion.

6. Many small islands (cover) _____ by the wave.

7. More than 160 villages (destroy) _____.

8. Thousands of people (drown) _____ by the wave.

9. Dust from the explosion (carry) _____ to many parts of the world.

10. The weather around the world (affect) _____ for many years.

**An erupting volcano**

## 5 | Practice

**Jim and Berta saw an old house for sale one year ago, but they did not want to buy it because it needed too much work. They are looking at the house again, and they are noticing some changes. Complete the sentences with the subjects and verbs given. Use the present perfect passive.**

1. the outside walls/paint

   _The outside walls have been painted._ _____

2. the front door/change

   _____

3. the big trees/cut down

   _____

4. a lot of flowers/plant

   _____

5. a new garage/build

   _____

6. the kitchen/modernize

   _____

**7.** the windows/repair

_____

**8.** a new bathroom/put in

_____

**9.** the old gate/replace

_____

## 6 Practice

**Rewrite the sentences in the passive voice when possible. Use the correct tense. If a sentence cannot be passive, write "No change."**

**1.** German immigrants introduced the hamburger to the United States.

_The hamburger was introduced to the United States by_
_German immigrants._

**2.** The word _hamburger_ comes from the German city of Hamburg.

_____

**3.** In 1904 at the St. Louis Fair, they served hamburgers on buns.

_____

**4.** McDonald's® made hamburgers a popular American food.

_____

**5.** The McDonald brothers opened the first McDonald's® restaurant in California in 1949.

_____

**6.** The restaurant served only three things: hamburgers, French fries, and milkshakes.

_____

**7.** People waited outside the restaurant to eat.

_____

**8.** The business became too big for the McDonald brothers.

_____

**9.** The brothers sold McDonald's®.

_____

**10.** Ray Kroc bought the restaurant.

_____

**11.** Since then, the company has opened over 25,000 McDonald's® restaurants around the world.

_____

**12.** People eat more than 40 million hamburgers every day.

_____

**13.** Ray Kroc became a millionaire.

_____

# 11b The *By* Phrase

The telephone was invented **by Alexander Graham Bell.**

We use a prepositional phrase with *by* in a passive sentence to express the agent when it is important to know who does the action.

The telephone was invented **by Alexander Graham Bell**. (The person who invented it is important to the writer's meaning.)

*Hamlet* was written **by Shakespeare**. (The person who wrote it is important to the writer's meaning.)

## 7 Practice

**Rewrite the sentences in the passive voice. Use the *by* phrase only when necessary. Use the correct tense.**

**1.** Someone built this store in 1920.

_This store was built in 1920._

**2.** An artist painted the ceiling by hand.

_____

**3.** The famous architect George Emery designed the building.

_____

**4.** Today, they sell beauty products in the store.

_____

**5.** They make their creams from plants.

_____

**6.** They grow the plants in Brazil.

_____

**7.** They do not test their products on animals.

_____

**8.** Many famous people use their products.

_____

**9.** The actress Karen Krone advertises their products on television.

_____

**10.** They will open another store in New York next month.

_____

_____

## 8 | Practice

**Rewrite the sentences in the passive voice. Use the *by* phrase only when necessary. Use the correct tense.**

**1.** People sell billions of bottles of Coca-Cola® every year.

_Billions of bottles of Coca-Cola® are sold every year._

**2.** People drink Coca-Cola® all over the world.

_____

**3.** Dr. John Pemberton invented Coca-Cola® in 1886, in Atlanta, Georgia.

_____

**4.** He sold it as medicine.

_____

**5.** In the first year, he only sold a few drinks a day.

_____

**6.** A man named Asa Candler bought the business from Pemberton.

_____

**7.** He opened the first factory in Texas in 1895.

_____

**8.** They still make Coca-Cola® there.

_____

**9.** People do not know the ingredients of Coca-Cola®.

_____

**10.** The company keeps them a secret.

_____

**11.** World War I made Coca-Cola® popular outside the U.S.

_____

**12.** They sent Coca-Cola® to soldiers.

_____

**13.** In 1982, they introduced Diet Coke®.

_____

**14.** They use many advertisements to make Coca-Cola® popular.

_____

## 9 | Practice

**Complete the sentences with the correct form of the verb in parentheses. Use the active and passive voice when necessary. Some verbs are intransitive.**

### The Olympic Games

The first Olympic games (hold) _____*were held*_____ in the town of
                                            1

Olympia in ancient Greece. They (hold) _____ in 776 B.C. The
                                                        2

games (continue) _____ until about A.D. 394. Then the
                              3

games (ban) _____ by a Roman emperor.
                        4

A winner of a race in ancient Greece (receive) _____ a
                                                                      5

wreath. The wreath (made) _____ of the branches of a special
                                        6

olive tree. Only the winner of a race (recognize) _____.
                                                                7

A runner in second or third place (not, be) _____.
                                                            8

In 1875, parts of the Olympic stadium (discover) _____
                                                                      9

and people (become) _____ interested in the Olympic games
                                  10

again. The French educator Pierre de Coubertin (renew) _____
                                                                            11

the Olympic games in the 1890s. The first modern Olympic games

(hold) _____ in Athens in 1896. After more than
                  12

1500 years, Athens (choose) _____ by the organizers
                                          13

to be the place for the first modern Olympics. As in ancient times, the athletes were men.

Women (admit) _____ in 1900. Even in 1932, women
                            14

(not, allow) _____ 15 to participate in more than three events.

Since 1896, the Olympic games (hold) _____ 16 every four years.

The games (cancel) _____ 17 in 1916, 1940, and 1944

because of World Wars. However, in ancient Greece, wars

(stop) _____ 18 for the Olympic games.

The Olympic flag (use) _____ 19 for the first time in 1920.

The first Olympic village (build) _____ 20 in 1932. Today, before

the games, the Olympic torch (light) _____ 21 at Mt. Olympus

in Greece. Then it (carry) _____ 22 by runners to the city

where the games (hold) _____ 23. Sometimes, the torch

(carry) _____ 24 half way around the world. Millions of people

around the world (watch) _____ 25 the games. Every four years

the games (be) _____ 26 in a different country. Do you know

where the next Olympic games (hold) _____ 27?

# 11c The Passive Form of the Present Progressive and Past Progressive Tenses

**Form / Function**

At the airport, tickets **are being checked.** Questions **are being asked.**

| | Subject | Am/Is/Are | (Not) Being | Past Participle |
|---|---|---|---|---|
| **Present** | I | **am** | | **asked** questions. |
| **Progressive** | He/She/It | **is** | **(not) being** | **understood.** |
| **Passive** | We/You/They | **are** | | **cheated.** |
| **Past** | I/He/She/It | **was** | | **asked** questions. |
| **Progressive** **Passive** | We/You/They | **were** | **(not) being** | **understood.** |

1. The present progressive passive shows that something is taking place right now.

      ACTIVE:     Someone **is asking** him questions.
      PASSIVE:   He **is being asked** questions.

2. The past progressive passive shows that something was taking place at a specific time in the past.

      ACTIVE:     Someone **was asking** him questions.
      PASSIVE:   He **was being asked** questions.

3. We can use the *by* phrase if we want to say who or what did the action.

      He was being asked questions **by the airline clerk.**

## 10 Practice

**What is happening at the airport? Complete the sentences with the present progressive passive of the verbs in parentheses.**

1. Arriving and departing flights (show) _____*are being shown*_____ on television screens.

2. Departing flights (announce) _____

3. One flight (cancel) _____

4. Other flights (delay) _____

5. Passports (check) _____

6. Luggage (x-ray) _____

7. People (search) _____

8. Passengers (tell) _____ to wait in lines for their boarding passes.

9. Labels (attach) _____ to luggage.

10. Luggage (take) _____ away on a conveyor belt.

**11.** Passengers (tell) _____ to wait in the airport lounge.

**12.** Gate numbers (show) _____ on screens 30 minutes before flight departure.

II Practice

**A. At four o'clock yesterday many preparations were being made at the Grand Hotel for the big reception for the president. Complete the sentences with the past progressive passive of the verbs in the list.**

| bring | decorate | rehearse | tell |
|-------|----------|----------|------|
| cook | make | set | practice |

**1.** A cake _____ *was being made* _____.

**2.** Food _____.

**3.** Tables _____.

**4.** More tables _____ because there weren't enough.

**5.** The reception hall _____ with flowers.

**6.** Security guards _____ what to do.

**7.** Music _____ by the band.

**8.** Speeches _____.

**B. What other things do you think were being done? Give five more examples.**

**1.** *Flowers were being arranged.* _____

**2.** _____

**3.** _____

**4.** _____

**5.** _____

# 11d The Passive Forms of Modals

Toxic gases **must not be put** into the air.

Dangerous chemicals **must be removed** from the water.

We form the passive of modals with modal + *be* + past participle. We form the passive of modal negatives with modal + *not* + *be* + past participle.

| ACTIVE VOICE MODAL | | | PASSIVE VOICE MODAL | |
|---|---|---|---|---|
| Subject | Active Modal | Object | Subject | Passive Voice Modal |
| We | will clean | the air. | The air | will be cleaned. |
| | can clean | | | can be cleaned. |
| | should clean | | | should be cleaned. |
| | ought to clean | | | ought to be cleaned. |
| | must clean | | | must be cleaned. |
| | have to clean | | | has to be cleaned. |
| | may clean | | | may be cleaned. |
| | might clean | | | might be cleaned. |
| | must not pollute | | | must not be polluted. |
| | don't have to pollute | | | doesn't have to be polluted. |

## 12 Practice

**A. People are talking about the environment. Rewrite the sentences in the passive voice.**

1. We must not throw waste from factories into the oceans.

   *Waste from factories must not be thrown into the oceans.*

2. We should not cut down the forests.

   _____

**3.** We should protect animals in danger.

_____

**4.** We must not spray food plants with chemicals.

_____

**5.** We should recycle bottles and paper.

_____

**6.** We should save energy.

_____

**7.** We could use electric cars.

_____

**8.** We can use other kinds of natural energy.

_____

**9.** The government ought to ban leaded gasoline.

_____

**10.** We have to prevent oil spills.

_____

**11.** We will destroy our planet.

_____

**12.** We must take action now.

_____

**B. Work with a partner. Think of five other things we can do to help our environment.**

**1.** _Paper, metal, and plastic should be recycled._

**2.** _____

**3.** _____

**4.** _____

**5.** _____

# 11e *Have* Something *Done*

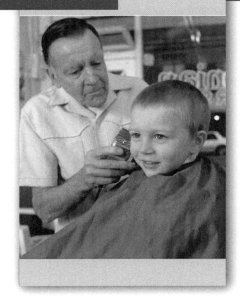

Bobby **is having his hair cut.**

1. We use *have* + object + past participle to say somebody does a job for us. We do not do it ourselves.

| Tense | Subject | Form of *Have* | Object | Past Participle |
|---|---|---|---|---|
| Simple Present | | has | | |
| Present Progressive | | is having | | |
| Simple Past | | had | | |
| Past Progressive | | was having | | |
| Simple Future | He | will have | his hair | cut. |
| | | is going to have | | |
| Future Progressive | | will be having | | |
| Present Perfect | | has had | | |
| Present Perfect Progressive | | has been having | | |
| Past Perfect | | had had | | |
| Past Perfect Progressive | | had been having | | |

2. We can use a *by* phrase to say who performed the action.

   He had his hair cut **by a very good barber.**

## 13 Practice

**This is a busy week for Helen. Write sentences with _have_ something _done_ and the words in parentheses. Use the correct tense.**

1. Yesterday, she (her checks/deposit) to her bank account.

   _Yesterday, she had her checks deposited to her bank account._

2. Right now, she (her oil/change).

   _____

3. Yesterday, she (her suit/dry clean).

   _____

4. Tomorrow, she (her teeth/clean).

   _____

5. The day after tomorrow, she (her washing machine/fix).

   _____

6. Yesterday, she (her eyes/test) for new glasses.

   _____

7. Tomorrow, she (her new sofa/deliver).

   _____

8. In two days, she (a tree/cut) down in the back yard.

   _____

9. Yesterday, she (some photos/take) for a passport.

   _____

10. Tomorrow, she (some new business cards/make).

    _____

## 14 Practice

**Karen Krone is a famous movie star. She is very rich and has everything done for her. Read the questions and write Karen Krone's answers. Use a _by_ phrase to say who performed the action.**

1. Do you style your hair yourself? (Lorenzo)

   _No, I have it styled by Lorenzo._

2. Do you drive your car yourself? (my chauffeur)

   _____

3. Will you design your next dress yourself? (Alfani)

   _____

4. Do you cook your food yourself? (my chef)

_____

5. Do you make your appointments yourself? (my assistant)

_____

6. Do you clean your house yourself? (my housekeeper)

_____

7. Did you plant these flowers yourself? (my gardener)

_____

8. Do you fly your plane yourself? (my pilot)

_____

9. Do you arrange for your interviews yourself? (my assistant)

_____

10. Do you buy your groceries yourself? (my housekeeper)

_____

## 11f  More Phrasal Verbs with Objects: Separable

### Form / Function

Remember that phrasal verbs are made of a verb and a particle. See page 180 for more information on phrasal verbs.

| Phrasal Verb | Meaning | Example |
|---|---|---|
| call off | cancel something (a meeting, a game, etc.) | They **called** the game **off** because of the storm. |
| call up | to telephone someone | If you want to go to the movies with Rosa, **call** her **up** and ask her! |
| pay back | return money to someone | Thanks for the twenty dollars. I'll **pay** you **back** tomorrow. |
| put back | return something to its original place | Please **put** the books **back** when you're finished with them. |
| shut off | stop a machine; turn off | How do you **shut off** this machine? |
| take back | return something (usually to a store) | This CD player doesn't work right. I'm going to **take** it **back**. |
| try on | put on clothing to see if it is the correct size | Be sure to **try** those shoes **on** before you buy them. |
| turn up | make the volume louder | I like that song. **Turn up** the radio, please. |
| turn down | make the volume softer | The television is too loud. **Turn** it **down**. |

**Replace the underlined words with a phrasal verb + an object. Put the object in the correct place. Remember that sometimes the object can go in two places.**

Tom: I can't hear you! Can you <u>make the volume of the television softer</u>?
Sue: Sure.

**1.** *turn the television down*

Mark: A man <u>telephoned you</u> when you were not here. His name was Thompson.

**2.** _____

Michele: Did he leave a message?
Mark: Yes, he <u>cancelled the meeting</u> for tomorrow.

**3.** _____

Janet: I'm going to the department store. I want to <u>return a blouse</u>.

**4.** _____

Mother: Did you <u>put it on to see if it is the correct size</u> before you bought it?

**5.** _____

Janet: Yes, I did but I don't like it now. Can I borrow twenty dollars from you? I'll <u>give the money to you</u> tomorrow.

**6.** _____

Mother: OK. But <u>put the milk in its place</u> before you go.

**7.** _____

Janet: Sure. Anything else?
Mother: Could you please <u>make the television louder</u> before you go so I can hear the news?

**8.** _____

Janet: Do you want me to <u>turn off the oven</u> as well? I think your cake is done.

**9.** _____

Mother: Yes, please. Thank you.

## 16 Practice

**Answer in complete sentences.**

1. What are some things you try on before you buy them?

   *I try shoes and pants on.*

2. What do you pay back?

   _____

3. What can you turn up and down?

   _____

4. What do you shut off?

   _____

5. Who do you call up often?

   _____

# WRITING: Describe a Place

Write a paragraph about a city or town.

**Step 1. Work with a partner. Think of a town or city (maybe your hometown or a city you know). Ask and answer questions using the passive voice as much as possible. These prompts may help you.**

1. Where is it located?
2. When was it founded?
3. Who/what was it named after?
4. What is/was it famous for?
5. What are some famous places in the city? Who are they visited by? Why?
6. How has your city changed?

**Step 2. Write answers to the questions in Step 1.**

**Step 3. Rewrite your answers in paragraph form. For more writing guidelines, see pages 407–411.**

**Step 4. Evaluate your paragraph.**

**Checklist**

_____ Did you write a title (the name of the city or town)?
_____ Did you write the title with a capital letter for each word?
_____ Did you indent the first line of your paragraph?
_____ Did you write any sentences in the passive voice?

**Step 5. Edit your work. Work with a partner to edit your sentences. Correct spelling, punctuation, vocabulary, and grammar.**

**Step 6. Write your final copy.**

**A   Choose the best answer, A, B, C, or D, to complete the sentence. Mark your answer by darkening the oval with the same letter.**

1. The house _____ recently.

   A. has been painted    Ⓐ Ⓑ Ⓒ Ⓓ
   B. has painted
   C. been painted
   D. was been painted

2. My car radio _____.

   A. was stole    Ⓐ Ⓑ Ⓒ Ⓓ
   B. stolen by someone
   C. was stolen
   D. is stolen by a person

3. _____ in the United States?

   A. People grow rice    Ⓐ Ⓑ Ⓒ Ⓓ
   B. They grow rice
   C. Is rice grown
   D. Is rice grow

4. When _____?

   A. did someone invent    Ⓐ Ⓑ Ⓒ Ⓓ
      paper
   B. was paper invented by someone
   C. someone invented paper
   D. was paper invented

5. Lillian is at the beauty salon. She
   _____.

   A. is having her hair cut   Ⓐ Ⓑ Ⓒ Ⓓ
   B. is cut her hair
   C. is cutting her hair by someone
   D. has her hair cut

6. Paul's jacket is dirty. He _____ at the dry cleaners.

   A. is cleaning it    Ⓐ Ⓑ Ⓒ Ⓓ
   B. was cleaned it
   C. is having it cleaned
   D. clean it

7. This machine _____ after 6:00 P.M.

   A. must not use    Ⓐ Ⓑ Ⓒ Ⓓ
   B. must not be used
   C. must not be use
   D. not be used

8. I can't hear you. Can you _____ the radio?

   A. turn up    Ⓐ Ⓑ Ⓒ Ⓓ
   B. turn down
   C. turn back
   D. turn it on

9. I always try _____ a pair of pants before I buy them.

   A. it on    Ⓐ Ⓑ Ⓒ Ⓓ
   B. them on
   C. up
   D. on

10. Vicky is at the optician. She is _____ by the doctor.

    A. testing her eyes    Ⓐ Ⓑ Ⓒ Ⓓ
    B. tested her eyes
    C. her eyes tested
    D. having her eyes tested

**B** Find the underlined word or phrase, A, B, C, or D, that is incorrect. Mark your answer by darkening the oval with the same letter.

1. An island <u>named</u> Easter Island <u>by</u>
             A              B
 the Dutch navigator Jacob Roggeveen in
 1772 because he <u>reached</u> <u>it</u>
                      C       D
 on Easter Sunday.

 Ⓐ Ⓑ Ⓒ Ⓓ

2. Many blind people can <u>use</u> <u>their</u> fingertips
                         A   B
 <u>to read</u> what <u>was written</u> on a page.
  C             D

 Ⓐ Ⓑ Ⓒ Ⓓ

3. The nurse Florence Nightingale <u>was call</u>
                                 A
 the Lady of the Lamp <u>because</u> she <u>walked</u>
                  B           C
 from bed to bed in the middle of the
 night <u>with</u> her lamp.
     D

 Ⓐ Ⓑ Ⓒ Ⓓ

4. The Royal Flying Doctor Service <u>in</u>
                              A
 Australia <u>is started</u> <u>by</u> John Flynn <u>in</u> 1928.
          B     C            D

 Ⓐ Ⓑ Ⓒ Ⓓ

5. Workers <u>was gathered</u> from all over Russia
           A
 <u>to build</u> <u>the</u> city <u>of</u> St. Petersburg.
  B    C      D

 Ⓐ Ⓑ Ⓒ Ⓓ

6. <u>When</u> Marco Polo <u>returned</u> from China, he
    A                 B
 <u>was written</u> a book about <u>his travels</u>.
    C                  D

 Ⓐ Ⓑ Ⓒ Ⓓ

7. The Taj Mahal <u>is consider</u> to be one of the
                A
 <u>most beautiful</u> <u>buildings</u> <u>in the world</u>.
   B          C       D

 Ⓐ Ⓑ Ⓒ Ⓓ

8. Special diets <u>is</u> <u>needed</u> <u>by people</u> who
               A   B     C
 suffer from <u>certain diseases</u>.
            D

 Ⓐ Ⓑ Ⓒ Ⓓ

9. Moby Dick was <u>a great white</u> whale <u>whose</u>
               A            B
 story <u>was wrote</u> <u>by the American novelist</u>
      C          D
 Herman Melville.

 Ⓐ Ⓑ Ⓒ Ⓓ

10. Frozen foods, such as frozen <u>fish</u> and
                           A
 vegetables, <u>introduced</u> in the 1920s when
           B
 people <u>began</u> to buy freezers for
        C
 <u>their homes</u>.
  D

 Ⓐ Ⓑ Ⓒ Ⓓ

# UNIT 12

## CONJUNCTIONS AND NOUN CLAUSES

# 12a The Conjunctions *And, But,* and *Or*

Doctors **and** nurses work in hospitals.

Conjunctions are words that join sentences or parts of a sentence.

1. We use the conjunction *and* to join sentences that are alike. *And* can also join one sentence that gives extra information to the other. We use a comma before *and* when it joins sentences.

   > I saw the doctor. He gave me some medicine.
   > I saw the doctor, **and** he gave me some medicine.

2. We use the conjunction *but* to give opposite or contrasting information. *But* can also join a positive sentence and a negative sentence that talk about the same subject. We use a comma before *but* when it joins sentences.

   > A doctor can prescribe medicine. A nurse cannot prescribe medicine.
   > A doctor can prescribe medicine, **but** a nurse cannot prescribe medicine.

3. We use the conjunction *or* to join sentences that give a choice. We use a comma before *or* when it joins sentences.

   > You can see the doctor at the hospital. You can see her in her private office.
   > You can see the doctor at the hospital, **or** you can see her in her private office.

4. When *and, but,* and *or* connect two things (for example, two nouns, two adjectives, two adverbs, etc.) that are not sentences, we do not use a comma.

   > You can see a doctor **or** a nurse. (two nouns)
   > Nurses must be hard-working **and** patient. (two adjectives)
   > The surgeon operated quickly **but** carefully. (two adverbs)

5. When we use *and, but,* and *or* to connect three or more items in a series, we use a comma after each item before the conjunction.

> I had a sore throat, a headache, a stomachache, **and** a temperature.

> The doctor told me not to drink tea, coffee, **or** soda.

> The nurse took my temperature, my pulse, **but** not my blood pressure.

6. Do not use a comma when the verb in the second part of the sentence does not have its own subject in that part of the sentence.

> **I wanted** to see a doctor, but **I saw** a nurse. (Each verb has its own subject. Use a comma.)

> **I wanted** to see a doctor but **saw** a nurse. (The subject of *saw* in the second part of the sentence is *I*. There is no subject in the second part of the sentence. Do not use a comma.)

## 1 Practice

**Complete the sentences about the body and health with *and, but,* or *or*. Add commas where necessary.**

1. We need to eat fruit _____*and*_____ vegetables for good health.

2. We need vitamins for good health _____ we need only very small amounts.

3. Blood takes food _____ oxygen to the organs of our body.

4. Everyone's blood is one of four basic types: A, B, AB _____ O.

5. O is the most common group _____ there are more people with group A in some countries like Norway.

6. We can live without food for a few days _____ we will die in a few minutes without air.

7. The scalp has about 10,000 hairs _____ about 60 of them fall out every day.

8. The skin is thickest on the palms of our hands _____ the bottoms of our feet.

9. Vitamin A is found in carrots, green vegetables, liver _____ milk.

10. Newborn babies can drink milk _____ they cannot eat vegetables.

11. In the first eight months of its life, a baby cannot sit up, feed itself _____ walk.

12. Our eyelashes _____ eyebrows grow more slowly than the hair on our heads.

13. A newborn baby can see _____ it cannot see things far away.

14. Hair grows faster in the summer _____ when we sleep.

Add commas where necessary. Some sentences do not need commas.

1. At Mount Rushmore, the heads of Presidents George Washington, Thomas Jefferson, Abraham Lincoln, and Theodore Roosevelt are carved into a mountain.
2. They are the work of Gustave Borglum. He began work in 1927 and died in 1941.
3. Borglum and his workers went up the mountain and they worked even in bad weather.
4. They went on foot or on horseback.
5. Borglum and his helpers went up thousands of times.
6. They used drills and dynamite to remove the rock.
7. The work was difficult and it was also dangerous.
8. In 1941, Borglum died but the work was not complete.
9. His son took over the work and finished it in 1941.

**3** Your Turn

**What things do you like or not like? Talk about them with a partner.**

**Example:**
I like to eat broccoli, peas, and carrots, but I don't like cabbage.

I like to eat _____, but I don't like _____.

My favorite television shows are _____ and _____,

but I don't like _____.

# 12b The Conjunction *So*

It started to rain, **so** he opened his umbrella.

*So* is a conjunction that connects two sentences. *So* gives us the result. We use a comma before *so*.

| | Cause | Result |
|---|---|---|
| **Two Sentences** | It started to rain. | He opened his umbrella. |
| **One Sentence** | It started to rain, | **so** he opened his umbrella. |

## 4 Practice

**Complete the sentences with *but* or *so*.**

1. I was tired, _____*so*_____ I went to bed early.

2. I went to bed early, _____ I couldn't sleep.

3. I couldn't sleep, _____ I got up.

4. I turned on the television, _____ there was nothing good on.

5. I decided to have a glass of milk, _____ I went to the refrigerator.

6. There was no milk in the refrigerator, _____ there was some juice.

7. I drank the juice, _____ it gave me a stomachache.

8. My stomachache got really bad, _____ I took some medicine for it.

9. I was feeling pretty bad, _____ I went to bed.

**10.** I didn't know what time it was, _____ I looked at the clock. It was 6:00 in the morning.

**11.** I usually get up at 6:00 to go to work, _____ I got up.

**12.** I usually feel energetic in the morning, _____ I didn't feel energetic at all!

## 5 | Practice

**Complete the sentences with *and, but, or,* and *so*. Put commas where necessary.**

Thomas Edison was a great inventor. He went to school ___*but*___ didn't enjoy it.
<sub>1</sub>

He didn't do his school work _____ the principal of the school told him not to
<sub>2</sub>

come back. He only went to school for three _____ four months _____ he
<sub>3</sub> <sub>4</sub>

never stopped learning. His mother wanted him to learn _____ she taught him at
<sub>5</sub>

home. She gave him science books. He stayed at home _____ read the books.
<sub>6</sub>

Edison needed money to buy more books _____ he started to work on a train. He
<sub>7</sub>

sold candy _____ newspapers. He loved to do experiments. One day he blew up the
<sub>8</sub>

office where he worked _____ he lost his job. Edison always worked long hours
<sub>9</sub>

_____ slept for only five _____ six hours a day. Edison invented over
<sub>10</sub> <sub>11</sub>

1,000 items and processes. His most important are sound recording _____ the
<sub>12</sub>

light bulb.

## 6 | Your Turn

**Say three things you need to do. Also say the result. Use *so*.**

**Example:**
I need to do my homework tonight, so I can give it to the teacher tomorrow.

## 12c *Too, So, Either,* and *Neither*

**Linda**

**Nancy**

Linda has curly hair. **So does** Nancy.
Linda has curly hair. Nancy **does too**.
Linda doesn't have straight hair. **Neither does** Nancy.

| AFFIRMATIVE STATEMENT | AGREEMENT WITH *TOO* | | | AGREEMENT WITH *SO* | |
|---|---|---|---|---|---|
| | Subject + Verb | *Too* | *So* | Auxiliary Verb | Subject |
| I like Ken. | I **do,**<br>I **like** him, | | | **do** | I. |
| I am a student. | I **am,***<br>a student, | | | **am** | I. |
| We are studying. | They **are,***<br>studying, | **too.** | **So** | **are** | they. |
| Bob went to Seoul last year. | Karen **did,**<br>Karen **went** there, | | | **did** | Karen. |
| Tina can drive. | Tom **can,**<br>Tom **can drive,** | | | **can** | Tom. |

*If no information is repeated from the affirmative statement, we do not contract auxiliary verbs with their subjects when expressing agreement with *too*.

| | | | |
|---|---|---|---|
| CORRECT: | I am, too. | She is too. | They are, too. |
| INCORRECT: | I'm, too. | She's, too. | They're, too. |

| NEGATIVE STATEMENT | AGREEMENT WITH *EITHER* | | AGREEMENT WITH *NEITHER* | | |
|---|---|---|---|---|---|
| | Subject + Verb + *Not* | *Either* | *Neither* | Auxiliary Verb | Subject |
| I'm not hungry. | I'm **not,**<br>I'm **not** hungry, | | | am | I. |
| I don't like football. | Paul **doesn't,**<br>Paul **doesn't like** it, | | | does | Paul. |
| I didn't enjoy the movie. | They **didn't,**<br>They **didn't enjoy** it, | either. | Neither | did | they. |
| They won't go. | We **won't,**<br>We **won't go,** | | | will | we. |
| I can't do that. | I **can't,**<br>I **can't do it,** | | | can | I. |

1. When the main verb is a form of *be* (*am, is, are, was,* or *were*), we use the main verb in the agreement.

   A: I **am** not hungry.     B: Neither **am** I.

2. When the main verb is any other verb in the simple present or simple past tense, we use the auxiliary verbs *do, does,* or *did* in the agreement.

   A: Casey **liked** the movie. B: So **did** I.

3. When the verb is an auxiliary verb + another form of a verb, we use the auxiliary verb in the agreement.

   A: I **am studying.**     B: We **are,** too.

4. When we use *so* or *neither,* we put the auxiliary verb before the subject.

   A: Susan **wasn't** in class.  B: Neither **was I.**

5. When we use *too* or *either,* we can also use the entire verb and other information from the original statement.

   A: I **don't like** football.   B: I **don't like it,** either.

## Function

1. We use *too* and *so* to agree with or add information to affirmative ideas.

   A: I'm tired.
   B: I'm tired, **too.** OR **So** am I.

   A: Ken is strong.
   B: Ben is, **too.** OR **So** is Ben.

2. We use *either* and *neither* to agree with or add information to negative ideas.

    A: Ken doesn't have a moustache.
    B: Ben does**n't** have a moustache, **either.** OR **Neither** does Ben.

3. In informal conversation, we often use *me too* and *me neither*.

    A: I like Ken.
    B: **Me too.**

    A: I'm not hungry.
    B: **Me neither.**

---

## 7   Practice

**Ken met Monica at a party. They are finding out that they have a lot in common. Write sentences showing agreement using *so* and *neither*.**

**1.** Monica: I love this kind of music.

    Ken: _So do I._

**2.** Monica: I haven't been to a party for a long time.

    Ken: _____

**3.** Monica: I am very shy.

    Ken: _____

**4.** Monica: I am not good at making conversation.

    Ken: _____

**5.** Monica: I love to read.

    Ken: _____

**6.** Monica: I play tennis.

    Ken: _____

**7.** Monica: I live alone.

    Ken: _____

**8.** Monica: I came to this city a few years ago.

    Ken: _____

**9.** Monica: I don't have many friends.

    Ken: _____

**10.** Monica: I would like to make new friends.

    Ken: _____

## 8 | Practice

**Judy and Laura went to a new restaurant. They always agree. Complete the sentences.**

1. Judy: I haven't been here before.

   Laura: And I _____ *haven't* _____, either.

2. Judy: I like the décor and atmosphere.

   Laura: And I _____, too.

3. Judy: I don't like this dish.

   Laura: And I _____, either.

4. Judy: My food isn't fresh.

   Laura: And neither _____.

5. Judy: My meal is cold.

   Laura: And _____, too.

6. Judy: I can't eat this.

   Laura: And _____, either.

7. Judy: I don't have a napkin.

   Laura: And neither _____.

8. Judy: I didn't ask for a salad.

   Laura: And _____, either.

9. Judy: I am disappointed.

   Laura: And so _____.

10. Judy: I won't come here again.

    Laura: And _____, either.

## 9 | Practice

**Fill in the blanks with the names of students in your class and the correct auxiliary.**

1. _*Berta*_ wears eyeglasses, and so _____ *does Kim.* _____

2. _____ is wearing black shoes, and so _____

3. _____ doesn't have a car, and neither _____

4. _____ always sits in the front row, and so _____

5. _____ wasn't late to class, and neither _____

6. _____ is absent from class today, and so _____

7. _____ answered in class yesterday, and so _____

8. _____ didn't make any mistakes, and neither _____

9. _____ has never been to London, and neither _____

10. _____ wants to learn English, and so _____

**How do you feel about television, holidays, and music? Make statements. Your partner will agree or disagree. Use** *so, neither, too,* **and** *not ... either.*

**Example:**
You:            I like game shows.
Your partner:  So do I, but I don't like police shows.
You:            Neither do I.

# 12d Noun Clauses Beginning with Wh- Words

**Form / Function**

Mr. Brown, I know **what the answer is.**

**INTRODUCTION TO NOUN CLAUSES**

1.  A noun clause is a dependent clause. It cannot stand on its own. It is connected to a main clause. A noun clause has a subject and a verb.

| Main Clause | Noun Clause |
|---|---|
| I know | what the answer is. |

2.  There are three kinds of noun clauses.

| Type of Clause | Main Clause | Noun Clause |
|---|---|---|
| **Wh- Clauses** (see below) | The students know | what the answer is. |
| *If* **Clauses** (see section 12e) | I don't know | if it's cold outside or not. |
| *That* **Clauses** (see section 12f) | She explained | that she had to leave. |

3.  We often use a noun clause after expressions like these:

| I know | I believe |
|---|---|
| I don't know | I wonder |
| Do you know | Can/Could you tell me |

## NOUN CLAUSES BEGINNING WITH WH- WORDS

| MAIN CLAUSE | | WH- NOUN CLAUSE | | |
|---|---|---|---|---|
| Subject | Verb | Wh- Word | Subject | Verb |
| I | don't know | where | she | is. |
| | | when | | arrives. |
| | | how | | knew. |
| We | wondered | where | he | was. |
| | | what | | was doing. |
| | | why | | called. |

1. The word order in a wh- noun clause is the same as in a statement: subject + verb.

    CORRECT:     I don't know where **he is** going.
    INCORRECT: I don't know where ~~is he~~ going.

2. We use a period at the end of a sentence if the main clause is a statement. We use a question mark at the end of a sentence if the main clause is a question.

    CORRECT:     I wonder where she is going. ("I wonder" is a statement.)
    INCORRECT: I wonder where she is going~~?~~

    CORRECT:     Can you tell me what time it is? ("Can you tell me" is a question.)
    INCORRECT: Can you tell me what time it is~~.~~

## Function

1. We often use wh- noun clauses after verbs such as *know, understand, remember, wonder,* and *believe*. Most of these verbs express thinking, uncertainty, or curiosity.

    Peter left for work this morning. I don't know **when he left.**

2. We use sentences with wh- noun clauses in place of direct questions because they can make a question more indirect, and therefore more polite.

    Direct question:  What time is it?
    Wh-clause:        Can you tell me what time it is?

# 11 Practice

A police officer is asking you questions about an accident. You can't remember much and are not sure. Complete the sentences with noun clauses.

1. Police Officer: What color was the car?

   You: I can't remember _what color it was._

2. Police Officer: Who was driving the car?

   You: I am not sure _____

3. Police Officer: How many people were there in the car?

   You: I don't know _____

4. Police Officer: How fast was the car going?

   You: I don't know _____

5. Police Officer: What was the license plate number?

   You: I don't know _____

6. Police Officer: Where were you standing?

   You: I can't remember _____

7. Police Officer: How many other witnesses were there?

   You: I don't know _____

8. Police Officer: When did the accident happen?

   You: I am not certain _____

9. Police Officer: Where was the pedestrian*?

   You: I'm not sure _____

10. Police Officer: How fast was she walking?

    You: I don't know _____

    Police Officer: Thank you. You have been a great help!

    *A *pedestrian* is a person on foot.

# 12 Practice

A young child is asking his mother a lot of difficult questions. She does not know the answers to them. Complete the sentences with noun clauses.

1. Child: Why is the sky blue?

   Mother: I don't know _why the sky is blue._

2. Child: Who is that girl?

   Mother: I don't know _____

**3.** Child:   What am I going to be when I grow up?

Mother: I don't know _____

**4.** Child:   Where does our water come from?

Mother: I don't know _____

**5.** Child:   Why do stars shine?

Mother: I don't know _____

**6.** Child:   How can a fly walk upside down?

Mother: I don't know _____

**7.** Child:   When do fish sleep?

Mother: I don't know _____

**8.** Child:   How big is the sky?

Mother: I don't know _____

**9.** Child:   What makes the sea blue?

Mother: I don't know _____

**10.** Child:   When am I going to get married?

Mother: I don't know _____

## 13 Your Turn

**Work with a partner to ask and answer polite questions for these situations.**

**Example:**
You:             Excuse me. Can you tell me where the restroom is?
Your partner:  I'm sorry. I don't know where it is.

1. You are in a department store. You are looking for the restroom.
2. You are in a train station. You are looking for platform 15.
3. You are at the airport. You are looking for the baggage claim area.
4. You are in a supermarket. You are looking for the eggs.

# 12e Noun Clauses Beginning with *If* or *Whether*

I wonder **if I locked the door.**

| MAIN CLAUSE | | NOUN CLAUSE WITH *IF* OR *WHETHER* | | |
|---|---|---|---|---|
| Subject | Verb | *If/Whether* | Subject | Verb |
| I | don't know<br>can't remember | **if**<br>**whether** | I | **locked the door (or not).** |

1. *If/whether* clauses have a subject and a verb. There is no comma between the *if/whether* clause and the main clause.

2. When we change a yes/no question to a noun clause, we use *if* or *whether* to introduce the clause. *If/whether* clauses are like yes/no questions, but the word order is like a statement (subject + verb).

   Yes/No Question:      **Did** I **lock** the door?
   Noun Clause:          I don't know **if** I **locked** the door.

3. The phrase *or not* often comes at the end of the *if/whether* clause.

   I don't know **if** I locked the door **or not.**
   I wonder **whether** the flight has arrived **or not.**

   We can put *or not* immediately after *whether,* but not immediately after *if.*

   CORRECT:      I wonder **whether or not** the flight has arrived.
   INCORRECT:  I wonder if ~~or not~~ the flight has arrived.

1. *If* and *whether* have the same meaning when they begin noun clauses.

2. As with wh- clauses, we often use *if/whether* clauses after verbs that express mental activity such as thinking, uncertainty, or curiosity.

> I **can't remember** if I locked the door.
> I **don't know** whether he is coming or not.

## 14 Practice

**Brenda was in a hurry this morning. She can't remember certain things she did or didn't do. Rewrite the questions as noun clauses with *if* or *whether*.**

1. Did I lock the door? I wonder _if I locked the door._
2. Did I turn off the gas? I'm not sure _____
3. Is the TV still on? I don't know _____
4. Did I mail my bills? I'm not sure _____
5. Did I take my medicine? I can't remember _____
6. Did I feed the cat? I can't remember _____

## 15 Practice

**You have met someone you like, but you are worrying about it. Complete the questions with noun clauses with wh- words or with *if/whether*.**

1. What kind of job does he/she have?

   I wonder _what kind of job she has._
2. Does he/she like movies?

   I wonder _____
3. Where does he/she live?

   I wonder _____
4. Is he/she neat and tidy?

   I wonder _____
5. Can he/she play tennis?

   I wonder _____
6. How old is he/she?

   I'd like to know _____
7. Is he/she at home right now?

   I wonder _____

**8.** Is he/she thinking about me?

I wonder _____

**9.** Should I call him/her?

I don't know _____

**10.** Is it too late to call him/her?

I don't know _____

**11.** Did he/she say he/she would call me?

I can't remember _____

**12.** Does he/she want me to call?

I wonder _____

## 16 Practice

**You are meeting some people at the airport. Rewrite the questions using noun clauses starting with wh- words or with *if/whether*.**

**1.** Where can I park my car?

*Can you tell me where I can park my car?* _____

**2.** What time does the flight arrive?

Do you know _____

**3.** Is it flight 206 or 208?

I wonder _____

**4.** Do the passengers come out here?

Can you tell me _____

**5.** Why aren't they here?

I wonder _____

**6.** Is the flight delayed?

I wonder _____

**7.** Do they know I'll be waiting?

I wonder _____

**8.** Will they recognize me?

I don't know _____

**9.** How long is the flight?

Can you tell me _____

**10.** Did they have a good flight?

I wonder _____

**Your Turn**

This is the first day of your new class. Write four statements about things that you are not sure about. Use *if* or *whether* to begin the noun clause.

1.  *I wonder if the teacher is nice.*
2.  _____
3.  _____
4.  _____

## 12f Noun Clauses Beginning with *That*

**Form**

John realized **that he made a mistake.**
He hopes **that people don't notice.**

| MAIN CLAUSE | | NOUN CLAUSE WITH *THAT* | | |
|---|---|---|---|---|
| Subject | Verb | *That* | Subject | Verb |
| John | realized | (that) | he | had made a mistake. |
| He | hopes | | people | will not notice. |

A noun clause can begin with *that*. Like other clauses, *that* clauses have a subject and a verb. We can usually omit *that*.

1. We use *that* clauses after certain verbs that express feelings, thoughts, and opinions. Here are some of these verbs.

| | | | | |
|---|---|---|---|---|
| agree | expect | hope | presume | remember |
| assume | fear | imagine | pretend | show |
| believe | feel | know | prove | suppose |
| decide | figure out | learn | read | suspect |
| discover | find | notice | realize | teach |
| doubt | forget | observe | recognize | think |
| dream | guess | predict | regret | understand |

2. We often omit *that,* especially when we speak. The meaning of the sentence does not change.

> Mary:  I know (that) she is coming soon.
> John:  I hope (that) she does.

3. When the introductory verb is in the present tense, the verb in the noun clause can be in the present, past, or future. It depends on the meaning of the sentence.

> I know she is here.
> I know she will be here.
> I know she was here a few hours ago.

4. To avoid repeating information in giving answers to questions, we can use *so* after verbs like *think, believe, hope, be afraid,* and *guess.*

> Ken:  Is Nancy here today?
> Pat:  I **think so.** (*So* = "that Nancy is here today")

Negative answers can be formed with *so* or with *not,* depending on the verb.

| Question | Affirmative Answer | Negative Answer |
|---|---|---|
| Is Nancy here today? | I think **so.** | I don't think **so.**<br>I think **not.*** |
| Did the rain stop? | I believe **so.** | I don't believe **so.** |
| Are we having dinner soon? | I hope **so.** | I hope **not.** |
| Is Tony going with us? | I guess **so.** | I guess **not.** |
| Did you get your grade on the test? | I'm afraid **so.** | I'm afraid **not.** |

*"I think not" is formal.

## 18 Practice

**Work with a partner or a group. Write sentences that give your own opinion about each statement. Start your sentences with *I believe/think that* or *I don't believe/think that*.**

1. People can live without light.

   *I don't believe that people can live without light.*

2. It is difficult for some people to learn languages.

   _____

3. There are too many talk shows on television.

   _____

4. Men have shorter lives than women.

   _____

5. People will drive cars with atomic power in our lifetime.

   _____

6. Computers will have emotions.

   _____

7. People will be happy all the time.

   _____

8. We will stop having zoos in fifty years.

   _____

**Write two more opinions.**

9. _____

10. _____

## 19 Practice

**Complete the sentences with the verbs in parentheses and *so* or *not*.**

1. Ken: Do we have class today?

   Sue: (think) *I think so* _____. There is no change that I know of.

2. Ken: Can you lend me your book until tomorrow?

   Sue: (be afraid) _____. I need it tonight.

3. Pat: Is John coming to class today?

   Lillian: (think) _____. I just saw him. He was walking

   this way.

**4.** Pat:     Are we going to have a test today?

Lillian:  (believe) _____. The teacher just told me to be ready

for it.

**5.** Pat:     Is it going to be an essay?

Lillian:  (guess) _____. The other tests have been essays.

**6.** Pat:     Are you ready for it?

Lillian:  (hope) _____. I studied all night.

**7.** Janet:   Do you have an extra pen?

Ben:     (think) _____. I always carry an extra one.

**8.** Janet:   Can we use a dictionary during the test?

Ben:     (afraid) _____. Our teacher never lets us do that.

---

**20** **Your Turn**

**Work with a partner. Take turns asking and answering the following questions. Add
some questions of your own. Answer with the verbs in this section.**

**Example:**
You:            Is your English improving?
Your partner:  I think so. It's improving very slowly.
                OR No, I don't think so. I still don't understand the present perfect.

**1.** Is your English improving?
**2.** Would you like to be a teacher?
**3.** Would you like to live in a different country from the one you grew up in?
**4.** Do you think you will change in the future?

# 12g Expressions that Introduce Noun Clauses with *That*

## Form / Function

**It is true** that a cat is not able to taste sweet things.

1. We can use *that* clauses after expressions with *be* + an adjective, or with *be* + a past participle. These expressions show feeling. We can omit the word *that*.

| Main Clause | *That* Clause |
|---|---|
| **I am sorry** | (that) you couldn't come. |
| **I am disappointed** | (that) I failed the test. |

2. Here is a list of some of the adjectives and past participles that can introduce *that* clauses.

| | | | | |
|---|---|---|---|---|
| be afraid | be delighted | be happy | be proud | be terrified |
| be amazed | be disappointed | be horrified | be sad | be thrilled |
| be angry | be fortunate | be impressed | be shocked | be worried |
| be aware | be furious | be lucky | be sure | it is a fact |
| be convinced | be glad | be pleased | be surprised | it is true |

## 21 Practice

**Look at the following facts and write your opinion about each one. Use a *that* clause and one of the expressions from the list.**

I am (not) aware that       I am (not) surprised that
It is (not) a fact that        It is (not) true that

1. There is a town called "Chicken" in Alaska.

   *I am surprised that there is a town called Chicken in Alaska.*

2. Rice is the chief food for half the people in the world.

   _____

**3.** There are 15,000 different kinds of rice.

_____

**4.** Women live longer today than they did 100 years ago.

_____

**5.** Women live longer than men.

_____

**6.** Clouds are higher during the day than during the night.

_____

**7.** Men laugh longer, more loudly, and more often than women.

_____

**8.** Everyone dreams.

_____

**9.** The elephant is the largest animal on land.

_____

**10.** People in India drink tea with a lot of milk, sugar, and spices.

_____

**11.** Hair grows faster at night.

_____

**12.** The smallest country in the world is Vatican City.

_____

| 22 | **Your Turn** |

**Give your opinion about five things or five people. Use a _that_ clause with one of the following expressions or others from this section.**

**Example:**
I am pleased that I passed the test.

| | |
|---|---|
| I'm angry | I'm proud |
| I'm glad | I'm surprised |
| I'm pleased | |

## WRITING: Describe an Event

Write a personal letter that describes something that happened to you in your life.

**Step 1.** Write sentences about an event that happened to you recently that made you feel sad, happy, upset, etc. Use conjunctions and noun clauses in your answers.

1. When did it happen?
2. Where did it happen?
3. What happened?

4. What was the result?
5. How did you feel about it?

**Step 2.** Write a letter to a friend or family member about this experience. Use the sentences from Step 1 and the following model as a guide. For more writing guidelines, see pages 407–411.

> *January 3, 20XX*
>
> *Dear Meg,*
>
> *Happy New Year! We had a good holiday season here. I feel especially happy because of a great thing that happened to me last week.*
>
> *You know that I have been seeing Joe for about a year. Well, on Tuesday, he came over to our house and* _____
> _____
> _____
> _____
> _____
>
> *You can imagine how I felt. Please write back and let me know what you think.*
>
> *Your friend,*
> *Cathy*

**Step 3. Evaluate your letter.**

**Checklist**

_____ Did you put the date at the top of your letter?

_____ Did you start your letter with "Dear" and the person's name?

_____ Did you write an introductory paragraph?

_____ Did you describe the event that happened to you?

_____ Did you write a concluding paragraph?

_____ Did you end your letter with a phrase such as "Yours truly" or "Love" and your name?

**Step 4. Edit your work.** Work with a partner or your teacher to edit your paragraph. Check spelling, vocabulary, and grammar.

**Step 5. Write your final copy.**

**A** Choose the best answer, A, B, C, or D, to complete the sentence. Mark your answer by darkening the oval with the same letter.

1. Tom: I hate fish.
   Jack: I _____. I don't like the smell.

   **A.** too     Ⓐ Ⓑ Ⓒ Ⓓ
   **B.** either
   **C.** neither
   **D.** do, too

2. Ken was born in Hong Kong. So _____ his sister.

   **A.** didn't     Ⓐ Ⓑ Ⓒ Ⓓ
   **B.** did
   **C.** was
   **D.** wasn't

3. I wonder _____ the movie.

   **A.** if liked she     Ⓐ Ⓑ Ⓒ Ⓓ
   **B.** if did she like
   **C.** if she liked
   **D.** if or not she liked

4. I don't know _____.

   **A.** what job she does     Ⓐ Ⓑ Ⓒ Ⓓ
   **B.** if job she does
   **C.** what does she job
   **D.** what job does she

5. It is a fact _____ everybody dreams.

   **A.** that     Ⓐ Ⓑ Ⓒ Ⓓ
   **B.** if
   **C.** what
   **D.** whether

6. He had a rash, a headache, _____ a temperature from the bad food.

   **A.** but     Ⓐ Ⓑ Ⓒ Ⓓ
   **B.** so
   **C.** and
   **D.** or

7. I have a computer, _____ I read the news on the Internet.

   **A.** so     Ⓐ Ⓑ Ⓒ Ⓓ
   **B.** and
   **C.** or
   **D.** but

8. Bill: Are we having a test today?
   Lisa: _____.

   **A.** I hope not     Ⓐ Ⓑ Ⓒ Ⓓ
   **B.** I don't hope so
   **C.** I don't guess so
   **D.** I don't think

9. Chris: Is the teacher here today?
   Pat: _____.

   **A.** I think     Ⓐ Ⓑ Ⓒ Ⓓ
   **B.** I don't hope
   **C.** I guess so
   **D.** I believe

10. Ken doesn't have a car and _____.

    **A.** neither does not     Ⓐ Ⓑ Ⓒ Ⓓ
    John
    **B.** neither does John
    **C.** neither John does
    **D.** John doesn't neither

**B** **Find the underlined word or phrase, A, B, C, or D, that is incorrect. Mark your answer by darkening the oval with the same letter.**

1. It is a fact what about two-thirds of your
     A        B
   body is water.
       C  D

   Ⓐ Ⓑ Ⓒ Ⓓ

2. Chimpanzees are very intelligent creatures
             A       B
   and too are dolphins.
       C  D

   Ⓐ Ⓑ Ⓒ Ⓓ

3. I asked that salt water freezes at a
         A         B
   lower temperature than fresh water.
    C            D

   Ⓐ Ⓑ Ⓒ Ⓓ

4. Most vegetarians eat dairy products, such
                 A
   as cheese and milk, and vegans avoid all
      B      C
   animal products.
       D

   Ⓐ Ⓑ Ⓒ Ⓓ

5. Many island people in Indonesia and the
                    A
   Philippines live on boats but in houses
          B      C
   made of wood over the water.
       D

   Ⓐ Ⓑ Ⓒ Ⓓ

6. I think if the most popular sport
         A   B       C
   in Japan is baseball.
        D

   Ⓐ Ⓑ Ⓒ Ⓓ

7. I don't know if makes the sky blue,
             A   B   C
   do you?
    D

   Ⓐ Ⓑ Ⓒ Ⓓ

8. I wonder if or not a person can grow after
            A     B     C     D
   the age of eighteen?

   Ⓐ Ⓑ Ⓒ Ⓓ

9. Picasso was a painter who painted in
          A        B
   several different styles, but greatly
                   C
   influenced other painters of his time.
            D

   Ⓐ Ⓑ Ⓒ Ⓓ

10. Can you tell me how far is it from here to
              A   B   C        D
    the train station?

    Ⓐ Ⓑ Ⓒ Ⓓ

# UNIT 13

## ADJECTIVE AND ADVERB CLAUSES

# 13a Adjective Clauses with *Who, Whom,* and *That* Referring to People

A pilot is a person **that flies airplanes.**
I know a man **who is a pilot.**

1. An adjective clause is used with a main clause. An adjective clause describes or gives information about a noun in the main clause.

| MAIN CLAUSE | ADJECTIVE CLAUSE |
|---|---|
| A pilot is a person | **that flies airplanes.** |
| I know a man | **who is a pilot.** |

2. *Who* and *that* are relative pronouns. Relative pronouns begin adjective clauses.

3. We use *who* or *that* to refer to people. *Who* and *that* can be the subject of an adjective clause.

| MAIN CLAUSE | ADJECTIVE CLAUSE | | |
|---|---|---|---|
| | Subject | Verb | |
| There is the woman | **who** | flew | the plane. |
| There's the flight attendant | **that** | helped | us. |

4. *Whom* also refers to people. In an adjective clause, *whom* is always an object.

| MAIN CLAUSE | ADJECTIVE CLAUSE | | |
|---|---|---|---|
| | Object | Subject | Verb |
| That's the pilot | **whom** | I | know. |

*Whom* is very formal English. When writing, we use *whom* only in formal situations such as writing for school. When speaking, we use *whom* only in formal situations such as giving a speech. We use *that* or *who,* not *whom,* as an object relative pronoun in ordinary speech and writing.

5. An adjective clause comes after the noun it describes. Sometimes the main clause comes in two parts.

> The pilot whom I know is young.
> Main Clause:        The pilot is young
> Adjective Clause:   whom I know
>
> CORRECT:        The **pilot whom** I know is young.
> INCORRECT:      The pilot is young ~~whom I know~~.

## 1 Practice

**Match the definitions with the correct adjective clause.**

_e_  **1.** A pilot is a person      **a.** who rides bikes.

_____ **2.** A jockey is a person      **b.** who sails ships.

_____ **3.** A sailor is a person      **c.** who rides racehorses.

_____ **4.** A race car driver is a person      **d.** who travels into space.

_____ **5.** An astronaut is a person      **e.** who flies planes.

_____ **6.** A cyclist is a person      **f.** who drives fast cars.

## 2 Practice

**Complete the definitions with an adjective clause using *who* or *that*. Use the phrases from the list.**

| | |
|---|---|
| cuts men's hair | serves people in a restaurant |
| fixes cars | trains athletes |
| fixes teeth | works in a bank |
| helps sick people | writes for a newspaper |

**1.** A mechanic _is a person who fixes cars._

**2.** A barber _____

**3.** A doctor _____

**4.** A coach _____

**5.** A waiter _____

**6.** A journalist _____

**7.** A dentist _____

**8.** A teller _____

## 3 Practice

**Read the first two sentences. Then complete the third sentence with an adjective clause. Use *who* if the relative pronoun is the subject. Use *whom* if it is the object.**

1. That's the woman. I dated her a few times last year.

    That's the woman _whom I dated a few times last year._

2. She's the one. She had a lot of money.

    She's the one _____

3. She had an assistant. The assistant did everything for her.

    She had an assistant _____

4. She had a driver. She paid him to take care of her three cars.

    She had a driver _____

5. She had a cook. He made fantastic food.

    She had a cook _____

6. Unfortunately, she wasn't the woman. I wanted to marry her.

    Unfortunately, she wasn't the woman _____

7. I found another woman. She works as a librarian.

    I found another woman _____

8. She says I'm the man. She wants to marry me.

    She says I'm the man _____

9. She's the woman. She will be my wife.

    She's the woman _____

10. We'll be two people. We won't have much money.

    We'll be two people _____

11. But we'll be two people. We will be happy.

    But we'll be two people _____

## 4 Practice

**Combine the two sentences into one sentence. Use *who* if the relative pronoun is a subject. Use *whom* if it is an object.**

1. Grace Kelly was an actress. This actress became Princess Grace of Monaco.

    _Grace Kelly was an actress who became Princess Grace_
    _of Monaco._

2. The Beatles were four young men. These young men became famous all over the world.

    _____

**3.** Brad Pitt is an actor. This actor stars in a lot of popular movies.

_____

**4.** The man was a movie director. We saw him in the restaurant.

_____

**5.** James Dean was an actor. This actor died young.

_____

**6.** The opera singer isn't Spanish. We heard him last night.

_____

**7.** Louis Armstrong was a famous jazz musician. This musician played the trumpet.

_____

**8.** There was a beautiful actress. We met her at the party.

_____

**9.** The singer is giving a concert here next week. I like her so much.

_____

**10.** Celine Dion is a singer. I'm sure you have heard her.

_____

**11.** Who is that detective on TV? He always solves the problem.

_____

**12.** Sophia Loren is a famous movie star. Everybody knows her.

_____

## 5 | Your Turn

**Make sentences with adjective clauses to describe these people.**

**Example:**

a friend
A friend is someone who tells you the truth.

a friend
a teacher
a leader
a grandfather

# 13b Adjective Clauses with *That* and *Which* Referring to Things

An orange is a kind of fruit
**that** has a lot of vitamin C.

1. We use *who (whom)/that* to refer to people. We use *that/which* to refer to things.

   Casimir Funk was the man **who/that** invented the word "vitamin".
   An orange is a fruit **that/which** has a lot of vitamin C.

2. *That* and *which* can be subject relative pronouns or object relative pronouns.

   You must get the vitamins **that/which** are important to your health.
   (*That/which* is the subject of the verb *are*.)

   The vitamins **that/which** I take are expensive.
   (*That/which* is the object of the verb *take*.)

3. When an adjective clause has a subject relative pronoun, its verb agrees with the
   word that the relative pronoun refers to.

   A fruit that **is** healthy is the orange.

   A person who **plays** sports needs a lot of energy.

   It is important to eat vegetables that **are** good for you.

   People who **play** sports need a lot of energy.

## 6 Practice

**Complete the sentences with *who* or *which*. Then check whether you think the sentences are true or false.**

1. A person __who__ drinks a lot of water is healthy.    T _____    F _____
2. Food _____ is fresh is good for you.    T _____    F _____
3. Onions are vegetables _____ make you cry.    T _____    F _____
4. Carrots are vegetables _____ make your hair red.    T _____    F _____
5. Children _____ eat a lot of butter and sugar grow tall.    T _____    F _____
6. People _____ drink a lot of coffee sleep a lot.    T _____    F _____
7. Foods _____ have a lot of sugar and fat can make you fat.    T _____    F _____
8. People _____ eat a lot of vegetables are healthy.    T _____    F _____
9. A person _____ exercises is healthy.    T _____    F _____
10. A child _____ eats a lot of candy can develop bad teeth.    T _____    F _____
11. Spinach is a food _____ is good for you.    T _____    F _____
12. Milk is a food _____ is important for babies.    T _____    F _____

## 7 Practice

**Underline the correct verb in parentheses.**

1. Australia is a country that (have / <u>has</u>) some special animals.
2. Kangaroos are animals that (live / lives) in Australia.
3. A kangaroo is an animal that (carry / carries) its baby in a pouch.
4. The ostrich is also a bird that (live / lives) in Australia.
5. Ostriches are birds that (run / runs) very fast.
6. An ostrich is a bird that (doesn't / don't) fly.
7. I met some people who (have / has) ostrich farms.
8. Ostriches have feathers that (is / are) beautiful.
9. Some animals that (live / lives) in New Zealand are special too.
10. Kiwis are birds that (live / lives) in New Zealand.
11. A kiwi is a bird that (have / has) very small wings and cannot fly.
12. People who (live / lives) in New Zealand are often called Kiwis.

# 13c Omission of *Who*, *That*, and *Which*

**Form / Function**

That's the funny tourist we met yesterday.

1. When the relative pronoun *who (whom)*, *which,* or *that* is the object of an adjective clause, we can leave it out.

   He's the funny tourist **that** we met yesterday.
   OR He's the funny tourist we met yesterday. (*That* is left out.)

2. We cannot leave out *who, which,* and *that* when they are the subject of the sentence.

   CORRECT:     The man who talked to us yesterday is funny.
   INCORRECT:  ~~The man talked to us yesterday is funny.~~ (*Who* cannot be left out.)

## 8 Practice

**Complete the sentences with the relative pronouns *who, that,* or *which*. If the relative pronoun can be left out, write *X*.**

1. Albert Einstein is a name _____ *X* _____ everybody knows.

2. Albert Einstein was a genius _____ *who* _____ started to speak when he was three years old.

3. Albert was a boy _____ hated school, but he loved to read at home.

4. Science was the subject _____ he loved the most.

5. He had a violin _____ he played often.

6. After his graduation from college in 1900, Einstein was a young man _____ could not find a job.

7. After Einstein graduated from college in 1900, he had a friend _____ helped him get a job.

8. He got a job in a government office _____ he didn't like very much.

9. Einstein was a man _____ wanted to find answers to many difficult questions.

10. Einstein had many ideas _____ changed the world.

11. He was a man _____ people didn't understand.

12. Einstein was a man _____ often forgot things.

13. He wore a coat _____ was old.

14. Clothes were things _____ were not important to him.

15. In 1922, he received a prize _____ made him famous. It was the Nobel Prize.

16. Princeton, New Jersey, was the town in the United States _____ became Einstein's home.

17. When Einstein died at the age of 76 in New Jersey, scientists _____ admired his work were sad.

18. Because of Einstein, scientists have important knowledge _____ they can use to help us understand the universe.

# 13d Adjective Clauses with *Whose*

**Form / Function**

A: What's a mermaid?
B: That's a legendary woman **whose** body is like a fish from the waist down.

1. We use the relative pronoun *whose* to show possession. We use *whose* instead of possessive adjectives like *my, your,* and *his* with people, animals, and things.

   A mermaid is a legendary woman. **Her** body is like a fish from the waist down.
   A mermaid is a legendary woman **whose** body is like a fish from the waist down.

   I know the man. **His** house is by the river.
   I know the man **whose** house is by the river.

2. We use *whose* to refer to people. In informal English, we also use *whose* to refer to things.

   New York is a city **whose** restaurants are very good.

3. Do not confuse *whose* with *who's*. They sound the same, but their meanings are different.

|  | Form | Example |
|---|---|---|
| **Who's** | A contraction of *who is* | A: **Who's** that? <br> B: It's Jack. |
| **Whose** | A relative pronoun | That's the man **whose** car was stolen. |

## 9 Practice

**Combine the sentences using *whose*.**

1. The student will win the prize. The student's essay is the best.

   *The student whose essay is the best will win the prize.*

2. I know a man. His brother is a guitarist in a pop group.

   _____

3. I won't go out with a man. His hair is always a mess.

   _____

4. I hear someone. Her voice is beautiful.

   _____

5. Those are the girls. Their Portuguese is almost perfect.

   _____

6. I once met someone. His conversations were always about food.

   _____

**7.** I have a friend. Nobody can pronounce his last name.

_____

**8.** I like people. Their lives are organized.

_____

## 10 Practice

**Complete the questions with _who_ for people, _that_ for things, and _whose_ to show possession. Then circle the answer that you think is correct.**

**1.** Who was the person _____who_____ invented the light bulb?

    **a.** George Washington    **b.** Thomas Edison    **c.** Vincent Van Gogh

**2.** What is the name of the long river _____ is in Africa?

    **a.** The Nile    **b.** The Mississippi    **c.** The Seine

**3.** What is the name of the painter _____ most famous painting is the _Mona Lisa_?

    **a.** Pablo Picasso    **b.** Leonardo da Vinci    **c.** Jean Renoir

**4.** What is the name of the writer _____ wrote _Hamlet_?

    **a.** Charles Dickens    **b.** William Shakespeare    **c.** Ernest Hemingway

**5.** What's the name of the country _____ capital city is Buenos Aires?

    **a.** Mexico    **b.** Spain    **c.** Argentina

**6.** What is the name of the South American country _____ people speak Portuguese?

    **a.** Argentina    **b.** Chile    **c.** Brazil

**7.** What is the name of the woman _____ helped the poor and sick in India?

    **a.** Mother Teresa    **b.** Florence Nightingale    **c.** Princess Diana

**8.** What is the name of the country _____ has the most people in the world?

    **a.** The United States    **b.** Japan    **c.** China

**9.** What is the name of the man _____ was the first to walk on the moon?

    **a.** Neil Armstrong    **b.** Frank Sinatra    **c.** John Kennedy

**10.** What is the name of the man _____ home was Graceland, in Memphis, Tennessee?

    **a.** John Lennon    **b.** Mick Jagger    **c.** Elvis Presley

# 13e Adjective Clauses with Prepositional Phrases

A measuring tape is something you measure things **with**.

1. The relative pronouns *who (whom), that,* and *which* can be the objects of prepositions in an adjective clause.

   I was sitting on a chair. It was uncomfortable. The chair **that I was sitting on** was uncomfortable.

2. There are two structures for prepositional phrases with relative pronoun objects. In informal English, we can also use different relative pronouns.

| THE RELATIVE PRONOUN REFERS TO A THING | | | |
|---|---|---|---|
| Rules | Main Clause | Adjective Clause | End of Main Clause |
| **Informal English:** The preposition goes at the end of the adjective clause. | The chair | **that** I was sitting **on** | was uncomfortable. |
| | | **which** I was sitting **on** | |
| | | I was sitting **on** | |
| **Formal English:** The preposition goes at the beginning of the adjective clause. The relative pronoun must be *which*. | The chair | **on which** I was sitting | was uncomfortable. |

| THE RELATIVE PRONOUN REFERS TO A PERSON | | | |
|---|---|---|---|
| Rules | Main Clause | Adjective Clause | End of Main Clause |
| **Informal English:** The preposition goes at the end of the adjective clause. | The woman | **that** I was talking **to** | was interesting. |
| | | **who** I was talking **to** | |
| | | I was talking **to** | |
| **Formal English:** The preposition goes at the beginning of the adjective clause. The relative pronoun must be *whom*. | The woman | **to whom** I was talking | was interesting. |

3. The choices of relative pronouns are the same as for other kinds of objects. In informal English, you can omit the relative pronoun because it is an object.

> The woman **that/who** I was talking **to** was interesting.
> OR The woman I was talking **to** was interesting.

But when we use formal English and put the preposition first, we must use the relative pronoun.

> CORRECT:     The woman **to whom** I was talking was interesting.
> INCORRECT:   The woman ~~to I was talking~~ was interesting.

## II Practice

**First complete the definitions using informal English. Then write the definitions again using formal English. Use the phrases in the list.**

| | | |
|---|---|---|
| are honest with | get information from | sleep in |
| care for | laugh at | travel in |
| climb on | look through | work toward |
| drink from | play with | write with |
| eat with | sit on | |

1. Informal: A pen is something you _write with._

   Formal: _A pen is something with which you write._

2. Informal: A bed is something you _____

   Formal: _____

3. Informal: A cup is something you _____

   Formal: _____

4. Informal: A goal is something you _____

   Formal: _____

5. Informal: A chair and a stool are things you _____

   Formal: _____

6. Informal: A spoon is something you _____

   Formal: _____

7. Informal: A best friend is a person you _____

   Formal: _____

8. Informal: A ladder is something you _____

   Formal: _____

9. Informal: The Internet is something you _____

   Formal: _____

**10.** Informal: A circus clown is someone you _____

　　　Formal: _____

**11.** Informal: A car is something you _____

　　　Formal: _____

**12.** Informal: A ball is a thing you _____

　　　Formal: _____

**13.** Informal: A telescope is something you _____

　　　Formal: _____

**14.** Informal: A sick person is someone you _____

　　　Formal: _____

---

## 12 | Your Turn

**Choose one of the following objects for the class to guess. The class asks questions about the object. Use informal English, and do not use *which* or *that*.**

**Example:**

Your classmate:　　Is it something you speak into?

You:　　Yes, it is. OR No, it isn't.

| | | |
|---|---|---|
| a can opener | a notebook | an umbrella |
| a cushion | a telephone | |

---

# 13f Adverb Clauses with *Because*

**Form**

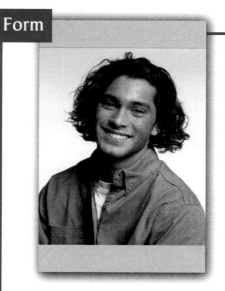

Carlos is happy **because he passed the test.**

1. A main clause has a subject and a verb and can stand alone as a complete sentence.

    Carlos is happy.

2. An adverb clause also has a subject and a verb, but it is not a complete sentence. We must use it with a main clause.

| MAIN CLAUSE | | | ADVERB CLAUSE | | | |
|---|---|---|---|---|---|---|
| Subject | Verb | | Conjunction | Subject | Verb | |
| Carlos | is | happy | because | he | passed | the test. |

3. *Because* is a conjunction that can begin an adverb clause.

4. An adverb clause can come at the beginning or at the end of a sentence. It has the same meaning. If the adverb clause comes at the beginning, we put a comma after the adverb clause.

    Carlos is happy **because he passed the test.**
    **Because Carlos passed the test,** he is happy.

## Function

We use the conjunction *because* to give a reason for something or to say why something happens. *Because* answers the question *why*.

    Carlos is happy. **Why** is he happy? He's happy **because he passed the test.**

## 13 Practice

**Combine the sentences with *because* in two different ways as in the example. Use correct punctuation.**

1. Pete failed the test. He didn't study.

    *Pete failed the test because he didn't study.*

    *Because Pete didn't study, he failed the test.*

2. Pete didn't have time to study. He was working.

    _____

    _____

3. Pete worked. He needed money.

    _____

    _____

**4.** Pete needed money. He wanted to help his family.

_____

_____

**5.** Pete's family had problems. His father lost his job.

_____

_____

**6.** His father lost his job. The company closed down.

_____

_____

**7.** His father couldn't find another job. The economy was bad.

_____

_____

**8.** Today, Pete is happy. His father found a new job.

_____

_____

<u>14</u> **What Do You Think?**

**What do you think Pete will do now? Why?**

# 13g Adverb Clauses with _Although_ and _Even Though_

<table>
<tr>
<td>**Form**</td>
<td></td>
</tr>
</table>

**Although** he has a car, he uses inline skates in the city.

1. _Although_ and _even though_ are conjunctions that can begin an adverb clause.

2. Like clauses with _because,_ clauses with _although_ and _even though_ can come at the beginning or at the end of a sentence. If they come at the beginning of a sentence, we put a comma after the clause.

   He went to work **although he was sick.**
   **Although he was sick,** he went to work.

1. *Although* and *even though* have the same meaning.

   **Although** he was sick, he went to work.
   **Even though** he was sick, he went to work.

2. We use *although* and *even though* to show contrast or an unexpected result.

   **Even though** it was snowing, the road was clear.
   **Although** it was cold, he wasn't wearing a coat.

15  Practice

**Complete the sentences using *who* for people, *that* for things, *because*, and *although*. Add commas where necessary.**

J. Paul Getty became a millionaire when he was 24. ___*Although*___ his father
                                                              1
was rich he did not help his son. Getty was a hard worker _____ made his
                                                                   2
money from oil. _____ Getty was a millionaire he wasn't happy.
                      3
_____ he married five times he was not happy. _____ he
      4                                                          5
had five children he didn't love them.

For a man _____ was the richest man in the world at one time, he was
                  6
tight with his money. _____ he was an American he loved to live in
                            7
England. He bought a house in England _____ had 72 bedrooms, but it had
                                              8
pay phones in the bedrooms _____ Getty wanted to save money on phone
                                  9
bills. _____ he was very rich he wrote down every dollar he spent every
          10
evening. _____ he could eat anything he wanted he ate simple food.
              11
_____ Getty didn't like to spend money he bought beautiful and
      12
expensive pieces of art. _____ he loved art he didn't care about the price.
                              13
Today, the wonderful pieces of art _____ he bought are in a museum. It is
                                          14
a museum _____ is in California. It is one of the most famous museums in
              15
the United States. It is called the J. Paul Getty Museum.

# WRITING: Write a Description

Describe a photo of your family or friends.

**Step 1. Bring a photo of some of your family and/or friends to class. Tell your partner about the photo.**

**1.** Who is in the photo?

**2.** Where was the photo taken?

**3.** How are the people related to you/how do you know the people?

**4.** What are their physical characteristics?

**5.** What are their personalities like?

**6.** What are they studying, or what do they do for a living?

**Step 2. Write a sentence or two about the place in the photo.**

**Examples:**
The photo shows the house that I grew up in. Although it is small, we all like it.

**Step 3. Write a sentence or two about each person in the photo. Use *who, whom, whose, that, which, because, even though,* or *although*.**

**Examples:**
There is a cake because it is my birthday. The person who is next to me is my aunt. That's the aunt whose husband is a doctor.

**Step 4. Write a paragraph about the photo. Write a title in three or four words. For more writing guidelines, see pages 407–411.**

**Step 5. Evaluate your paragraph.**

**Checklist**

_____ Did you give your paragraph a title?

_____ Did you indent your paragraph?

_____ Did you describe the people and the place in the photo?

**Step 6. Work with a partner or your teacher to correct grammar, spelling, and punctuation.**

**Step 7. Write your final copy.**

# SELF-TEST

A  **Choose the best answer, A, B, C, or D, to complete the sentence. Mark your answer by darkening the oval with the same letter.**

1. Beethoven was a great composer _____ deaf for much of his life.

   **A.** who was    Ⓐ Ⓑ Ⓒ Ⓓ
   **B.** whose
   **C.** who's
   **D.** whom was

2. The largest animal _____ on land is the elephant.

   **A.** that live    Ⓐ Ⓑ Ⓒ Ⓓ
   **B.** that lives
   **C.** who lives
   **D.** whom live

3. Louis Pasteur was a French professor _____ showed that germs cause many diseases.

   **A.** whom    Ⓐ Ⓑ Ⓒ Ⓓ
   **B.** who was
   **C.** whose
   **D.** who

4. The panda is an animal _____ only food is the bamboo plant.

   **A.** that    Ⓐ Ⓑ Ⓒ Ⓓ
   **B.** which is
   **C.** whose
   **D.** which

5. People _____ money to charity are called donors.

   **A.** whom give    Ⓐ Ⓑ Ⓒ Ⓓ
   **B.** who gives
   **C.** which give
   **D.** who give

6. A barometer is an instrument _____ air pressure.

   **A.** who measures    Ⓐ Ⓑ Ⓒ Ⓓ
   **B.** that measures
   **C.** which measure
   **D.** whose measures

7. The blue whale is the largest animal _____.

   **A.** who lives    Ⓐ Ⓑ Ⓒ Ⓓ
   **B.** that live
   **C.** that lives
   **D.** whom lives

8. Biographies are books _____ the stories of people's lives.

   **A.** that tell    Ⓐ Ⓑ Ⓒ Ⓓ
   **B.** whom tell
   **C.** that tells
   **D.** who tells

9. Thomas A. Watson was the first person _____ Alexander Graham Bell talked on the first telephone call.

   **A.** whom    Ⓐ Ⓑ Ⓒ Ⓓ
   **B.** who to
   **C.** to whom
   **D.** whom to

10. We have seasons _____ the Earth goes around the sun.

    **A.** although    Ⓐ Ⓑ Ⓒ Ⓓ
    **B.** because
    **C.** who
    **D.** that

**B   Find the underlined word A, B, C, or D, that is incorrect. Mark your answer by darkening the oval with the same letter.**

1. There are many flowers who close up
   A      B              C
   at night.
   D

   Ⓐ Ⓑ Ⓒ Ⓓ

2. Because he was famous and talented,
   A        B
   Mozart died poor and alone.
          C    D

   Ⓐ Ⓑ Ⓒ Ⓓ

3. When people get older, their lungs get
                           A
   darker although they breathe dirty air.
          B       C         D

   Ⓐ Ⓑ Ⓒ Ⓓ

4. Picasso was a Spanish artist whom is the
                A        B      C
   best known 20th Century painter.
                      D

   Ⓐ Ⓑ Ⓒ Ⓓ

5. Egypt is a country in Africa who's capital
   A      B                   C
   is Cairo.
   D

   Ⓐ Ⓑ Ⓒ Ⓓ

6. Mark Twain was an American writer whom
                   A              B
   real name was Samuel Clemens.
   C        D

   Ⓐ Ⓑ Ⓒ Ⓓ

7. African elephants have large ears who
                      A            B
   help them to keep cool in the hot climate.
   C    D

   Ⓐ Ⓑ Ⓒ Ⓓ

8. The holiday who is on the fourth Thursday
              A      B
   in November is Thanksgiving Day.
   C        D

   Ⓐ Ⓑ Ⓒ Ⓓ

9. Because so much of the Amazon forest
   A
   has been destroyed, it is still the biggest
                       B         C
   forest in the world.
          D

   Ⓐ Ⓑ Ⓒ Ⓓ

10. Palm trees are not like other trees
               A      B
    although they do not grow side branches.
    C              D

    Ⓐ Ⓑ Ⓒ Ⓓ

# UNIT 14

# REPORTED SPEECH AND CONDITIONAL CLAUSES

# 14a Quoted Speech

Elvis said, "I don't know anything about music. In my line, you don't have to."

Quoted speech tells who said something and what they said.

1. We can put the name of the speaker at the beginning of the sentence.

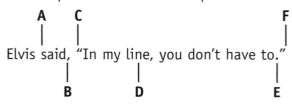

**A.** Mention the speaker and use a verb like *said*.
**B.** Put a comma after the verb.
**C.** Open the quotation marks (").
**D.** Write the quotation. Capitalize the first word.
**E.** End the quotation with a period, a question mark, or an exclamation point.
**F.** Close the quotation marks (").

2. We can also put the name of the speaker at the end of the sentence.

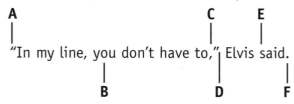

**A.** Open the quotation marks.
**B.** Write the quotation. Capitalize the first word.
**C.** If the original quotation ended in a period, use a comma at the end. If it ended in a question mark or an exclamation point, use those punctuation marks.
**D.** Close the quotation marks.
**E.** Mention the speaker and use a word like *said*.
**F.** End the sentence with a period.

3. We can also put the name of the speaker after *said*.

   "In my line, you don't have to," said Elvis.

4. If there is more than one sentence in the quotation, we put quotation marks only at the beginning and at the end of the whole quotation. We do not use separate quotation marks for each sentence.

   CORRECT:    My mother said, "Elvis was my favorite singer when I was young. He changed my world."

   INCORRECT:  My mother said, "Elvis was my favorite singer when I was young." "He changed my world."

## Function

We use quoted speech for the exact words someone uses. We use quoted speech in novels, stories, and newspaper articles.

| Source | Example |
|---|---|
| A newspaper article | "I'm retiring at the end of the season," the star player said. |
| A story about Thomas Edison | Edison said, "I have not failed. I've just found 10,000 ways that won't work." |

## 1 | Practice

**Nasreddin Hoca (Hodja) is a character in Turkish folktales. Write quoted speech for the speaker's words in this story. Use the verb *said* and the correct punctuation.**

*Nasreddin had a leaky ferry boat and used it to row people across the river. One day his passenger was a fussy schoolteacher, and on the way across the teacher decided to give Nasreddin a test to see how much he knew.*

1. The schoolteacher: Tell me, Nasreddin, what are eight times six?

   *The schoolteacher said, "Tell me, Nasreddin, what are eight times six?"*

2. Nasreddin: I have no idea.

   _____

3. The schoolteacher: How do you spell *magnificence?*

   _____

4. Nasreddin: I don't know.

   _____

**5.** The schoolteacher: Didn't you study anything at school?

_____

**6.** Nasreddin: No.

_____

**7.** The schoolteacher: In that case, half your life is lost.

_____

*Just then, there was a very bad storm, and the boat began to go down.*

**8.** Nasreddin: Tell me, schoolteacher, did you ever learn to swim?

_____

**9.** The schoolteacher: No.

_____

**10.** Nasreddin: In that case, your whole life is lost.

_____

# 14b Reported Speech

## Form

Muhammed Ali said that he was the greatest.

1. Reported speech has a main clause and a noun clause.

2. We use reporting verbs such as *say* or *tell* in the main clause.

| MAIN CLAUSE | | NOUN CLAUSE | |
|---|---|---|---|
| Speaker | Reporting Verb | (That) | Reported Speech |
| Muhammad Ali | said | (that) | he was the greatest. |
| Mary | says | (that) | she is happy. |

3. We can leave out *that*.

> Muhammed Ali said **that** he was the greatest.
> OR Muhammed Ali said he was the greatest.

4. If the reporting verb is in the present tense, there is no change in tense of the verb in the noun clause.

> QUOTED SPEECH:     Mary says, "I **am** happy."
> REPORTED SPEECH: Mary **says** that she **is** happy.

5. If the reporting verb is in the past (for example, *said, told*) the verb tense in the noun clause changes when we report it. Some modal auxiliaries change, too.

> QUOTED SPEECH:     Muhammad Ali said, "I **am** the greatest."
> REPORTED SPEECH: Muhammad Ali **said** that he **was** the greatest.

This chart shows the tense changes.

| QUOTED SPEECH | | REPORTED SPEECH | |
| Verb Tense or Modal | Example | Verb | Example |
| --- | --- | --- | --- |
| Simple Present | He said, "I **do** the work." | Simple Past | He said that he **did** the work. |
| Present Progressive | He said, "I **am doing** the work." | Past Progressive | He said that he **was doing** the work. |
| Simple Past | He said, "I **did** the work." | Past Perfect | He said that he **had done** the work. |
| Past Progressive | He said, "I **was doing** the work." | Past Perfect Progressive | He said that he **had been doing** the work. |
| Present Perfect | He said, "I **have done** the work." | Past Perfect | He said that he **had done** the work. |
| Future with *Be Going To* | He said, "I **am going** to do the work." | Simple Past for *Be* (*Going To*) | He said that he **was going to do** the work. |
| Future with *Will* | He said, "I **will do** the work." | *Would* | He said that he **would do** the work. |
| *Can* | He said, "I **can do** the work." | *Could* | He said that he **could do** the work. |
| *Have to* | He said, "I **have to do** the work." | *Had to* | He said that he **had to do** the work. |
| *Must* | He said, "I **must do** the work." | *Had to* | He said that he **had to do** the work. |

6. There are many possible pronoun changes in reported speech. We use the logic of each situation to decide on the changes.

    QUOTED SPEECH:    Bob said to Alice, "**You** gave me the wrong book."
    REPORTED SPEECH: Bob said that **she** had given him the wrong book.

    QUOTED SPEECH:    Bob said to me, "**You** gave me the wrong book."
    REPORTED SPEECH: Bob said that **I** had given him the wrong book.

The following are some pronoun changes.

| PRONOUN CHANGES | | |
|---|---|---|
| **Subject Pronouns** | I, you (singular) | he, she, I |
| | we, you (plural) | they, we |
| **Object Pronouns** | me, you (singular) | him, her, me |
| | you (plural) | us, them |
| | us (plural) | them |

7. Time expressions can change in reported speech.

    QUOTED SPEECH:    Jim said, "**Tomorrow** is my birthday."
    REPORTED SPEECH: Jim said that his birthday was **the next day.**

| TIME EXPRESSION CHANGES | |
|---|---|
| Quoted Speech | Reported Speech |
| now | then, at that time |
| today, tonight | that day, that night |
| yesterday | the day before |
| tomorrow | the next day |
| this week | that week |
| last week | the week before |
| next week | the week after |
| two weeks ago | two weeks before |

## Function

We use reported speech when we report what someone says or said. We use it when we do not want to use the exact words. We use reported speech often in both speech and writing.

## 2 Practice

**Rewrite the sentences as reported speech. Make the necessary changes to verbs and pronouns. In some cases, there is no tense change.**

1. Ben says, "I love swimming."

   *Ben says that he loves swimming.*

2. Kate says, "I can't swim, but I can ride a bicycle."

   _____

3. The newspaper article says, "Swimming is an excellent sport."

   _____

4. Dr. Carter said, "You have to do some exercise every day."

   _____

5. He said, "Twenty minutes a day is enough."

   _____

6. My mother said, "I can walk a lot."

   _____

7. My father said, "I'll go to the gym tomorrow."

   _____

8. Alice said, "I can go with you."

   _____

9. Tony said, "I went to the gym yesterday."

   _____

10. Paul said, "I have been to the gym this week."

    _____

11. Suzy said, "I go every day."

    _____

## 3 Your Turn

**Make up two events that could happen in a country's government. They don't have to be true. They can be funny. Write them on a piece of paper and give it to the teacher. The teacher will distribute the pieces of paper to the class. Using reported speech, tell the class what the headlines say.**

**Example:**
The president's dog bit a reporter.
You: It says that the president's dog bit a reporter.

# 14c *Say* or *Tell*

A: **Tell me,** Sandy, what did he **say** on the show?

B: He didn't **say anything.** He **said good evening**. Then he **said a few words** about how happy he was to be the host of the show. Then he **told us** a funny story about his girlfriend.

A: That's me, Sandy. That's me!

1. We use *say* with or without a prepositional phrase with *to*.

    CORRECT:     Linda said that she was thirsty.
    CORRECT:     Linda said **to me** that she was thirsty.
    INCORRECT: Linda ~~said me~~ that she was thirsty.

2. We always use *tell* with an object. We do not use a propositional phrase with *to* after *tell*.

    CORRECT:     Linda told **me** that she was thirsty.
    INCORRECT: Linda ~~told that~~ she was thirsty.
    INCORRECT: Linda ~~told to me~~ that she was thirsty.

3. We use *say* and *tell* with some special expressions.

| Say | Tell |
|---|---|
| Say something/anything/nothing | Tell the truth/a lie |
| Say one's prayers | Tell a story/a secret |
| Say a few words | Tell the time |
| Say good morning/good afternoon/etc. | Tell the difference |

## 4 Practice

**Complete the sentences with _say_ or _tell_ in the correct tense.**

**A.**

"No talking Jimmy," the teacher ___*said*___. "I didn't _____ anything,"
                              1                              2

Jimmy _____ the teacher. "Don't _____ lies," the teacher _____.
         3                              4                              5

"I can _____ the difference when someone talks and when someone doesn't talk,"
          6

the teacher _____ the class. "Now, I don't want to hear a sound. Is that clear?"
               7

the teacher _____.
               8

**B.**

"Yesterday Meg _____ she was moving to Alaska," Karen _____. "She
                  1                                           2

_____ me that she had found a good job there."
    3

"I don't believe that," Mike _____. "Last month she _____ me she
                                4                              5

was going to Paris. She doesn't _____ the truth all the time, you know."
                                   6

**C.**

Today, my neighbor _____ good morning to me as usual. Then she
                      1

_____ me a story about a mouse in her bedroom last night. She _____
    2                                                                  3

that the mouse had run out of her apartment and into my apartment. Did she

_____ me the truth or did she _____ me a story as usual?
    4                                  5

## 5 Your Turn

**Work with a partner. Tell your partner a short sentence. It does not have to be true.
Your partner tells the class what you told him or her.**

**Example:**
You:            I have six children.
Your partner:  My partner told me she had six children.

# 14d Reported Questions

The president of the company **wanted to know why** everybody was sitting so far away from him.

1. Reported questions have a main clause and a noun clause.

| MAIN CLAUSE | | NOUN CLAUSE | | |
|---|---|---|---|---|
| Subject | Reporting Verb | Wh- Word | Subject | Verb |
| He | asked | why | everyone | had left. |

2. We use verbs like *ask, inquire,* and *wonder* or the expression *want to know* to report questions. We do not use *say* or *tell.*

   "Where do you live?" she **asked** me.
   She **asked** me where I lived.
   She **wanted to know** where I lived.
   She **wondered** where I lived.

3. When the question begins with a wh- word like *who, what, where, when,* and *how,* the noun clause in the reported question begins with the same word.

   He asked me, "**What** do you want?"
   He asked me **what** I wanted.

4. When the question is a yes/no question, we begin the noun clause in the reported question with *if* or *whether. If* and *whether* have the same meaning here.

   "Are you coming?" he asked.
   He asked **if** I was coming. OR He asked **whether** I was coming.

5. In reported questions, the words are in statement form. They are not in question form. We do not use question marks.

> He asked me, "How are you?"
> He asked me how I was.
>
> "Are you happy?" she asked us.
> She asked us if we were happy.
>
> "Where is your backpack?" she asked.
> She asked where my backpack was.

6. Reported questions use the same rules as reported speech for changing verb tenses, modal auxiliaries, and other words. Review these rules on pages 369–370.

## 6 Practice

**I was a tourist in London last summer. I met a woman who asked me some questions. Write her questions as reported questions.**

1. Can you speak English?

   _She asked me if I could speak English._

2. Where do you come from?

   _____

3. Where do you want to go?

   _____

4. Do you have a map?

   _____

5. Have you seen Buckingham Palace?

   _____

6. Did you visit the British Museum?

   _____

7. Is this your first time in London?

   _____

8. What is your name?

   _____

9. Are you married?

   _____

10. Are you on vacation here?

    _____

**11.** How long are you going to stay here?

_____

**12.** Would you like to have a cup of tea with me?

_____

## 7 | Practice

**Yesterday you saw a man who was lying on the sidewalk. You went to help him and asked some questions. You are reporting what you asked.**

1. Are you OK?

   _I asked if he was OK._

2. Do you need help?

   _____

3. How did you fall?

   _____

4. Can you stand up?

   _____

5. Were you on your way to work?

   _____

6. Where does it hurt?

   _____

7. What's your name?

   _____

8. Can I call someone for you?

   _____

9. Do you want me to call for an ambulance?

   _____

## 8 | Your Turn

**Write five questions to ask your partner. Your partner will answer your questions. Later, your partner will report to the class what you wanted to know and the answer.**

**Example:**
You:            Where do you live?
Your partner:  I live on Elm Street.
Your partner:  My partner wanted to know where I lived. I said that I lived on Elm Street.

# 14e Reported Commands, Requests, Advice, and Suggestions

The man said, "Stop."
The man **ordered me to stop.**

To report commands, requests, and advice, we can use reporting verb + someone + (*not*) infinitive.

1. We can report commands with the reporting verbs *tell* or *order* + someone + (*not*) infinitive.

   "Don't talk!" the teacher said to us.
   The teacher **told us not to talk.**
   OR The teacher **ordered us not to talk.**

   "Stay in the car," the police officer said.
   The police officer **ordered me to stay** in the car.
   OR The police officer **told me to stay** in the car.

   We can also use the reporting verb *warn* to report commands. We use *warn* to show that something is dangerous.

   "Don't go near the swimming pool!" she said to the little girl.
   She **warned the little girl not to go** near the swimming pool.

2. We can report requests with the reporting verb *ask*.

   "Wait a minute, please," Ted said.
   Ted **asked me to wait** a minute.

   "Would you help me?" he asked.
   He **asked me to help** him.

3. We can report advice with the reporting verb *advise*.

   The doctor said, "Helen, you should lose ten pounds."
   The doctor **advised Helen to lose** ten pounds.

4. There are other verbs that can use the verb + someone + (*not*) infinitive pattern. Here are some of them.

| Verb | Example |
|---|---|
| beg | "Please help me," he said.<br>He **begged me to** help him. |
| invite | "Will you come to the party?" she said.<br>She **invited me to** come to the party. |
| offer | "Shall I carry your suitcase?" he said.<br>He **offered to** carry my suitcase. |
| allow | "You can go early," the teacher said.<br>The **teacher allowed us to** go early. |

5. We can use two different structures for reporting suggestions.

| SUGGEST + VERB *-ING* | | | | |
|---|---|---|---|---|
| Quoted Speech | Subject | *Suggest* | Verb *-ing* | |
| "Let's start early," he said. | He | **suggested** | **starting** | early. |

| SUGGEST + NOUN CLAUSE | | | | |
|---|---|---|---|---|
| Quoted Speech | Subject | *Suggest* | (*That*) | Subject + a Base Verb |
| "Let's start early," he said. | He | **suggested** | (**that**) | **we start** early. |

When we use *suggest* + a noun clause, we always use a base verb in the main clause, even for the subjects *he, she,* and *it*.

   CORRECT:   The doctor suggested that she **get** more exercise.
   INCORRECT: The doctor suggested that she ~~gets~~ more exercise.

The verb *recommend* also uses these structures:

   The doctor **recommended drinking** a lot of water.
   The doctor **recommended that she drink** a lot of water.

Practice

Complete the sentences with one of the verbs in the list. Use the past tense of the verb. In some sentences, there is more than one correct answer.

advise            beg              warn
allow             invite
ask               order

1. "Don't sit on that chair!" the teacher said. "It might break," he added.

   The teacher _____warned_____ her not to sit on the chair.

2. "Write your essay," the teacher said.

   The teacher _____ us to write the essay.

3. "Please help me with this question," Kate said to her partner in class. "I really need your help."

   She _____ her partner to help her with that question.

4. "Would you like to have a cup of coffee with me after class?" Tony said to Nancy.

   Tony _____ Nancy to have a cup of coffee with him after class.

5. "You can use your dictionaries to write the essay," the teacher said.

   The teacher _____ us to use our dictionaries to write the essay.

6. "You should write a title for the essay," Tony told Kate. "The teacher likes us to write titles."

   Tony _____ Kate to write a title for the essay.

7. "Please, please, check this essay, " Suzy said to Kim.

   Suzy _____ Kim to check her essay.

8. "You should check the spelling of these words," Kim said to Suzy.

   Kim _____ Suzy to check the spelling of those words.

9. "Do you need any help?" the teacher said to Suzy.

   The teacher _____ Suzy if she needed any help.

10. "You can finish the essay at home," the teacher said.

    The teacher _____ us to finish the essay at home.

10 Practice

Choose a reporting verb and report the speaker's words.

1. "Let's go to the shopping mall," said Dick to Mary.

   _Dick suggested that they go to the shopping mall._

**2.** "Please, please, give me the keys to the car," Mary said to her brother Dick.

Mary _____

**3.** "OK, you can drive the car," Dick said to his sister.

Dick _____

**4.** "Don't drive too fast," Dick said.

_____

**5.** "Please don't tell Dad," Mary said.

Mary _____

**6.** "You should be very careful!" said Dick.

_____

**7.** "Take your driver's license with you," said Dick.

_____

**8.** "You can drive to the shopping mall," said Dick.

_____

**9.** "Please, please, let me drive back, too," said Mary.

_____

**10.** "Let's drive to the mall first," said Dick.

_____

## ⊞ Practice

**Paul is going on vacation for two weeks. He wants people to help him take care of things. Choose a reporting verb and report the speaker's words.**

**1.** Paul said to John, "Can you take care of my bird?"

   *Paul asked John to take care of his bird.*

**2.** Paul said, "Don't give the bird any cookies."

_____

**3.** Paul said to Linda, "Will you water my plants for me?"

_____

**4.** Paul said to Linda, "Don't water them too much."

_____

**5.** Paul said to his mother, "Please do my laundry."

_____

**6.** Paul said to his mother, "Don't clean my apartment."

_____

**7.** Paul said to his mother, "Don't touch my CD player."

_____

**8.** Paul said to Ken, "Will you give these papers to my boss?"

_____

---

**12** **Your Turn**

**What do you ask people to do for you when you go away? Say three things.**

**Example:**
I ask someone to take my mail into the apartment.

---

## 14f Wishes about the Present or Future

### Form / Function

I **wish** I **were** on vacation.

1. We use *wish* + the simple past to say that we would like something to be different in the present.

> I **wish** I **had** a credit card. (But I don't have a credit card.)
> I **wish** I **made** more money. (But I don't make more money.)

| MAIN CLAUSE | | NOUN CLAUSE | |
|---|---|---|---|
| Subject | *Wish* | *(That)* | Subject + Simple Past Verb |
| I | wish | | I **had** a car. |
| My brother | wishes | | he **spoke** Thai. |
| She | wishes | (that) | she **didn't need** to borrow money. |
| My parents | wish | | they **didn't live** in a small town. |
| Laura | wishes | | she **could go** to Florida for her vacation.* |

*We use *could* after *wish* to express ability.

2. For the verb *to be,* we use *were* for all subjects.*

| MAIN CLAUSE | | NOUN CLAUSE | | |
|---|---|---|---|---|
| Subject | *Wish* | *(That)* | Subject | *Were/Weren't* |
| I | wish | that | I | **were** on the beach now. |
| You | | | you | **weren't** in class now. |
| He/She/It | wishes | | he/she/it | |
| We | wish | | we | |
| They | | | they | |

*In informal English, many people use *was* for the subjects *I, he, she,* and *it.*

13 Practice

A. **Look at the information in the box. Then write sentences about Carol Brown's wishes.**

| Reality | Wish |
|---|---|
| 1. has curly hair | have straight hair |
| 2. is short | be tall |
| 3. is a student | be a model |
| 4. makes little money | make a lot of money |
| 5. shares a small apartment | live in a big house |
| 6. rides a bicycle | drive a sports car |
| 7. stays home on weekends | go out with friends on weekends |
| 8. wears regular clothes | wear designer clothes |

1. *Carol wishes she had straight hair.* _____
2. _____
3. _____
4. _____
5. _____
6. _____
7. _____
8. _____

B. **Write two more things she wishes.**

1. _____
2. _____

## 14 Practice

**Susan started studying at a college far from home. She is not very happy. She wishes things were different. Write sentences about what she wishes.**

1. Classes are so hard.

   *She wishes classes were not so hard.*

2. There are so many tests.

   _____

3. Books are so expensive.

   _____

4. Teachers are not friendly.

   _____

5. I don't have friends.

   _____

6. My roommate is not nice.

   _____

7. I have no time to have fun.

   _____

## 15 Practice

**Nick is a famous soap opera star on television. He doesn't like his present life. He wishes it were different. Write his wishes.**

1. Photographers follow me everywhere.

   _I wish photographers didn't follow me everywhere._

2. Newspapers write untrue stories about me.

   _____

3. I don't have privacy.

   _____

4. People touch me and pull my clothes.

   _____

5. I have to sign autographs all the time.

   _____

6. I have to smile all the time.

   _____

7. I can't wear anything I want.

   _____

8. I can't go to the store to get groceries.

   _____

## 16 Your Turn

**Do you wish things were different? Give two examples for each wish.**

**Example:**
I wish I had a million dollars.
I wish I had a girlfriend.

1. I wish I had ...
2. I wish I could ...
3. I wish I were ...

# 14g Wishes about the Past

I **wish** I **had called** yesterday!

We use *wish* + the past perfect tense to make a wish about something in the past that we regret. We cannot change what happened.

> I **wish** I **had listened** to you. (I didn't listen to you.)
> I **wish** I **had studied** for the test. (I didn't study for the test.)

## 17 Practice

**John went for an interview yesterday. He thinks he didn't get the job. Write sentences about what he wishes about the past.**

**1.** I was so nervous.

   *I wish I had not been so nervous.*

**2.** My hands were sweaty.

_____

**3.** I didn't look the interviewer in the eye.

_____

**4.** I asked about the pay.

_____

**5.** I didn't look confident.

_____

**6.** I didn't smile.

_____

**7.** I forgot the name of my last boss.

_____

**8.** I didn't tell the interviewer about my computer skills.

_____

## 18 | Practice

**Alice and Steve met at a party yesterday. Read the sentences about Alice and Steve and write sentences about what they wish they had or had not done.**

**Steve says to himself:**

**1.** I didn't give her my phone number.

_I wish I had given her my phone number._

**2.** I didn't ask her what her last name was.

_____

**3.** I told her that she looked sad.

_____

**4.** I didn't ask her to dance with me.

_____

**Alice says to herself:**

**5.** I didn't tell him my last name.

_____

**6.** I wasn't very friendly with him.

_____

**7.** I told him I was tired.

_____

**8.** I told him I was with a friend.

_____

**9.** I left early.

_____

**10.** I didn't give him a chance.

_____

## Your Turn

**What did you do or not do last week? Are there things you wish you had done or hadn't done? Say three things.**

**Example:**
I wish I hadn't spent so much money.
I wish I had seen that program on TV.

# 14h Present Real Conditional and Future Conditional Sentences

**Form**

If you see a koala bear outside of a zoo, you are in Australia.

1. We use two clauses in a conditional sentence, an *if* clause and a main clause. The *if* clause contains the condition and the main clause contains the result.

| Type of Sentence | Form | *If* Clause | Main Clause |
|---|---|---|---|
| Present Real Conditional | Simple present tense in both clauses | If you **see** a koala bear outside of a zoo, | you **are** in Australia. |
| | | If the temperature **doesn't fall** below 0° C, | water **won't freeze.** |
| Future Conditional | *If* clause: Simple present tense **Main clause:** Future tense | If I **miss** the bus, | I **will be** late. |
| | | If he **doesn't study,** | he **won't get** a good grade. |

2. We can put the *if* clause first or the main clause first. There is no difference in meaning. When we put the *if* clause first, we put a comma after it.

> **If I miss the bus,** I will be late.
> OR I will be late **if I miss the bus.**

3. In the main clause of a future conditional sentence, we can use any verb form that refers to the future.

> If I finish my homework soon, I **can go** to bed.
> If my sister visits me, we**'re going to travel** around the country.

## Function

1. We use the present real conditional to talk about what happens when there is a definite situation.

> If I have a big lunch, it makes me sleepy.
> If she hears his name, she gets angry.

2. We use the present real conditional to talk about general facts that are always true.

> If an elephant has big ears, it comes from Africa.
> If you mix oil and water, the oil stays on top.

3. We use the present real conditional to talk about habits or things that happen every day.

> If I go to work by car, it takes thirty-five minutes.
> I always walk to the store if it doesn't rain.

4. We use the future conditional to make predictions about what will happen in the future.

> If it rains tomorrow, we'll visit a museum.
> If he comes early, we'll go out.

## 20 Practice

**Complete the sentences with the correct tense of the verb in parentheses.**

1. If people sneeze, they (close) _____*close*_____ their eyes.
2. If you (exercise) _____ a lot, you lose weight.
3. You die if you (not/get) _____ oxygen.
4. If you (break) _____ a nail, it grows back again.
5. People (sweat) _____ if they exercise.
6. If you (cut) _____ your finger, it bleeds.

## 21 Practice

**What will you see if you and your family go to these places? Write sentences with the prompts. Use the correct punctuation.**

1. London/Buckingham Palace

   _If we go to London, we will see Buckingham Palace._

2. Paris/the Eiffel Tower

   _____

3. Rome/the Coliseum

   _____

4. New York/the Statue of Liberty

   _____

5. Egypt/the pyramids

   _____

6. Los Angeles/the movie studios

   _____

7. Sydney/the Sydney Opera House

   _____

8. Venice/gondolas

   _____

9. Tokyo/the Imperial Gardens

   _____

10. Mexico City/the Archaeological Museum

   _____

## 22 Practice

**What will happen if...? Sandra's mother always worries about her when she is away from home. Match the sentence parts. Then write the sentences below. Use the correct punctuation.**

___c___ **1.** eat too much      **a.** feel better

_____ **2.** lie in the sun      **b.** catch a cold

_____ **3.** drink too much coffee      **c.** gain weight

_____ **4.** don't eat breakfast      **d.** not be tired in the morning

_____ **5.** go without a coat      **e.** get sunburned

_____ **6.** go to sleep early      **f.** not sleep

_____ **7.** take this medicine      **g.** be hungry

**1.** _If she eats too much, she will gain weight._

**2.** _____

**3.** _____

**4.** _____

**5.** _____

**6.** _____

**7.** _____

## 23 Practice

**Use the verb form for the present real conditional (simple present) if it is possible in the sentence. If it is not possible, use the verb form for the future conditional (future tense).**

René's parents are coming to visit him in the United States.

**1.** My parents are coming for a visit next week. If we have enough time, we (visit)

_____will visit_____ the art museum.

**2.** If they don't like the art museum, we (go) _____ shopping at a mall.

**3.** We can't stay at the mall for a long time because my mother has problems with her feet. If she walks too much, her feet (hurt) _____.

**4.** If it doesn't rain, we (rent) _____ a boat and row on the lake.

**5.** My father likes boats. If he is on a boat, he (be) _____ happy.

**6.** As for me, if I don't take a pill, I (get) _____ sick when I'm on a boat.

**7.** There is a concert at the university. If I can get tickets, we (go)

_____ .

**8.** My parents like trying new food. If they have a choice, they (eat)

_____ food from different countries.

**9.** If we go to Chinatown, they (love) _____ the food there.

**10.** If they have a good time this year, they (come) _____ back

next year.

**11.** If I get to see my parents once a year, I (be) _____ lucky.

---

| 24 | **Your Turn** |
|---|---|

**Answer what you will do if the following things happen.**

**Example:**
if you pass this class with an A
If I pass this class with an A, I'll have a big party.

**1.** if you pass this class with an A
**2.** if it rains tomorrow
**3.** if there is no class tomorrow

# 14i  Present Unreal Conditional Sentences

If I **had** a million dollars, I **would buy** an island in the sun.

| IF CLAUSE | | | MAIN CLAUSE | | |
|---|---|---|---|---|---|
| If | Subject | Past Tense Verb | Subject | Would/ Could | Base Verb |
| If | I | | I | **would** | |
| | you | | you | **'d** | |
| | he | **had** a lot of money, | he | **wouldn't** | |
| | she | **were** very rich, | she | | **buy** that big house. |
| | we | | we | **could** | |
| | they | | they | **couldn't** | |

Remember, after *if,* we use *were* for all persons.

If she **were** a millionaire, would she be happy?

## Function

We use *if* + simple past + *would/could* + base verb for an unreal situation in the present. The statement is contrary to fact. We imagine a result in the present or future.

**If** I **had** a million dollars, **I'd be** very happy. (I don't have a million dollars.)
**If** you **wrote** things down, you **wouldn't forget** them. (You don't write things down, and you always forget them.)

## 25 Practice

**Complete the sentences with the correct form of the present unreal conditional verb in parentheses.**

**A.**

If my car (break) _____*broke*_____ down on the highway at night, I
                              1

(lock) _____ the doors. Then, I (call) _____ for emergency
           2                                              3

services on my cell phone. If I (not have) _____ a cell phone, I
                                                     4

(walk) _____ to the nearest emergency call box. If the emergency call box
           5

(be) _____ too far away, I (wait) _____ in my car with my
          6                                              7

doors locked.

**B.**

If someone (steal) _____ my purse with all my money and credit cards
                         1

in it, I (report) _____ it to the police. Then, I (call) _____
                       2                                                      3

the credit card company. If I (think) _____ I could find it,
                                        4
I (go) _____ back to all the places to look for it.
            5

C.

If I (see) _____ a big spider in my bed, I
                    1
(scream) _____ . If I (be) _____ alone, I
                2                            3
(find) _____ a friend or neighbor to do something about it. If I
            4
(not/find) _____ anyone, I (sleep) _____ in another
                5                                        6
room or maybe not sleep at all!

D.

If I (wake) _____ up in the night and (hear) _____
                1                                                    2
something in my house, I (go) _____ to the phone and call the police. If I
                                3
(be) _____ alone, I (lock) _____ the door of the room, and
        4                            5
wait for the police to come.

26 Practice

**What would you do if these things happened to you? Write your own sentences.**

1. If someone called you in the middle of the night

   *If someone called me in the middle of the night, I'd get out*

   *of bed and answer the phone.*

2. If all the lights suddenly went out

   _____

   _____

3. If you found a snake in your closet

   _____

   _____

4. If you saw a strange person breaking into your neighbor's house

   _____

   _____

5. If you smelled smoke in your house

   _____

   _____

## 27 | Your Turn

**Ask and answer the questions with a partner.**

**Example:**

You:        If you could be someone else, who would you like to be? Why?

Your partner:  I'd be Bill Gates because I love computers, and I want to be rich.

1. If you could be someone else, who would you like to be? Why?
2. If you could live somewhere else, where would you like to live? Why?
3. If you could interview someone, who would you like to interview? What questions would you like to ask?

# 14j Past Unreal Conditional Sentences

**Form**

If we **had lived** one hundred years ago, we **would have dressed** differently.

| | IF CLAUSE | | MAIN CLAUSE | |
|---|---|---|---|---|
| *If* | Subject | Past Perfect Tense | Subject | *Would/Could/Might +*<br>*Have* + Past Participle |
| If | I | **had lived** 100 years ago, | I | **would have worn** different clothes. |
| | he | **hadn't driven** so fast, | he | **would have passed** the driving test. |
| | she | **had been** here, | she | **might have gotten** the job. |

1. We use the past unreal conditional to talk about what might have been the result if things had been different in the past.

> If I **had studied** harder, I **would have passed** the test.
> (I didn't study harder, and I didn't pass the test.)

> If it **hadn't snowed,** we **might not have had** the accident.
> (It snowed, and we had the accident.)

> If they **had sent** the letter, it **would have arrived** last week.
> (They didn't send the letter, and it didn't arrive last week.)

2. We can use *would, might,* and *could* in the main clause.

We use *would have* + past participle in the main clause if we think the past action was certain.

> If I had heard the telephone ring, I **would have answered** it.
> (I think I would definitely have answered it.)

We use *might have* + past participle in the main clause if we think the past action was possible.

> If you had paid more attention, you **might not have burned** the food.
> (I think it's possible that you wouldn't have burned it.)

We use *could have* + past participle to say that someone would have been able to do something in the past.

> If you had brought your CDs, we **could have danced.**
> (We would have been able to dance.)

## 28 Practice

**Complete the sentences with the correct tense of the verb in parentheses.**

1. If I (not/get up) _____*hadn't gotten up*_____ late, I
   (not/miss) _____*wouldn't have missed*_____ the train.

2. If I (not/miss) _____ the train, I
   (not/be) _____ late for work.

3. If I (not/be) _____ late for work, my boss
   (not/get) _____ angry with me.

**4.** If my boss (not/get) _____ angry with me, he

(not/yell) _____ at me.

**5.** If he (not/yell) _____ at me, I

(not/yell) _____ at him.

**6.** If I (not/yell) _____ at him, I

(not/lose) _____ my job.

## 29 Practice

**Harold is thinking about his past. There are things in his life he wanted to do but did not do.**

**A. Write sentences to express what he would, might, or could have done if things had been different. You can use _would, might,_ or _could_.**

**1.** I wanted to go to the university, but my parents didn't have the money.

_If his parents had had the money, he could have gone to the_
_university._

**2.** I wanted to buy a farm, but I didn't have the money.

_____

_____

**3.** I asked Nina to marry me, but she didn't like my nose.

_____

_____

**4.** I wanted to be an actor, but I didn't have enough talent.

_____

_____

**5.** I wanted to go to Brazil, but I couldn't speak Portuguese.

_____

_____

**6.** I wanted to work for my uncle, but he died.

_____

_____

**7.** My uncle was a thoughtful man, so he left a will.

_If my uncle hadn't been a thoughtful man, he_

_____

**8.** My uncle left a will, and I became a millionaire.

_____

_____

**9.** I became a millionaire, and Nina married me.

_____

_____

**B.** Write five sentences about yourself if you had lived 100 years ago. Write about what you would, might, or could (not) have done or had.

**1.** _If I had lived one hundred years ago, I wouldn't have had a_ _telephone._

**2.** _____

**3.** _____

**4.** _____

**5.** _____

## 30 Your Turn

Think about your past. Do you wish that any things had been different? Write five sentences with *wish,* and then write a sentence using the unreal past conditional.

**Example:**
I wish I had learned to play the guitar. If I had learned how to play the guitar, I could have joined a band.

**1.** _____

_____

**2.** _____

_____

**3.** _____

_____

**4.** _____

_____

**5.** _____

_____

# WRITING: Write a Personal Narrative

**Write a diary entry about your mistakes.**

**Step 1. Imagine that you didn't pass your classes. Think about these questions.**
1. Would you have passed if you had studied harder?
2. Why didn't you study harder? What do you regret?
3. What would happen if your parents knew? What would you say to them?
4. What do you wish you could do?

**Step 2. Write your answers to these or other questions.**

**Step 3. Look at the following diary entry. Use your answers in Step 2 to write your diary entry. Use some past unreal conditional sentences in your diary entry. For more writing guidelines, see pages 407–411.**

### Diary

December 22, 20XX

Dear Diary,

    I feel terrible. Everything has gone wrong in the last few months. I wish I had studied harder for my class. If I had studied harder, I would

Yours truly,
Yvonne

**Step 4. Evaluate your diary entry.**

**Checklist**

_____ Did you write a date for your diary entry?

_____ Did you start your entry with "Dear Diary" followed by a comma?

_____ Did you indent your paragraphs?

_____ Did you use some past unreal conditional sentences?

_____ Did you end your entry with a closing such as "Yours truly" and a comma?

_____ Did you sign your name at the end?

**Step 5. Work with a partner to edit your diary entry. Check spelling, punctuation, vocabulary, and grammar.**

**Step 6. Write your final diary entry.**

**A Choose the best answer, A, B, C, or D, to complete the sentence. Mark your answer by darkening the oval with the same letter.**

1. I wish the sun _____.

   A. is shining    Ⓐ Ⓑ Ⓒ Ⓓ
   B. was shining
   C. were to shine
   D. were shining

2. Kim _____ a funny story last night.

   A. said me    Ⓐ Ⓑ Ⓒ Ⓓ
   B. to me said
   C. told me
   D. tell me

3. Ben said that he _____ with us next week.

   A. will go    Ⓐ Ⓑ Ⓒ Ⓓ
   B. would go
   C. is go
   D. will to go

4. He asked _____.

   A. whether I am coming    Ⓐ Ⓑ Ⓒ Ⓓ
   B. if I am coming
   C. whether I was coming
   D. if I come

5. If I could afford the plane ticket, I _____ on the next plane to Hawaii.

   A. would be    Ⓐ Ⓑ Ⓒ Ⓓ
   B. could have been
   C. will be
   D. were

6. If my father _____ the opportunity, he would have gone to the university.

   A. have    Ⓐ Ⓑ Ⓒ Ⓓ
   B. had
   C. had had
   D. have had

7. She _____ happy, but I wasn't.

   A. asked to me if I was    Ⓐ Ⓑ Ⓒ Ⓓ
   B. asked me if I were
   C. said to me if I was
   D. told me if I was

8. He suggested _____.

   A. going early    Ⓐ Ⓑ Ⓒ Ⓓ
   B. to going early
   C. to go early
   D. us going early

9. I didn't give him my card. I wish I _____ him my card.

   A. give    Ⓐ Ⓑ Ⓒ Ⓓ
   B. have give
   C. had given
   D. had given to

10. If you don't have air to breathe, you _____.

   A. would die    Ⓐ Ⓑ Ⓒ Ⓓ
   B. die
   C. would have died
   D. died

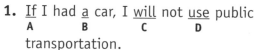

**B** **Find the underlined word or phrase, A, B, C or D, that is incorrect. Mark your answer by darkening the oval with the same letter.**

1. If I had a car, I will not use public
   A     B       C    D
   transportation.

   Ⓐ Ⓑ Ⓒ Ⓓ

2. The teacher warned to us not to talk
             A   B C     D
   during the test.

   Ⓐ Ⓑ Ⓒ Ⓓ

3. If we had lived a hundred years ago, we
            A             B
   wouldn't had problems with air pollution.
           C             D

   Ⓐ Ⓑ Ⓒ Ⓓ

4. When I was a child, my father told me to
                         A   B
   always say the truth.
    C    D

   Ⓐ Ⓑ Ⓒ Ⓓ

5. The doctor recommended to using less
                    A      B
   salt and sugar and drinking more water.
          C      D

   Ⓐ Ⓑ Ⓒ Ⓓ

6. I will have health problems if I won't
       A                B   C
   follow this diet.
        D

   Ⓐ Ⓑ Ⓒ Ⓓ

7. My manager said me that he was going on
             A    B       C
   vacation next week.
     D

   Ⓐ Ⓑ Ⓒ Ⓓ

8. The school counselor advised me taking
                    A   B   C
   an English writing class next semester.
    D

   Ⓐ Ⓑ Ⓒ Ⓓ

9. I didn't study English when I was in high
                         A
   school, but now I wish I have studied it.
              B    C       D

   Ⓐ Ⓑ Ⓒ Ⓓ

10. If I knew how to speak French, I will go
    A          B            C
    to France with you.
       D

    Ⓐ Ⓑ Ⓒ Ⓓ

# APPENDICES

## Appendix 1    Grammar Terms

### Adjective
An adjective describes a noun or a pronoun.

My cat is very **intelligent**. He's **orange** and **white**.

### Adverb
An adverb describes a verb, another adverb, or an adjective.

Joey speaks **slowly**. He **always** visits his father on Wednesdays.

His father cooks **extremely** well. His father is a **very** talented chef.

### Article
An article comes before a noun. The definite article is *the*. The indefinite articles are *a* and *an*.

I read **an** online story and **a** magazine feature about celebrity lifestyles.

**The** online story was much more interesting than **the** magazine feature.

### Auxiliary Verb
An auxiliary verb is found with a main verb. It is often called a "helping" verb.

Susan **can't** play in the game this weekend. **Does** Ruth play baseball?

### Base Form
The base form of a verb has no tense. It has no endings (*–ed*, *–s*, or *–ing*).

Jill didn't **see** the band. She should **see** them when they are in town.

## Comparative

Comparative forms compare two things. They can compare people, places, or things.

> This orange is **sweeter than** that grapefruit.
>
> Working in a large city is **more stressful than** working in a small town.

## Conjunction

A conjunction joins two or more sentences, adjectives, nouns, or prepositional phrases. Some conjunctions are *and, but,* and *or.*

> Kasey is efficient, **and** her work is excellent.
>
> Her apartment is small **but** comfortable.
>
> She works Wednesdays **and** Thursdays.

## Contraction

A contraction is composed of two words put together with an apostrophe. Some letters are left out.

> Frank usually **doesn't** answer his phone.    (doesn't = does + not)
>
> **He's** really busy.    (he's = he + is)
>
> Does he know what time **we're** meeting?    (we're = we + are)

## Imperative

An imperative gives a command or directions. It uses the base form of the verb, and it does not use the word *you.*

> **Go** to the corner and **turn** left.

## Modal

A modal is a type of auxiliary verb. The modal auxiliaries are *can, could, may, might, must, shall, should, will,* and *would.*

> Elizabeth **will** act the lead role in the play next week.
>
> She **couldn't** go to the party last night because she had to practice her lines.
>
> She **may** be able to go to the party this weekend.

## Noun

A noun is a person, an animal, a place, or a thing.

> My **brother** and **sister-in-law** live in **Pennsylvania**. They have three **cats**.

## Object

An object is the noun or pronoun that receives the action of the verb.

> Georgie sent **a gift** for Johnny's birthday.
>
> Johnny thanked **her** for the gift.

## Preposition

A preposition is a small connecting word that is followed by a noun or pronoun. Some are a*t, above, after, by, before, below, for, in, of, off, on, over, to, under, up,* and *with*.

> Every day, Jay drives Chris and Ally **to** school **in** the new car.
> **In** the afternoon, he waits **for** them **at** the bus stop.

## Pronoun

A pronoun takes the place of a noun.

> Chris loves animals. **He** has two dogs and two cats.
> His pets are very friendly. **They** like to spend time with people.

## Sentence

A sentence is a group of words that has a subject and a verb. It is complete by itself.

> Sentence:         Brian works as a lawyer.
> Not a sentence:  Works as a lawyer.

## Subject

A subject is the noun or pronoun that does the action in the sentence.

> **Trisha** is from Canada.
> **She** writes poetry about nature.

## Superlative

Superlative forms compare three or more people, places, or things.

> Jennifer is **the tallest** girl in the class.
> She is from Paris, which is **the most romantic** city in the world.

## Tense

Tense tells when the action in a sentence happens.

| | | |
|---|---|---|
| Simple present | – | The cat **eats** fish every morning. |
| Present progressive | – | He **is eating** fish now. |
| Simple past | – | He **ate** fish yesterday morning. |
| Past progressive | – | He **was eating** when the doorbell rang. |
| Future with *be going to* | – | He **is going to eat** fish tomorrow morning, too! |
| Future with *will* | – | I think that he **will eat** the same thing next week. |

## Verb

A verb tells the action in a sentence.

> Melissa **plays** guitar in a band.
> She **loves** writing new songs.
> The band **has** four other members.

# Appendix 2    Irregular Verbs

| Base Form | Simple Past | Past Participle | Base Form | Simple Past | Past Participle |
|---|---|---|---|---|---|
| be | was, were | been | keep | kept | kept |
| become | became | become | know | knew | known |
| begin | began | begun | leave | left | left |
| bend | bent | bent | lend | lent | lent |
| bite | bit | bitten | lose | lost | lost |
| blow | blew | blown | make | made | made |
| break | broke | broken | meet | met | met |
| bring | brought | brought | pay | paid | paid |
| build | built | built | put | put | put |
| buy | bought | bought | read | read | read |
| catch | caught | caught | ride | rode | ridden |
| choose | chose | chosen | ring | rang | rung |
| come | came | come | run | ran | run |
| cost | cost | cost | say | said | said |
| cut | cut | cut | see | saw | seen |
| do | did | done | sell | sold | sold |
| draw | drew | drawn | send | sent | sent |
| drink | drank | drunk | shake | shook | shaken |
| drive | drove | driven | shut | shut | shut |
| eat | ate | eaten | sing | sang | sung |
| fall | fell | fallen | sit | sat | sat |
| feed | fed | fed | sleep | slept | slept |
| feel | felt | felt | speak | spoke | spoken |
| fight | fought | fought | spend | spent | spent |
| find | found | found | stand | stood | stood |
| fly | flew | flown | steal | stole | stolen |
| forget | forgot | forgotten | swim | swam | swum |
| get | got | gotten/got | take | took | taken |
| give | gave | given | teach | taught | taught |
| go | went | gone | tear | tore | torn |
| grow | grew | grown | tell | told | told |
| hang | hung | hung | think | thought | thought |
| have | had | had | throw | threw | thrown |
| hear | heard | heard | understand | understood | understood |
| hide | hid | hidden | wake up | woke up | woken up |
| hit | hit | hit | wear | wore | worn |
| hold | held | held | win | won | won |
| hurt | hurt | hurt | write | wrote | written |

# Appendix 3    Spelling Rules for Endings

**Adding a Final –s to Nouns and Verbs**

| Rule | Example | -s |
|---|---|---|
| 1. For most words, add –s without making any changes. | book<br>bet<br>save<br>play | books<br>bets<br>saves<br>plays |
| 2. For words ending in a consonant + *y*, change the *y* to *i* and add –es. | study<br>party | studies<br>parties |
| 3. For words ending in *ch, s, sh, x,* or *z*, add –es. | church<br>class<br>wash<br>fix<br>quiz | churches<br>classes<br>washes<br>fixes<br>quizzes |
| 4. For words ending in *o*, sometimes add –es and sometimes add –s. | potato<br>piano | potatoes<br>pianos |
| 5. For words ending in *f* or *lf*, change the *f* or *lf* to *v* and add –es. For words ending in *fe*, change the *f* to *v* and add –s. | loaf<br>half<br>life | loaves<br>halves<br>lives |

## Adding a Final *-ed, -er, -est,* and *-ing*

| Rule | Example | -ed | -er | -est | -ing |
|---|---|---|---|---|---|
| 1. For most words, add the ending without making any changes. | clean | cleaned | cleaner | cleanest | cleaning |
| 2. For words ending in silent *e*, drop the *e* and add *–ed*, *–er*, or *–est*. | save<br>like<br>nice | saved<br>liked | saver<br><br>nicer | nicest | saving<br>liking |
| 3. For words ending in a consonant + *y*, change the *y* to *i* and add the ending.<br><br>Do not change or drop the *y* before adding *–ing*. | sunny<br>happy<br>study<br>worry | studied<br>worried | sunnier<br>happier | sunniest<br>happiest | studying<br>worrying |
| 4. For one-syllable words ending in one vowel and one consonant, double the final consonant, then add the ending.<br><br>Do not double the last consonant if it is a *w, x,* or *y*. | hot<br>run<br>bat<br>glow<br>mix<br>stay | batted<br>glowed<br>mixed<br>stayed | hotter<br>runner<br>batter | hottest | running<br>batting<br>glowing<br>mixing<br>staying |
| 5. For words of two or more syllables that end in one vowel and one consonant, double the final consonant if the final syllable is stressed. | begin<br>refer<br>occur<br>permit | referred<br>occurred<br>permitted | beginner | | beginning<br>referring<br>occurring<br>permitting |
| 6. For words of two or more syllables that end in one vowel and one consonant, do NOT double the final consonant if the final syllable is NOT stressed. | enter<br>happen<br>develop | entered<br>happened<br>developed | developer | | entering<br>happening<br>developing |

# Appendix 4    Capitalization Rules

## First words

1. Capitalize the first word of every sentence.

   **T**hey live in San Francisco.          **W**hat is her name?

2. Capitalize the first word of a quotation.

   She said, "**M**y name is Nancy."

## Names

1. Capitalize names of people, including titles of address.

   **M**r. **T**hompson          **A**lison **E**mmet          **M**ike **A**. **L**ee

2. Capitalize the word "I".

   Rose and **I** went to the market.

3. Capitalize nationalities, ethnic groups, and religions.

   **L**atino          **A**sian          **K**orean          **I**slam

4. Capitalize family words if they appear alone or with a name, but not if they have a possessive pronoun or article.

   He's at **A**unt Lucy's house.     vs.     He's at an **a**unt's house.

## Places

1. Capitalize the names of countries, states, cities, and geographical areas.

   **T**okyo          **M**exico          the **S**outh          **V**irginia

2. Capitalize the names of oceans, lakes, rivers, and mountains.

   the **P**acific **O**cean          **L**ake **O**ntario          **M**t. **E**verest

3. Capitalize the names of streets, schools, parks, and buildings.

   **C**entral **P**ark          **M**ain **S**treet          the **E**mpire **S**tate **B**uilding

4. Don't capitalize directions if they aren't names of geographical areas.

   She lives **n**ortheast of Washington. We fly **s**outh during our flight.

## Time words

1. Capitalize the names of days and months.

   **M**onday          **F**riday          **J**anuary          **S**eptember

2. Capitalize the names of holidays and historical events.

   **C**hristmas          **I**ndependence **D**ay          **W**orld **W**ar I

3. Don't capitalize the names of seasons.

   **s**pring          **s**ummer          **f**all          **w**inter

## Titles

1. Capitalize the first word and all important words of titles of books, magazines, newspapers, and articles.

   *The Sound and the Fury*      *Time Out*      *The New York Times*

2. Capitalize the first word and all important words of titles of films, plays, radio programs, and TV shows.

   *Star Wars*      "Friends"      *Mid Summer Night's Dream*

3. Don't capitalize articles (*a, an, the*), conjunctions (*but, and, or*) and short prepositions (*of, with, in, on, for*) unless they are the first word of a title.

   *The Story of Cats*      *The Woman in the Dunes*

# Appendix 5   Punctuation Rules

## Period

1. Use a period at the end of a statement or command.

   I live in New York.      Open the door.

2. Use a period after most abbreviations.

   Ms.      Dr.      St.      U.S.

   Exceptions:      NATO      UN      AIDS      IBM

3. Use a period after initials.

   Ms. K.L. Kim      F.C. Simmons

## Question Mark

1. Use a question mark at the end of questions.

   Is he working tonight?      Where did they use to work?

2. In a direct quotation, the question mark goes before the quotation marks.

   Martha asked, "What's the name of the street?"

## Exclamation Point

Use an exclamation point at the end of exclamatory sentences or phrases. They express surprise or strong emotion.

   Wow!      I got an A!

## Comma

1.  Use a comma to separate items in a series.

    John will have juice, coffee, and tea at the party.

2.  Use a comma to separate two or more adjectives that each modify the noun alone.

    Purrmaster is a smart, friendly cat. (*smart* and *friendly* cat)

3.  Use a comma before a conjunction (*and, but, or, so*) that separates two independent clauses.

    The book is very funny, and the film is funny too.

    She was tired, but she didn't want to go to sleep.

4.  Don't use a comma before a conjunction that separates a sentence from an incomplete sentence.

    I worked in a bakery at night and went to class during the day.

5.  Use a comma after an introductory clause or phrase.

    After we hike the first part of the trail, we are going to rest.

6.  Use a comma after *yes* and *no* in answers.

    Yes, that is my book.

    No, I'm not.

7.  Use a comma to separate quotations from the rest of a sentence. Don't use a comma if the quotation is a question and it is in the first part of the sentence.

    The student said, "I'm finished with the homework."

    "Are you really finished**?**" asked the student.

## Apostrophe

1.  Use apostrophes in contractions.

    don't (*do not*)    it's (*it is*)    he's (*he is*)    we're (*we are*)

2.  Use apostrophes to show possession.

    Anne's book (the book belongs to Anne)

## Quotation Marks

1.  Use quotation marks at the beginning and end of exact quotations. Other punctuation marks go before the end quotation marks.

    Burt asked, "When are we leaving?"

    "Right after lunch," Mark replied.

2. Use quotation marks before and after titles of articles, songs, stories, and television shows. Periods and commas are usually placed before the end quotation marks, while question marks and exclamation points are placed after them. If the title is a question, the question mark is placed inside the quotation marks, and appropriate punctuation is placed at the end of the sentence.

> Burt's favorite song is "Show Some Emotion" by Joan Armatrading.
> He read an article called "Motivating Your Employees."
> We read an interesting article called "How Do You Motivate Employees?".

## Italics and Underlining

1. If you are writing on a computer, use italic type (*like this*) for books, newspapers, magazines, films, plays, and words from other languages.

> Have you ever read *Woman in the Dunes*?
> How do you say *buenos dias* in Chinese?

2. If you are writing by hand, underline the titles of books, newspapers, magazines, films, and plays.

> Have you ever read <u>Woman in the Dunes</u>?
> How do you say <u>buenos dias</u> in Chinese?

# Appendix 6  Writing Basics

## 1. Sentence types

There are three types of sentences: declarative, interrogative, and exclamatory. Declarative sentences state facts and describe events, people, or things. We use a period at the end of these sentences. Interrogative sentences ask yes/no questions and wh- questions. We use a question mark at the end of these sentences. Exclamatory sentences express surprise or extreme emotion, such as joy or fear. We use an exclamation point at the end of these sentences.

## 2. Indenting

We indent the first line of a paragraph. Each paragraph expresses a new thought, and indenting helps to mark the beginning of this new thought.

## 3. Writing titles

The title should give the main idea of a piece of writing. It should be interesting. It goes at the top of the composition and is not a complete sentence. In a title, capitalize the first word and all of the important words.

## 4. Writing topic sentences

The topic sentence tells the reader the main idea of the paragraph. It is always a complete sentence with a subject and a verb. It is often the first sentence in a paragraph, but sometimes it is in another position in the paragraph.

## 5. Organizing ideas

Information can be organized in a paragraph in different ways. One common way is to begin with a general idea and work toward more specific information. Another way is to give the information in order of time using words like *before, after, as, when, while,* and *then.*

## 6. Connecting ideas

It is important to connect the ideas in a paragraph so that the paragraph has cohesion. Connectors and transitional words help make the writing clear, natural, and easy to read. Connectors and transitional words include *and, in addition, also, so, but, however, for example, such as, so ... that,* and *besides.*

## 7. The writing process

Success in writing generally follows these basic steps:

❖ Brainstorm ideas.
❖ Organize the ideas.
❖ Write a first draft of the piece.
❖ Evaluate and edit the piece for content and form.
❖ Rewrite the piece.

# Index

## L

## M

## N

## O

## P